WITHDRAWN

Policy Framework for Investment

A REVIEW OF GOOD PRACTICES

OECD

ORGANISATION FOR ECONOMIC CO-OPERATION AND DEVELOPMENT

ORGANISATION FOR ECONOMIC CO-OPERATION AND DEVELOPMENT

The OECD is a unique forum where the governments of 30 democracies work together to address the economic, social and environmental challenges of globalisation. The OECD is also at the forefront of efforts to understand and to help governments respond to new developments and concerns, such as corporate governance, the information economy and the challenges of an ageing population. The Organisation provides a setting where governments can compare policy experiences, seek answers to common problems, identify good practice and work to co-ordinate domestic and international policies.

The OECD member countries are: Australia, Austria, Belgium, Canada, the Czech Republic, Denmark, Finland, France, Germany, Greece, Hungary, Iceland, Ireland, Italy, Japan, Korea, Luxembourg, Mexico, the Netherlands, New Zealand, Norway, Poland, Portugal, the Slovak Republic, Spain, Sweden, Switzerland, Turkey, the United Kingdom and the United States. The Commission of the European Communities takes part in the work of the OECD.

OECD Publishing disseminates widely the results of the Organisation's statistics gathering and research on economic, social and environmental issues, as well as the conventions, guidelines and standards agreed by its members.

This work is published on the responsibility of the Secretary-General of the OECD. The opinions expressed and arguments employed herein do not necessarily reflect the official views of the Organisation or of the governments of its member countries.

Also available in French under the title:
Cadre d'action pour l'investissement
UN PANORAMA DES BONNES PRATIQUES

Foreword

The Policy Framework for Investment: A Review of Good Practices *is published as a companion volume to the* Policy Framework for Investment. *It reproduces the analytical background reports which supported the development of the ten chapters of the* Framework. *The objective of the* Policy Framework for Investment *is to mobilise private investment that supports economic growth and sustainable development. It thus aims to contribute to the prosperity of countries and their citizens and the fight against poverty.*

Drawing on good practices from OECD and non-member economies, the Framework *proposes guidance in ten policy fields identified in the 2002 United Nations Monterrey Consensus on Financing for Development as critically important for improving the quality of a country's environment for investment. It enables policy makers to ask appropriate questions about their economy, their institutions and their policy settings in order to identify priorities, to develop an effective set of policies and to evaluate progress.*

The Framework *was developed by OECD and non-member participants in a task force established under the aegis of the OECD Investment Committee as part of the OECD Initiative on Investment for Development launched in Johannesburg in November 2003.*

The Framework *was adopted and declassified by the OECD Council, the governing board of the Organisation, and welcomed by Ministers at their annual OECD meeting in May 2006. The OECD and its non-member partners will continue to work together, in co-operation with the World Bank, the United Nations and other interested institutions and with the active engagement of business, labour and other civil society organisations, to support effective use and future development of the* Framework.

How the *Policy Framework for Investment* and the *Review of Good Practices* were developed

The task force which developed the *Framework* consisted of officials from some 60 governments. In addition to the 30 member countries, non-OECD economies who participated in the task force's meetings were Argentina, Bahrain, Brazil, Chile, China, Chinese Taipei, Egypt, Estonia, India, Indonesia, Israel, Jordan, Latvia, Lithuania, Malaysia, Morocco, Mozambique, Pakistan, Philippines, Romania, Russian Federation, Senegal, Slovenia, South Africa, Tanzania and Viet Nam. Chile (Mr. Luis Eduardo Escobar, Senior Advisor to the Finance Minister) and Japan (Mr. Shuichiro Megata, Deputy Permanent Representative of Japan to the OECD) chaired jointly the task force. Together with the Investment Committee, nine other OECD bodies were involved in developing the *Framework* and in reviewing individual chapters of the *Review of Good Practices*: the Development Assistance Committee, the Trade Committee, the Competition Committee, the Committee on Fiscal Affairs, the Steering Group on Corporate Governance, the Education Committee, the Employment, Labour and Social Affairs Committee, the Working Group on Bribery in International Business Transactions, and the Public Governance Committee.

The World Bank, UNCTAD and other international organisations participated in task force meetings and discussions of the *Review*'s individual chapters. The Business and Industry Advisory Committee (BIAC), the Trade Union Advisory Committee (TUAC) and representatives of non-governmental organisations also participated in these discussions and made submissions. The task force conducted broader public consultations on the *Framework*, as well as the *Review*'s chapters, under the auspices of the OECD Global Forums on International Investment held in India and Brazil, and of OECD and other regional investment initiatives.

The *Review of Good Practices* was finalised under the OECD Secretariat's responsibility. Co-ordinated by Michael Gestrin and Jonathan Coppel of the Investment Division headed by Pierre Poret, in the Directorate for Financial and Enterprise Affairs, the *Review* was prepared by: for the investment policy and investment promotion and facilitation chapters, Michael Gestrin; for the trade policy chapter, Dale Andrew, Jonathan Gage and Sebastien Miroudot; for the competition policy chapter, Michael Gestrin, Patricia Heriard-Dubreuil and Jeremy West; for the tax policy chapter, Steven Clark; for the corporate governance chapter, Daniel Blume; for the responsible business conduct chapter, Kathryn Gordon; for the human resource development and infrastructure and financial sector development chapters, Jonathan Coppel; and for the public governance chapter, Janos Bertok, Elodie Beth, Nicola Ehlermann-Cache, Josef Konvitz, Delia Rodrigo and Christian Vergez. The World Bank contributed background material on human resource development and infrastructure and financial sector development.

Table of contents

5

Boxes

Tables

Figures

ISBN 92-64-02586-3
Policy Framework for Investment
A review of Good Practices
© OECD 2006

Chapter 1

Investment Policy*

* This background document was prepared by Michael Gestrin, Investment Division, OECD Directorate for Financial and Enterprise Affairs.

1.1. Introduction

This chapter addresses one of the policy areas covered in the *Policy Framework for Investment* within the context of the OECD *Initiative on Investment for Development* – investment policy. The purpose of this chapter is to examine how investment policy contributes to an environment that is attractive to investors and that enhances the benefits of investment to societies. It serves as background documentation for the investment chapter of the *Policy Framework for Investment*.

Sections 1.2 and 1.3 examine two principal aspects of investment policy that support an attractive investment environment; transparency and protection. Section 1.4 focuses on international investment issues, with particular attention to non-discrimination and the role of international investment agreements.

One of the concerns sometimes associated with investment policy in the context of international agreements dealing with investment has been over the implications of such agreements for the sovereign right to regulate. This chapter takes as a starting point the right to regulate in the public interest. Indeed, the principles of transparency, protection, and non-discrimination that are the focus of this chapter are important features of a healthy business environment not because they place limitations on the right to regulate but rather because they underpin government efforts to regulate well.

1.2. Transparency

> **What steps has the government taken to ensure that the laws and regulations dealing with investments and investors, including small and medium sized enterprises, and their implementation and enforcement are clear, transparent, readily accessible and do not impose unnecessary burdens?**

The Monterrey Consensus calls upon countries to strive for "a transparent, stable and predictable investment climate, with proper contract enforcement and respect for property rights, embedded in sound macroeconomic policies and institutions that allow businesses, both domestic and international, to operate efficiently and profitably and with maximum development impact. Special efforts are required in such priority areas as economic policy and regulatory frameworks for promoting and protecting investments…" (paragraph 21).

Transparent information on how governments implement and change rules and regulations dealing with investment is a critical determinant in the investment decision. Transparency and predictability are especially important for small- and medium-sized enterprises that tend to face particular challenges to entering the formal economy. It is also important for foreign investors who may have to function with very different regulatory systems, cultures and administrative frameworks from their own. A transparent and

Box 1.1. **The OECD Framework for Investment Policy Transparency**

The OECD Framework for Investment Policy Transparency was developed by the OECD Investment Committee to assist both OECD and non-OECD governments to enhance transparency of their investment policy frameworks and to serve as a basis for experience sharing among public officials. While the focus is on the information gaps and special needs of foreign investors, they apply, in most instances, to domestic investors as well. The Framework poses fifteen questions that are supportive of a level playing field for all investors.

1. Are the economic benefits of transparency for international investment adequately recognised by public authorities? How is this being achieved?

2. What information pertaining to investment measures is made "readily available", or "available" upon request to foreign investors?

3. What are the legal requirements for making this information "public"? Do these requirements apply to primary and secondary legislation? Do they apply to both the national and sub-national levels? Is this information also made available to foreign investors in their countries of origin?

4. Are exceptions/qualifications to making information available clearly defined and delimited?

5. What are the main vehicles of information on investment measures of interest to foreign investors? What may determine the choice of publication avenues? What efforts are made to simplify the dissemination of this information?

6. Is this information centralised? Is it couched in layman's terms? In English or another language? What is the role of Internet in disseminating essential/relevant information to foreign investors?

7. Have special enquiry points been created? Can investment promotion agencies fulfil this role?

8. How much transparency is achieved via international agreements or by international organisations?

9. Are foreign investors normally notified and consulted in advance of the purpose and nature of regulatory changes of interest to them? What are the main avenues? Are these avenues available to all stakeholders?

10. Are the notice and comment procedures codified? Do they provide for timely opportunities for comment by foreign investors and accountability on how their comments are to be handled?

11. Are exceptions to openness and accessibility to procedures clearly defined and delimited?

12. What are the available means for informing and assisting foreign investors in obtaining the necessary licensing, permits, registration or other formalities? What recourse is made to "silent and consent" clauses or *a posteriori* verification procedures?

13. What are foreign investors' legal rights in regard to administrative decisions?

14. To what extent "one-stop" shops may assist foreign investors fulfil administrative requirements?

15. What efforts are being made to address capacity building bottle-necks?

predictable regulatory framework dealing with investment helps businesses to assess potential investment opportunities on a more informed and timely basis, shortening the period before investment becomes productive. The importance of transparency and predictability has thus motivated a number of initiatives, such as the OECD Framework for Investment Policy Transparency, that aim to help governments to achieve greater transparency. Transparency provisions have also been enshrined in virtually all modern international investment agreements, including the agreements of the WTO, regional agreements such as the NAFTA and most bilateral investment treaties of recent vintage.

The growing consensus about the importance of transparency does not imply that transparency-enhancing reforms are easy to enact and implement. All countries – developed and less developed – face significant obstacles to reform. OECD work finds that the difficulties stem from three areas:

- *Politics.* The main obstacles to transparency-enhancing reform are political. Attempting to overcome the natural political dynamic in favour of "concentrated benefits" is an ongoing struggle for all political systems. Lack of transparency also shields government officials from accountability. Thus, many actors – both inside and outside the public sector – can have a stake in non-transparent practices. It is for this reason that, despite the broad apparent agreement in principle about their benefits, actual implementation of transparency-enhancing reforms are likely to involve painful shifts in the way policies are made and implemented, especially in countries with highly opaque policy environments. The difficulty will be to develop the political momentum for pro-transparency reform and to prevent backsliding.

- *Institutions.* All countries' institutional structures make certain transparency measures possible and make others more difficult. International agreements tend to focus on core transparency measures. These are the starting points for other communication processes that are closely linked to national institutions that usually evolve slowly and incrementally. The challenge is to create the conditions that help countries move forward on core measures, while also working with and enhancing the distinctive national characteristics of transparency practices.

- *Technological, financial and human resources.* Transparency requires access to resources and entails administrative costs. It involves the creation of registers, Web sites, the development of "plain language" texts and other mechanisms for making the language of legal and regulatory codes accessible to target audiences. For foreigners, translation of the host country's texts into relevant foreign languages would also require resources and entail costs. However, most studies suggest that the costs of opacity far outweigh the costs of transparency-enhancing reforms.

There are many options for promoting transparency-oriented reform. Some important elements for implementing regulatory transparency include:

- *Consultation with interested parties.* The widespread use of consultations reflects a growing recognition that effective rules cannot rely solely on command and control – the individuals and organisations, including from civil society, who have a stake in the rules need to be recruited as partners in their implementation. Consultation is the first phase of this recruitment process. It can also generate information and ideas that would not otherwise be available to public officials. Consultation mechanisms are becoming more standardised and systematic. This enhances effective access by improving predictability and outside awareness of consultation opportunities. There is a trend toward adapting forms of consultation to the stage in the regulatory process. Consultation tends to start earlier in the policy making process, is conducted in several stages and employs different mechanisms at different times. Problems have been noted as well. For example, consultation fatigue – where some organisations are overwhelmed by the volume of material on which their views are requested – has been noted in several countries.

- *Legislative simplification and codification.* There is increased use of legislative codification and restatement of laws and regulations to enhance clarity and identify and eliminate inconsistency.

- *Plain language drafting.* OECD work has documented that twenty-three member countries require the use of "plain language drafting" of laws and regulation. Sixteen member countries issue guidance materials and/or offer training programmes to help with clearer drafting.

- *Registers of existing and proposed regulation.* The adoption of centralised registers of laws and regulations enhances accessibility. OECD work documents that eighteen member countries stated in end-2000 that they published a consolidated register of all subordinate regulations currently in force and nine of these provided that enforceability depended on inclusion in the register. Many countries now also commit to publication of future regulatory plans.

- *Electronic dissemination of regulatory material.* Three quarters of OECD countries now make most or all primary legislation available via the Internet.

- *Review of administrative decisions.* Transparency in the implementation or enforcement of rules and regulations is as important as the transparency of the rules and regulations themselves. Clear criteria and transparent procedures for administrative decisions, including with respect to investment approval mechanisms, and their possible review can serve to bolster confidence in the regulatory framework for investment.

OECD surveys on progress with respect to regulatory reform have found that performance is still far from satisfactory. The twelve OECD countries surveyed had problems with legal texts that were difficult to understand and with overly complex regulatory structures. Biased participation in public consultation was noted for 8 countries and a tendency to exclude less powerful groups from consultation was cited for 4 countries. Other problems included lack of systematic policy analysis (often called regulatory impact analysis, or RIA) as a tool for improving the quality of consultations and a lack of clear standards in licensing and concessions (7 countries). Despite these challenges, the growing recognition of the importance of transparency for the investment climate has been reflected in considerable progress and efforts across virtually all countries, including through innovative new approaches to regulation specifically for investors.

Common transparency-related problems and possible solutions are outlined in Box 1.2. These provide policy-makers with more detailed, operational criteria for consideration in answering the overarching question posed at the beginning of this section.

Box 1.2. **Transparency and predictability in investment policy: from principles to action**

What steps have been taken to ensure that laws and regulations dealing with investment, as well as the processes associated with their implementation and enforcement, are clear and transparent?

Policy issue: some form of public consultation is used when developing new regulations, but not systematically and with no minimum standards of access. Participation biased or unclear.

Possible action: adopt minimum standards, with clear rules of the game, procedures, and participation criteria, applicable to all organs with regulatory powers. Use "notice and comment" as a safeguard against regulatory capture. Reduce use of "informal" consultations with selected partners.

Policy issue: regulatory reform programme and strategy are not transparent to affected groups.

Possible action: develop coherent and transparent reform plans, and consult with major affected interests in their development.

Policy issue: information on existing regulations not easily accessible (particularly for SMEs and foreign traders and investors).

Possible action: creation of centralised registries of rules and formalities with positive security, use one-stop shops, use information technologies to provide faster and cheaper access to regulations.

Policy issue: legal text difficult to understand.

Possible action: adopt principle of plain language drafting.

Policy issue: complexity in the structure of regulatory regimes.

Possible action: codification and rationalisation of laws.

Policy issue: RIA is never or not always used in public consultation.

Possible action: integrate RIA at an early stage of public consultation.

Policy issue: inadequate use of communications technologies.

Possible action: use Internet more frequently in making drafts and final rules available as a consultation mechanism.

Policy issue: lack of transparency in government procurement.

Possible action: adopt explicit standards and procedures for decision-making.

Policy issue: lack of transparency in ministerial mandates and roles of regulators

Possible action: clarify responsibilities between regulators.

Policy issue: too much administrative discretion in applying regulations.

Possible action: strengthen administrative procedures and accountability mechanisms. Publish criteria for administrative decisions and require decisions to be motivated against these criteria.

Policy issue: inadequate use of international standards.

Possible action: encourage the use of international standards government-wide, and track the use of uniquely national standards. Issue guidance for translation of international standards into national practice.

> ### Box 1.2. **Transparency and predictability in investment policy:**
> ### **from principles to action** (*cont.*)
>
> **Policy issue:** lack of clear standards in licensing and concessions decisions, such as in telecommunications.
>
> **Possible action:** reduce the use of concessions and licences to the extent possible by moving to generalised regulation, announce clear criteria for decisions on concessions and licenses, use public consultation for changes in existing licenses and concessions.
>
> **Policy issue:** decisions of independent regulators not transparent enough.
>
> **Possible action:** apply RIA to independent regulators, ensure that independent regulators also use public consultation processes with regulated and user groups.

1.3. Protection of property and contractual rights

As quoted from the Monterrey Consensus in the introduction to the previous section, the protection of investment (including physical and intellectual property rights) is widely accepted as a necessary condition for the development of a healthy investment environment. Indeed, investment protection, which is a sub-category of the more general protection of property, is closely associated with fundamental human rights. Article 17 of the United Nations Universal Declaration of Human Rights states that "1) Everyone has the right to own property alone as well as in association with others" and "2) No one shall be arbitrarily deprived of his property". Article 27(2) of the Declaration also holds relevance from a broader investment perspective: "Everyone has the right to the protection of the moral and material interests resulting from any scientific, literary or artistic production of which he is the author."

The protection of such rights, within the broader context of efforts aimed at developing a sound legal framework and judiciary system,[1] including with respect to private investment, have also been closely linked to economic development. Research by the World Bank in Poland, Russia, Slovakia and Ukraine shows that entrepreneurs who believe their property rights are secure reinvest between 14 and 40 per cent more of their profits than those who do not enjoy secure property rights. Likewise, farmers in Ghana and Nicaragua invest up to 8 per cent more in their land when their rights to it are secure. Indeed, the development literature strongly supports a positive relationship between property rights and growth.[2] With respect to the protection of investment, two broad policy areas stand out.[3] These are; 1) the promotion and protection of property rights, and 2) contract enforcement, including timely and adequate compensation for expropriations.

1.3.1. *The promotion and protection of physical property rights*

> **What steps has the government taken towards the progressive establishment of timely, secure and effective methods of ownership registration for land and other forms of property?**

Secure, transferable rights to agricultural and other types of land and other forms of property are an important pre-requisite for a healthy investment environment and an important incentive for investors and entrepreneurs to shift into the formal economy. They are also a fundamental element in building a credible corporate governance framework (for further details, see the chapter on corporate governance). They entitle the investor to participate in the eventual profits that derive from an investment and reduce the risk of fraud in transactions. These rights carry an intrinsic economic value and investors need to be confident that their entitlement to these rights are properly recognised and protected. Well-defined and secure ownership, including effective register of what constitute public properties, encourages new investment and the upkeep of existing investments. Land titles, for example, give an incentive to owners to promote productivity enhancing investments. Reliable land titling and property registrars also help individuals and businesses to seek legal redress in case of violation of property rights and offers a form of collateral that investors can use to improve access to credit. Improved access to credit lowers one of the main obstacles to new investment, especially among small and medium-sized enterprises.

According to the World Bank, the value of rural land in Brazil, Indonesia, the Philippines, and Thailand increased by anywhere from 43 per cent to 81 per cent after being titled. For urban land, titling increased the value by 14 per cent in Manila, by almost 25 per cent in both Guayaquil, Ecuador, and Lima, Peru, and by 58 per cent in Davao, Philippines. Titling land has also been shown to increase productivity. The output by farmers in Thailand who enjoyed clear ownership was 14-25 per cent higher than those working untitled land.[4]

Titling can also improve access to credit since registered title allows lenders to verify ownership for the purposes of collateral. For example, in Thailand, farmers with title borrowed anywhere from 50 per cent to five times more from banks and other institutional lenders than farmers with identical land in quality but without title. For people living in urban areas, the access to credit afforded by title provides important support for entrepreneurs and micro-enterprises. In this regard, the titling of automobiles, equipment, machinery and other valuable forms of "movable" property can help to bolster credit and investment in the same way as the titling of land. In 2000, Indonesia established a title registry for movable assets. In 2003, 12 000 interests in vehicles, machinery and other forms of property covered by the new law were registered.[5]

On a larger scale, the example of the Compania Peruana de Teléfonos (CPT) provides an indication of the potential economic impact of proper title. In 1990, the company was valued on the Lima stock exchange at $53 million. The company could not be sold or privatised however due to a lack of clarity with respect to the company's title over many of its assets. After a concerted effort to reform the title system and to establish clear title over CPT's assets lasting 3 years, CPT was sold for $2 billion, 37 times its previous market valuation.[6]

The main conclusion from the above is that governments should maintain land and property registries with a view to encouraging investment and increasing efficiency across all segments of the economy, from rural farmers to large-scale manufacturing. In countries that do not have well developed land registries, the challenges can be significant and long-term political commitment is required (see, for example, Box 1.3 on Thailand's 20-year program to title rural land). Nevertheless, the experiences of many countries attest to the importance of promoting and protecting ownership rights to land and other property.

POLICY FRAMEWORK FOR INVESTMENT: A REVIEW OF GOOD PRACTICES – ISBN 92-64-02586-3 – © OECD 2006

Box 1.3. Thailand's 20-year program to title rural land

In 1982, the Thai government began a 20-year project to title and register farmland throughout the kingdom. The aim was to enhance farmers' access to institutional credit and increase their productivity by giving them an incentive to make long-term investments.

Just over 8.5 million titles were issued during the life of the project. Along with those issued outside the project, the number of registered titles increased from 4.5 million in 1984 to just over 18 million by September 2001. Studies conducted during the project show that it met both its objectives: titled farmers secured larger loans on better terms than untitled farmers, and productivity on titled parcels rose appreciably.

The success in Thailand is attributed to several factors;

1. There was a clear vision for the project, a long-term plan to achieve it, and a commitment by the government and key stakeholders to project implementation.

2. A strong policy, legal, and institutional framework was in place for land administration.

3. The project built on earlier efforts to issue documents recognising holders' rights to their land.

4. Registration procedures developed by the Department of Lands were efficient and responsive to public demand.

5. The public had confidence in the land administration system and actively participated in the reform process.

6. The interests that can complicate projects in other countries – public notaries, private lawyers, and private surveyors – were not present.

Source: World Bank (2004), p. 83.

1.3.2. *The promotion and protection of intellectual property rights*

Has the government implemented laws and regulations for the protection of intellectual property rights and effective enforcement mechanisms? Does the level of protection encourage innovation and investment by domestic and foreign firms? What steps has the government taken to develop strategies, policies and programs to meet the intellectual property needs of SMEs?

Intellectual property rights give businesses an incentive to invest in research and development, and ultimately lead to the creation of innovative products and processes. They also give the holders of such rights the confidence to share new technologies, such as in the context of joint ventures. Successful innovations are in time diffused within and across economies, bringing higher productivity and growth. Investment is thus, both a pre-condition for the creation and diffusion of innovation activity. The intellectual property right protection instruments used by governments to encourage investment in research and development include patent and copyright laws, which give the owner, for a pre-determined period of time exclusive right to exploit the innovation. How effective these instruments are in terms of encouraging investment in innovation activity also depends on how well the rights are enforced. Efforts to curb non-compliance, for instance counterfeiting, are therefore an important feature of any intellectual property regime. At the same time, intellectual property right regimes need to strike a balance between society's interests in fostering innovation and in keeping markets competitive and, especially in the case of essential medicines, in sufficient supply (see also chapter 4 on competition policy and question 8.5 of the chapter on human resource development).

A modest increase in the value managers expect to realise from patenting new products has been found to boost R&D by anywhere from 11 per cent in the biotech industry to 8 per cent in the pharmaceutical industry to 7 per cent in the chemical industry. This stimulus comes at a price. Intellectual property rights give their holders the exclusive rights to products and processes. During this period, holders are free to determine prices and output as would a monopoly. Intellectual property rights thus need to strike a balance between society's interests in fostering innovation and in keeping prices to consumers low and, especially in the case of essential medicines, in sufficient supply. (On the evolving debate over intellectual property rights, see Box 1.4.)[7]

Furthermore, different areas of intellectual property present their own distinct challenges. For example, with the rise of modern biotechnology, genetic resources have taken on increasing economic, scientific and commercial value for a wide range of

---

Box 1.4. **The benefits of intellectual property rights in developing countries: the shifting debate**

Traditionally, a limited number of developed countries in which a high proportion of the world's R&D was concentrated were the main "demandeurs" of strong intellectual property rights internationally. Four recent developments are helping to broaden acceptance of the benefits of intellectual property rights.

First, more firms in more developing countries are now producing innovative products and thus have a direct stake in the protection of intellectual property rights. In Brazil and the Philippines short-duration patents have helped domestic firms adapt foreign technology to local conditions, while in Ghana, Kuwait, and Morocco local software firms are expanding into the international market. India's vibrant music and film industry is in part the result of copyright protection, while in Sri Lanka laws protecting designs from pirates have allowed manufacturers of quality ceramics to increase exports.

Second, a growing number of developing countries are seeking to attract FDI, including in industries where proprietary technologies are important. But foreign firms are reluctant to transfer their most advanced technology, or to invest in production facilities, until they are confident their rights will be protected.

Third, there is growing recognition that consumers in even the poorest countries can suffer from the sale of counterfeit goods, as examples ranging from falsely branded pesticides in Kenya to the sale of poisoned meat in China attest. Consumers usually suffer the most when laws protecting trademarks and brand names are not vigorously enforced.

Fourth, there is a trend toward addressing intellectual property issues one by one, helping to identify areas of agreement and find common ground on points of difference. Although the issue is not yet resolved, an agreement at the WTO ministerial meeting in November 2001 reflects developing countries' need for access to medicine. Discussion is also under way on policies that would give manufacturers of patented goods greater flexibility to sell at lower prices in poor countries than in wealthier ones.

Source: World Bank (2004), Chapter 4.

---

stakeholders. At the same time, tradition-based creations, like folklore and the many forms in which it is expressed, have acquired a new economic and cultural potential, thanks to the multitude of commercial and dissemination options made available by the Internet and the global information society. Issues such as these have often called for international solutions. For example, WIPO has been working closely with its member States to clarify the intellectual property dimensions of these subjects. In order to identify and address the relevant intellectual property issues, WIPO member States established, in September 2000, a WIPO Intergovernmental Committee on Intellectual Property and Genetic Resources, Traditional Knowledge and Folklore (IGC). Questions addressed in the IGC include, *e.g.* access to genetic resources and benefit-sharing, protection of traditional knowledge, whether or not associated with those resources, and protection of expressions of folklore.

● The intellectual property rights regime is not only a matter of concern to large firms and multinational enterprises with significant research and development programmes, but also to small and medium-sized enterprises (SME). SMEs are a driving force behind innovation, yet their potential to invest in innovation activities is not always fully exploited. SMEs tend to under utilise the intellectual property system, partly due to their lack of awareness. (On the promotion of investment by SMEs, see also the chapter on Investment Promotion and Facilitation.) Measures that extend access to the intellectual property regime system may thus help to attract investment in research and development and to transmit the positive spillovers to society that such investment embodies. Governments can help by, for example: promoting a greater use of the intellectual property system; developing specific strategies, policies and programs to meet the intellectual property needs of SMEs; improving the capacity of relevant public, private and civil society institutions, such as business and industry associations, to provide intellectual property-related services to SMEs; and by providing information and advice on intellectual property issues to SME support organisations.

1.3.3. Contract enforcement[8]

> **Is the system of contract enforcement effective and widely accessible to all investors? What alternative systems of dispute settlement has the government established to ensure the widest possible scope of protection at a reasonable cost?**

Protecting and promoting property rights, including through the establishment of an efficient land registry system and a framework for the protection of intellectual property, encourages investment in part by giving owners confidence in the value of what they own (as well as confidence that they will be able to reap the rewards from any investments aimed at increasing values). This dynamic applies whether the property owner is a subsistence rural farmer or a Fortune Global 500 MNE. However, the value of property is only realised when it is involved in a transaction. This transaction could involve using the property as collateral in order to obtain a loan or it could involve the outright sale of the property in question. Indeed, it is ultimately the *possibility* of using an asset in a given market transaction that gives the asset its value. Therefore, just as it is important for the investment climate that title to assets be clear, it is equally important that investors have trust in the channels through which transactions involving these assets take place.

A strong link exists between the quality of the institutions through which transactions involving assets take place and the investment environment. The World Bank's Investment Climate Surveys, for example, show that in some countries the average time required to enforce a contract through the local court system can exceed four years (compared, for example, to an average of less than 50 days in the Netherlands). Bureaucratic and cumbersome procedures for dealing with commercial transactions effectively serve to undermine the benefits to the investment environment of any established property rights.

One solution to this problem has involved combining procedural reform, reform of the management systems in courts, and the increased use of information technology. In a pilot test case in Ecuador, this approach reduced the average time to process a case by 85 per cent (World Bank, 2004, p. 86). Another option that has yielded positive results in some cases is the establishment of separate courts specialising in only commercial transactions. However, such specialised courts require strong political support in order not to be "captured" by special interest groups or powerful vested interests. In Tanzania, this approach has worked well, in part because the new courts deal with banks and other financial institutions that provide strong support. Furthermore, this initiative was accompanied by concerted and successful efforts to gain the support of key members within the legal establishment.[9]

Another source of friction with respect to contract enforcement concerns impediments to alternative forms of dispute settlement. This is particularly important in countries in which the court system is characterised by the types of problems outlined above. In many countries, arbitration, mediation, and conciliation have played an important role in improving efficiency, providing parties to disputes a choice of the most appropriate avenue, lessening the burden on courts, allowing a broader cross-section of property holders access to some form of dispute settlement, and lowering costs. Both Colombia and Peru have established successful arbitration chambers through the Bogotá and Lima Chambers of Commerce, respectively. Courts continue to play an important role however, especially with respect to the enforcement of awards handed down by less formal dispute settlement bodies that lack the full legal authority of the judicial system. Conversely, it is also important that limits be placed on the possibility of "forum shopping", whereby every time someone loses a case in arbitration they simply take the complaint to the formal court system to try again, thus negating the benefits that less formal dispute settlement channels can bring.

Irrespective of the actual channels through which disputes are handled and judgements enforced, it remains that an effective system that deals with these issues in a timely manner goes hand in hand with clear property rights themselves in support of a healthy investment environment.

1.3.4. Timely and adequate compensation for expropriation

> Does the government maintain a policy of timely, adequate, and effective compensation for expropriation also consistent with its obligations under international law? What explicit and well-defined limits on the ability to expropriate has the government established? What independent channels exist for reviewing the exercise of this power or for contesting it?

A natural corollary of the protection of property rights is the need for compensation when a government expropriates private property in the broader public interest. This need is uncontested and, indeed, is reflected in many international agreements dealing with investment. The 1992 World Bank Guidelines section IV(1) on "Expropriation and Unilateral Alterations or Termination of Contracts", state that: "A state may not expropriate or otherwise take in whole or in part a foreign private investment in its territory, or take *measures which have similar effects*, except where this is done in accordance with applicable legal procedures, in pursuance in good faith of a public purpose, without discrimination on the basis of nationality and against the payment of appropriatecompensation."

Notwithstanding the widespread acceptance of the need for timely, adequate and effective compensation, the power of government to expropriate raises policy issues that

---

Box 1.5. **The evolution of the expropriation issue in international law**

It is a well recognised rule in international law that the property of aliens cannot be taken, whether for public purposes or not, without adequate compensation. Two decades ago, the disputes before the courts and the discussions in academic literature focused mainly on the standard of compensation and measuring of expropriated value. The divergent views of the developed and developing countries raised issues regarding the formation and evolution of customary law. Today, the more positive attitude of countries around the world toward foreign investment and the proliferation of bilateral treaties and other investment agreements requiring prompt, adequate and effective compensation[*] for expropriation of foreign investments have largely deprived that debate of practical significance for foreign investors.

Disputes on direct expropriation – mainly related to nationalisation that marked the 70s and 80s – have been replaced by disputes related to foreign investment regulation and "indirect expropriation". Largely prompted by the first cases brought under NAFTA, there is increasing concern that concepts such as indirect expropriation may be applicable to regulatory measures aimed at protecting health, safety, and environmental interests of society. The question that arises is to what extent a government may affect the value of property by regulation, either general in nature or by specific actions in the context of general regulations, for a legitimate public purpose without effecting a "taking" and having to compensate for this act.

[*] Some agreements use alternative wording when it comes to compensation, often with a view to providing clearer guidance on what should be considered prompt (*e.g.* without undue delay), adequate (*e.g.* fair market value), and effective (*e.g.* fully realisable and freely transferable).

Source: OECD (2005), "Indirect Expropriation" and the "Right to Regulate", *International Investment Law: A Changing Landscape.*

---

usually involve a careful balancing of interests and judgement on the part of policy makers, in addition to the inherent negative impact of expropriation on the investment climate. To avoid negative effects on the investment climate, governments are encouraged to consider whether similar results can be achieved through other public policy means. If a government decides to expropriate land or other property, this decision ought to be motivated by a public purpose, observe due process of law, be non-discriminatory and guided by transparent rules that define the situations in which expropriations are justified and the process by which compensation is to be determined.

Some recent agreements provide that except in rare circumstances, non-discriminatory regulatory actions that are designed and applied to protect legitimate public welfare objectives, such as public health, safety and the environment, are not considered to constitute expropriations. However, governments need to remain mindful that, consistent with longstanding international norms, certain regulatory action may constitute expropriation.

1.4. The international dimension of investment policy

In addition to the level of transparency and protection afforded to investors in the context of the domestic regulatory and legal framework, the quality of a country's investment environment is also strongly influenced by its international investment-related commitments. This section considers first the issue of non-discrimination before turning to some of the specific contributions of international investment agreements (IIAs) to the quality of a country's investment environment.

1.4.1. Non-discrimination

Non-discrimination, as a general principle, is generally perceived as being a laudable feature of public policy. In social policy, most governments have laws, often enshrined in national constitutions, against discrimination based on gender, religion, or race. In economic policy, most governments generally do not discriminate based on nationality and, indeed, the core principles that underpin the multilateral trading system concern non-discrimination. However, it remains that, with respect to investment, States' exercise of the right to regulate sometimes involves discriminating against foreign investors.[10] While the right to regulate is not in question, policy makers need to consider, beyond commitments to non-discrimination undertaken in international agreements, instances where discrimination in investment policy is either inadvertent or, when it is intended, whether it is the best option for meeting particular policy objectives. A core principle that underpins non-discrimination in investment policy is national treatment.

National treatment and MFN

> **Has the government taken steps to establish non-discrimination as a general principle underpinning laws and regulations governing investment? In the exercise of its right to regulate and to deliver public services, does the government have mechanisms in place to ensure transparency of remaining discriminatory restrictions on international investment and to periodically review their costs against their intended public purpose? Has the government reviewed restrictions affecting the free transfer of capital and profits and their effect on attracting international investment?**

The non-discrimination principle provides that all investors, both foreign and domestic, are treated equally.

The concept of "national treatment" provides that a government treat enterprises controlled by the nationals or residents of another country no less favourably than domestic enterprises in like situations. The OECD Code of Liberalisation of Capital Movements, for instance, provides that non-resident investors be allowed to establish a subsidiary or branch or take participation in an existing domestic enterprise on conditions equivalent to those offered to resident investors. The OECD National Treatment Instrument applies a similar principle for operations by foreign controlled enterprises once established in the country. Beyond this straightforward definition, however, the national treatment principle has been applied in very different ways by different countries and in different contexts. One of the reasons for this is that, while most countries generally acknowledge the benefits of openness and non-discrimination, all countries maintain exceptions to the national treatment principle and, depending upon the country in question, these exceptions vary. Exceptions to national treatment include across-the-board special screening procedures for FDI entry, more burdensome licensing requirements for foreign investors than for domestic investors, sectoral foreign equity ownership ceilings, denial of access for foreign controlled-established enterprises to local finance and incentives, etc. Common examples of sectors where many countries maintain exceptions to national treatment concern investment in financial services, land, and international transport.

The divergent approaches to national treatment across countries reflect governments' "right to regulate". Subject to specific commitments made in international agreements (see Box 1.7), governments decide which industries will be subject to national treatment and those that will not. Usually this choice is motivated by some combination of development, equity, and national interest considerations, all of which can be completely valid. However, as argued in the chapter on competition policy, and aside from the delivery of some public services, any policies that favour some firms over others (*i.e.* any policies that derogate from national treatment) come at a cost, namely a reduction in competition. The question is therefore not whether or not a government can discriminate between domestic and foreign producers, but rather whether the potential benefits of this discrimination are outweighed by the costs borne by consumers. Exceptions from national treatment need to be evaluated to ensure that this is not the case, as well as with a view to determining whether the original reasoning behind an exception (*e.g.* infant industry protection for an industry that is no longer an infant) remains valid. Such considerations are especially important in service sectors that play an intermediary role supporting a wide range of economic activities and that contribute to productivity and growth across the economy (*e.g.* telecommunications).

Like national treatment, MFN is a relative concept insofar as it entails a comparison of the treatment of firms based on nationality. To provide MFN treatment under investment agreements means that an investor or investment from one country is treated by the host country "no less favourably" with respect to a given subject matter than an investor or investment from any third country. As with the application of the national treatment principle, MFN commitments towards investment vary considerably across countries (Box 1.6). As in the case of national treatment, one of the main issues with respect to MFN pertains to the impact of exceptions on competition and the possible negative impact this can have on the investment environment.

Box 1.6. **Non-discrimination in international agreements**

With respect to foreign investment, national treatment and MFN are the cornerstones of non-discrimination in most international agreements dealing with investment. Indeed, it is only in international investment agreements that national treatment and MFN take the form of binding obligations. However, the ways in which these principles are treated in international treaties varies significantly from one agreement to another. For example, some agreements take a top-down or negative list approach, whereby the commitment to national treatment and MFN applies except in specifically identified exceptions (*e.g.* NAFTA). Alternatively, some agreements are characterised by a bottom-up or positive list approach whereby national treatment or MFN only apply to scheduled sectors (*e.g.* GATS). Distinctions are also made concerning pre- and post-establishment coverage of non-discrimination provisions. Many bilateral investment treaties have emphasised the post-establishment application of national treatment and MFN. In other words, governments have reserved their right to screen prospective foreign investments and to maintain approval procedures to determine whether these will be allowed. However, some governments have also started to include pre-establishment national treatment and MFN obligations in their international agreements (*e.g.* NAFTA, Canadian and United States BITs and Japan's recent agreements).

One issue that is rarely considered concerns the harm that MFN exceptions can cause domestic firms. This harm is transmitted through two channels. First, MFN exceptions reduce the exposure of MNEs to their competitors. However, an MNE with control over a given national product market could be more harmful to local niche players in the same industry than an MNE that has to compete with international rivals. The second channel through which exceptions to MFN can hurt local enterprises concerns the supply chain. Any MNE that is uncontested in a local market will be able to exercise "hold up", the practice of squeezing suppliers through its monopsonistic position and squeezing buyers through its monopolistic position. In this case, exceptions to MFN can lead to a situation in which the often hoped for linkages between international business and the local economy actually become a negative factor. Exceptions from national treatment can also give rise to the same problems, the only difference being that the firm practicing "hold up" and extracting profits at the expense of the economy as a whole is home grown.

Policies that favour some firms over others (*i.e.* any policies that derogate from national treatment or MFN) involve a cost. They can, for instance, result in less competition and efficiency losses, thereby damaging the investment environment. For this reason, exceptions to non-discrimination need to be evaluated with a view to determining whether the original motivation behind an exception (*e.g.* protection based on the infant industry argument) remains valid, supported by an evaluation of the costs and benefits. A broad consideration of the costs and benefits is especially important in service sectors that support a wide range of economic activities across the economy (*e.g.* telecommunications).

For a firm to be able to make, operate, and maintain investments in another country, the ability to transfer investment-related capital, including repatriating earnings and liquidated capital, is important. Many governments allow such free transfers, albeit without prejudice to their ability to take measures to prevent evasion of tax and other applicable laws and regulations and policy measures aimed at addressing serious balance of payment difficulties in accordance with their rights and obligations under their international investment agreements. Measures that restrict transfers can adversely affect investor confidence and, concomitantly, inflows of international investment.

1.4.2. *Making the most of international investment agreements*

> **Are investment policy authorities working with their counterparts in other economies to expand international treaties on the promotion and protection of investment? Has the government reviewed existing international treaties and commitments periodically to determine whether their provisions create a more attractive environment for investment? What measures exist to ensure effective compliance with the country's commitments under its international investment agreements?**

International agreements containing investment provisions are an increasingly common form of international co-operation. Bilateral investment treaties in particular constitute an important pillar of the international investment architecture. By 2004 more than 2 332 such treaties had been concluded, the majority of them after 1990. Furthermore, most modern regional trade agreements also cover investment issues. For example, the NAFTA contains a chapter on investment as well as a separate chapter dealing with services. Bilateral and regional agreements dealing with investment issues increasingly involve developed and developing countries, reflecting the perceived mutual benefits of investment promotion and protection.

While regionalisation is often characterised as a second best solution compared with multilateral approaches to international trade and investment liberalisation, regional agreements do have a distinct advantage. Most countries that have entered into agreements containing high-standard rules on investment had either already been liberalising their investment regimes unilaterally or had experimented with investment rules in prior agreements. For example, a number of bilateral agreements recently negotiated by the North American Free Trade Agreement (NAFTA) signatories (such as Canada-Chile, United States-Jordan) contain provisions almost identical to NAFTA's chapter 11. Where countries have only recently begun to liberalise their investment regimes and where these have traditionally been relatively restrictive, the preference has been for less encompassing agreements covering limited rights of establishment and the movement of capital. In other words, the negotiation of investment rules in regional agreements could be characterised as taking place at the investment policy margin. Countries at similar levels on the investment liberalisation "trajectory" can scale their investment rule-making ambitions in line with historical local norms on international investment.

One of the most important contributions of international agreements to the investment climate consists in the enhanced confidence these can provide foreign and domestic investors beyond the level of confidence the government has already promoted through credible domestic commitments. International agreements promote investment in much the same way as the protection of title to property encourages investment (as described in sections 2 and 3 above). International agreements tend to make it more difficult for governments to change certain policies since these are now part of a broader package of international commitments (*e.g.* a "single undertaking" like the NAFTA contains binding commitments on trade, investment, services, and a range of other issues important to investors). This involves some foregone policy flexibility for the government that undertakes such commitments. However, it also makes the regulatory environment faced by investors (both domestic and foreign) more predictable. For example, many

---

Box 1.7. **Performance requirements in international agreements**

Provisions are often included in international agreements that place limits on the ability of governments to impose performance requirements on firms. The WTO TRIMs Agreement and the NAFTA investment chapter are two prominent examples which have influenced provisions in BITs and other agreements containing investment provisions.

The WTO's Agreement on Trade-Related Investment Measures (TRIMs) recognises that certain investment measures can restrict or distort trade and provides that "*no member shall apply any TRIM that is inconsistent with the provisions of Article III* [National Treatment and Internal Taxation and Regulation] *or Article XI* [General Elimination of Quantitative Restrictions] *of GATT 1994*".[1] The Agreement's Annex contains an illustrative list of prohibited measures which include, *inter alia*, local content requirements and trade-balancing requirements imposed on an enterprise.

BITs and investment provisions in trade agreements. Provisions on performance requirements included in IIAs have been generally based on the TRIMs Agreement and NAFTA. This latter agreement provides that the parties may not, either in the pre or post-establishment phase, impose or enforce any commitment or undertaking requiring investors to export a given level or percentage of goods or services; to achieve a level or percentage of domestic content; to purchase, use or accord preference to goods or services provided in the territory; to restrict sales of goods or services; to transfer technology; or to act as exclusive supplier of good or services to a specific region or world market. Other agreements such as Japan-Korea BIT prohibit additional measures such as requiring to locate the headquarters of the investor in its territory; to achieve a given level or value of research and development in its territory; or to hire a given level of its nationals.[2] Exceptions to the application of performance requirements may also be included in these agreements.

1. See WTO TRIMs Agreement Article 2
2. See Japan-Korea BIT Article 9.

---

international agreements dealing with investment contain limits on the use of trade-related investment measures (TRIMs), such as balance of payment or trade-balancing requirements. TRIMs tend to discourage investment by imposing costs on firms (indeed, this is why they often go hand in hand with various incentives to invest). By agreeing to limits on the use of TRIMs in international agreements, the risks and uncertainty associated with these policy instruments is reduced (see Box 1.7).

Another important feature of international agreements concerns the channels through which disputes are resolved. Many international agreements dealing with investment, including most recent BITs, contain provisions that allow disputes between investors and host country governments to be resolved through international arbitration. For example, the International Centre for Settlement of Investment Disputes (ICSID), established in 1966 and with 155 signatory states,[11] allows firms from one member state to pursue their investment disputes against other member states through binding international arbitration. Just as a sound domestic system for contract enforcement promotes investment by bolstering the confidence of investors that their contractual rights are secure (see the section on "Contract enforcement" above), commitments made in international agreements giving recourse to impartial channels of international arbitration provide an additional layer of protection to investors and, most importantly, signal a government's commitment to the rule of law. Also relevant in this regard is the United Nations Convention on the Recognition and Enforcement of Arbitral Awards (the New York Convention), which makes arbitral awards rendered in one party to the Convention enforceable in any other party to the Convention.

Has the government ratified and implemented binding international arbitration instruments for the settlement of investment disputes?

A key feature of international agreements concerns the channels through which disputes are heard and resolved. Most international investment agreements contain provisions by which governments consent to permit investors to seek the settlement of investment disputes with the host country government through binding international arbitration (sometimes in limited instances contingent upon provisions on the exhaustion of local remedies). These commitments, giving recourse to impartial channels of dispute settlement, provide an additional layer of protection to investors and, most importantly, signal a government's commitment to the rule of law, bolstering the confidence of investors that their property rights are secure (see also questions 1.2 and 1.4). International arbitration is carried out through *ad hoc* or institutional instruments, *e.g.* pursuant to the 1966 Washington Convention on the Settlement of Investment Disputes between States and Nationals of Other States (ICSID Convention). The Convention has been ratified by 143 states and is supported by the International Centre for Settlement of Investment Disputes (ICSID) which), which administers arbitration proceedings under international investment agreements. The ICSID Convention provides for a self-contained mechanism, including enforcement. For non-ICSID arbitral awards, the 1958 New York Convention for the Recognition and Enforcement of Foreign Arbitral Awards makes arbitral awards rendered in one party to the Convention enforceable in any other party to the Convention and has been ratified by 135 states. There is a need to extend support for government capacity building for treaty negotiation and handling to governments that lack experience in dispute settlement.

Governments, including those in all OECD member countries, also consider that additional transparency in investment arbitration, in particular in relation to the publication of arbitral awards, subject to necessary safeguards for the protection of confidential business and governmental information, is desirable to enhance effectiveness and public acceptance of international investment arbitration, as well as contributing to the further development of a public body of jurisprudence. They generally share the view that, especially insofar as proceedings raise important issues of public interest, it may also be desirable to allow third party participation, subject however to clear and specific guidelines.

Notes

1. Including civil law, commercial law, codes of civil procedures, company laws, civil execution laws, etc.

2. See World Bank (2004), p. 79.

3. As originally identified in World Bank (2004), p. 80.

4. World Bank (2004), p. 80.

5. World Bank (2004), p. 84.

6. See De Soto (2001), The Secrets of Non Success (www.cato.org).

7. The link between intellectual property protection and competition is also addressed in the competition policy chapter.

8. This section focuses on contract enforcement in the domestic context. Section 1.4 extends the discussion to contract enforcement through international channels.

9. World Bank (2004), p. 88.

10. Conversely, reverse or positive discrimination measures, whereby foreign investors are treated more favourably than domestic investors, are also frequent when countries compete by means of preferential financial and other incentives to attract FDI. The issue of incentives is addressed in the chapter investment promotion and facilitation.

11. Of which 142 had ratified the Convention as of 25 May 2005.

References and Further Policy Resources

APEC (1994), Non-Binding Investment Principles.

Foreign Investment Advisory Service (FIAS) (www.fias.net/).

FIAS, Investment Climate Surveys Database (http://rru.worldbank.org/InvestmentClimate/).

FIAS, Private Sector Toolkits (http://rru.worldbank.org/Toolkits/).

International Centre for Settlement of Investment Disputes (ICSID), ICSID Convention, Regulations and Rules (www.worldbank.org/icsid/).

OECD (2002), Forty Years' Experience with the OECD Code of Liberalisation of Capital Movements (www.oecd.org/daf/investment/instruments).

OECD (2002), Foreign Direct Investment: Maximising Benefits, Minimising Costs (www.oecd.org/daf/ investment).

OECD (2003), OECD Codes of Liberalisation of Capital Movements and Current Invisible Operations: User's Guide (www.oecd.org/daf/investment/instruments).

OECD (2003), "The Benefits of Public Sector Transparency for Investment and Beyond", Public Sector Transparency and the International Investor (www.oecd.org/daf/investment).

OECD (2003), A Framework for Investment Policy Transparency (www.oecd.org/daf/investment).

OECD (2003), Assessing FDI Incentive Policies: A Checklist (*www.oecd.org/daf/investment*).

OECD (2005), The National Treatment Instrument (*www.oecd.org/daf/investment/instruments*).

OECD (2005), "Transparency and Third Party Participation in Investor-State Dispute Settlement Procedures", International Investment Law: A Changing Landscape (*www.oecd.org/daf/investment*).

OECD (2005), "Fair and Equitable Treatment Standard", International Investment Law: A Changing Landscape (*www.oecd.org/daf/investment*).

OECD (2005), "Indirect Expropriation" and the "Right to Regulate", International Investment Law: A Changing Landscape (*www.oecd.org/daf/investment*).

OECD (2005), "Most-Favoured-Nation Treatment", International Investment Law: A Changing Landscape (*www.oecd.org/daf/investment*).

United Nations Commission on International Trade Law (UNCITRAL) (*www.uncitral.org*).

World Bank (2004), World Development Report 2005: A Better Investment Climate for Everyone (World Bank Group: Washington, DC).

World Bank (1992), Guidelines on the Treatment of Foreign Direct Investment.

World Bank, Doing Business database (*www.doingbusiness.org*).

World Intellectual Property Organisation (WIPO) (*www.wipo.org*).

World Trade Organisation (*www.wto.org*).

ISBN 92-64-02586-3
Policy Framework for Investment
A Review of Good Practices
© OECD 2006

Chapter 2

Investment Promotion and Facilitation*

---

* This background document was prepared by Michael Gestrin, Investment Division, OECD Directorate for Financial and Enterprise Affairs.

2.1. Introduction

Although domestic firms are by far the largest investors in developing and transition economies, foreign investors are often particularly sought after for their technology, skills and expertise and for their access to international markets. Most governments, including sometimes at the sub-national level, now actively promote foreign investment through agencies mandated to this effect and offer a range of inducements to link multinational enterprises (MNEs) more closely to the local economy. The traditional aims of foreign direct investment (FDI) policy in terms of employment, exports and, to a lesser extent, import substitution still exist, but the overall emphasis in now much more on the contribution of foreign MNEs to the overall development and competitiveness of the local business sector.

This background document focuses on what steps a government might take to promote and facilitate investment in the host country, including that of encouraging any potential spillovers from foreign investment to local enterprise development, based upon experience in both OECD and non-OECD economies. It serves as background documentation for the investment promotion and facilitation chapter of the *Policy Framework for Investment*.

2.2. Strategic investment promotion: the overall framework

> **Does the government have a strategy for developing a sound, broad-based business environment and within this strategy, what role is given to investment promotion and facilitation measures?**

Measures to promote and facilitate investment can be successful if they take place within the broader context of an overarching strategy for improving the investment environment, which involves mainstreaming investment across a broad range of policy areas that affect the investment climate, such as those covered in the PFI. Developing a broad strategy for investment requires strong political support and leadership, both from the highest levels of government as well as from front-line agencies and ministries responsible for implementing policy. One recent study suggests that, without an appropriate business climate for investment, promotional efforts might actually make foreign investment less likely. Morriset (2003) reviews the performance of investment promotion agencies in 58 developing and transition countries in terms of the level of FDI inflows. He finds that investment promotion is more effective in a country with a good investment climate and can even be counterproductive if the country offers only a poor investment climate. "It seems more difficult to convince an investor to come back if he was disillusioned during his first visit to a country. The disappointed investor is also likely to be vocal about his disenchantment and, so, discourage other potential investors."[1] He argues that countries with a poor investment climate would be better off spending limited resources on the climate itself rather than on promotion.

However, once a country is establishing a generally sound investment climate, governments can take additional steps to promote and facilitate investment. Foreign investors by themselves might be slow to perceive profitable opportunities in the host economy, especially in smaller, more remote markets or those with a history of political unrest. They might also prefer to deal with existing suppliers elsewhere rather than take the time and effort to establish contacts with local firms. Active promotional policies by the host government can encourage both investment and linkages with local firms. A common institutional approach to such promotion is to create an Investment Promotion Agency (IPA) or other institutional facility. Not only can the IPA help simplify administrative procedures, improve regulatory transparency and focus investment promotion, it can also serve as a conduit for private sector input into the reform process itself. In many cases, the IPA is also used as a vehicle for expanding linkages between foreign investors and domestic suppliers.

2.3. The investment promotion agency

As part of the South East Europe Compact for Reform, Investment, Integrity and Growth, the OECD has formulated Strategic Guidelines on Investment Promotion addressed to IPAs based on practices developed in some of the most successful host countries for foreign investment.[2] These include:

- the establishment of an IPA or other institutional facility,[3] as well as its objectives and the relevant legislative and governance structures;

- to inculcate within the IPA a professional management and service culture, result-oriented ethos and innovative marketing approach in order to compete successfully in attracting new investment and to ensure satisfactory continuity of the organisation culture; and

- to define strategic policy options and set out the corporate strategy and marketing plan of the IPA to build competitive strength and achieve selected policy options.

Has the government established an investment promotion agency (IPA)? To what extent has the structure, mission, and legal status of the IPA been informed by and benchmarked against international good practices?

Centralising many of the functions of government relating to foreign investment promotion and facilitation within a single agency is a popular method of organising and implementing a government's strategic investment promotion policies. The World Association of Investment Promotion Agencies (WAIPA) had 188 members as of February 2006, compared with the existence of only a handful two decades earlier.[4] The life cycle of an IPA can be summarised as follows: 1) image building; 2) investment generation; and 3) linkage promotion. At the same time, the IPA serves two additional functions at each stage of the life cycle: a) information dissemination and investment facilitation; and b) policy advocacy.

At any given time, an IPA will perform all of these functions to varying degrees, but over time the IPA tends to reorient its resources towards the latter phases as the level of foreign investment increases in the economy. The principal aim of an IPA, at least in the early stages, is to draw attention to profitable investment opportunities in the host economy. Low levels of foreign investment are not necessarily evidence of a lack of such opportunities.[5]

Owing to limited IPA resources and faced with the almost limitless supply of potential investors promotional efforts have in some cases focussed on those firms most likely to invest. This requires an understanding both of how geography influences investment patterns and of "what investors are seeking, their view of the country as an investment location, the needs of their particular sector and company, the country's competitive advantages for attraction of FDI and how it compares with other countries".[6] An UNCTAD survey of IPAs found that they are focussing more and more on such targeting, to a greater extent than on either additional incentives or further liberalisation.[7]

Targeting of industries or even individual firms usually involves promoting particular locations to investors in specific activities. Such an approach takes time and relatively sophisticated institutional capacities. Targeting of the most likely investors can sometimes give way to an implicit industrial policy whereby targets are chosen based on a desire to develop certain industries deemed to be strategic. A discussion of industrial policy would go beyond the scope of this chapter. However, there is a need for caution when targeting potential investors because identifying specific industries that might emerge as winners has always proven a difficult task. Furthermore, to the extent that targeting provides preferences for some firms over others, this could also have negative implications for competition. Nonetheless, proactive strategies based on sound analysis of the comparative advantages and market opportunities of a particular market or country, perhaps even taking into consideration the specific needs of different types of investors (*e.g.* market seeking, efficiency seeking and natural resource seeking) remains an important policy option, especially for countries that have particular advantages that the broader international investment community might not be aware of.

2.3.1. Characteristics of a successful IPA

> **Is the IPA adequately funded and is its performance in terms of attracting investment regularly reviewed? What indicators have been established for monitoring the performance of the agency?**

Experience suggests that unless there is a full commitment to investment promotion agencies by the government, they are less likely to succeed in attracting new investors. They need to be adequately funded in order to attract and retain qualified and motivated staff, ideally with private sector experience. Experience also suggests that agencies with links to the centre of government and with private sector representation on the board have higher visibility and credibility and hence a better record in attracting foreign investment. They are also more dynamic and adaptable to changing economic circumstances, a critical issue for countries undergoing major economic transformation.

Morriset (2003) provides a number of insights into the characteristics of a successful IPA. Agencies with links to the centre of government and with private sector representation on the board have higher visibility and credibility and hence a better record in attracting foreign investment. They are also more dynamic and adaptable to changing economic challenges and opportunities, a critical issue for countries undergoing major economic transformation. Size also matters: Morriset finds that "small agencies are not really effective in attracting FDI".[8] A minimum budget is essential if promotion is to yield results. Overall, the author finds that IPAs can help countries to attract FDI: every one per cent increase in the IPA budget yields an increase in FDI of 0.25 per cent.

2.3.2. Investment facilitation and the one-stop shop

> **How has the government sought to streamline administrative procedures to quicken and to reduce the cost of establishing a new investment? In its capacity as a facilitator for investors, does the IPA take full advantage of information on the problems encountered from established investors?**

Long delays and costly procedures to establish a new business entity is one of the obstacles to new investment and entrepreneurial activity. Many governments have introduced reforms to quicken and simplify the process of starting a new business. One common approach to this challenge has been the establishment of a "one-stop shop". These allow investors to access information on the necessary steps to start or expand a business and provide services to speed up the granting of necessary permits and licenses. "One-stop shops" also provide easy access to other information that helps to facilitate investment, both domestic and foreign, for instance, on legal and regulatory matters, on financing options, location choice, or recruitment and training. "One-stop shops" make it easier for the government to centralise the quality provision of these services. This can deliver substantial savings in time and cost to potential and existing investors, thereby facilitating new investment. (on the positive effects of easing business registration requirements, see Box 2.1).

Investment facilitation is not just about helping firms navigate administrative barriers. Once the country starts to attract the interest of investors, the "process of country visits, negotiations, advice, legal and regulatory matters, visits with existing investors, financing, location choice, property, recruitment, training, and post-investment facilitation must all be provided in a professional way to the investor".[9]

Because potential investors often seek out existing foreign investors, particularly from their own country or sector, to ascertain their experience in the host economy, IPAs should also facilitate ongoing operations and expansion by existing investors. In an extensive survey of investment promotion in sub-Saharan Africa, UNIDO found that investors indicated that they were far more likely to be attracted to a location based on the recommendation of an existing investor. For this reason, satisfying existing investors should be the "centrepiece of any promotion strategy".[10]

As well as providing information, one-stop shops are sometimes conceived as a way to centralise the approval process for foreign investment. This was particularly the case in the past when investments were screened. But allowing one agency to grant all licences, permits, approvals and clearances has often proved unworkable. In worst cases, the one-stop shop becomes one more stop, adding to the red tape facing the investor. Governments

---

Box 2.1. **Easing business registration requirements**

Opaque and complex business registration requirements discourage new firms from entering the formal economy. Viet Nam and Uganda illustrate successful strategies for reducing these costs through simpler, more transparent regulation.

Viet Nam: before a new Enterprise Law was enacted in January 2000, business registration and licensing requirements were extremely burdensome in Viet Nam. Entrepreneurs were required to submit detailed business plans, curricula vitae, character references, medical certificates, and other documents along with their applications for registration. On average, registering a business took about three months, and required visits to 10 different agencies and submissions of about 20 different documents with official seals. Additional licenses were often required before firms could start operating. Some of these licenses did not appear to serve vital public interests (such as those to operate photocopying machines). It took 6 to 12 months to fulfil the legal requirements to establish a business at a cost of $700 to $1 400. The new law reduced the costs of establishing a new business. The time to establish a new business came down to about two months – with business registration taking only 15 days – and total start-up costs were reduced to about $350. Viet Namese entrepreneurs responded. Fewer than 6 000 new businesses had registered in 1999, but the number shot up to more than 14 000 in 2000 and to more than 21 000 in both 2001 and 2002.

Uganda: a recent pilot program in Entebbe reduced the time and monetary costs to register a business. By streamlining licensing processes and reducing the number of previously required approvals and assessments, the time to register a business was reduced from two days to about 30 minutes. This reduced the cost of registering a business by 75 per cent. Although business registration is only one of several steps to start a new business in Uganda (businesses have to register for tax purposes and many need additional licenses), the cost can be significant because registration needs to be repeated annually for most businesses. The pilot program increased business registrations, with an estimated four times as many businesses registering in Entebbe the year after the pilot. Despite the lower fees, the higher number of registrations meant that revenue collections increased by 40 per cent. With administrative savings of 25 per cent in staff time and 10 per cent in financial resources, the program also benefited the municipal authority.

Source: From Box 5.4, World Bank, *World Development Report 2005*, p. 101, based upon Mallon, Raymond. 2004. "Managing Investment Climate Reforms: Viet Nam Case Study". Background paper for the WDR 2005 and Sander, Cerstin. 2004. "Less is More: Better Compliance and Increased Revenues by Streamlining Business Registration in Uganda." Case Study Commissioned by the UK Department for International Development for the 2005 World Development Report.

---

are rarely willing to vest decision-making authority within one single organisation, especially concerning an issue as politically sensitive as foreign direct investment. Line ministries also resist ceding their regulatory authority to another agency.

Because of these difficulties, many one-stop shops have failed to live up to expectations. UNIDO argues that "no research or evidence has been found that [the one-stop shop] is indeed the magic solution for sub-Saharan Africa".[11] It proposes instead that the IPA should liaise closely and effectively with relevant government administrative entities rather than trying to internalise all approval and implementation functions. Nevertheless, an IPA that is conceived as a one-stop shop from the investor's perspective (in the sense that it acts as a liaison between the investor and the various branches of government involved) can play a useful role as a facilitator or mediator in cases of difficulty.

2.3.3. *Image building*

Image building is a foundation block in the process of attracting FDI. Its role is primarily that of focusing investor interest on the location and overcoming negative perceptions rather than directly persuading a multinational company to invest. Indeed, it has been argued that "the perceived investment climate is as important as the actual one and so addressing negative perceptions is an important part of encouraging investment."[12] As with any brand, the Agency needs to create an image of the host country in the eyes of

---

Box 2.2. **Uganda: from pariah to paragon**

The example of Uganda demonstrates how persistence and political will can pay off even in what are seen as the most unfavourable circumstances and where much still remains to be done. The Ugandan experience highlights the following essential features:

- Investment promotion should be embedded in an overall framework of liberalisation.
- Political support is essential.
- Consistency and persistence are more important than the actual state of openness.
- Investors will come even if certain elements of the enabling environment are still "under construction".

History has not always been kind to Uganda. Once dubbed the pearl of Africa, Uganda fell prey to dictatorship and armed conflict in the 1970s and 1980s. The economy was crippled, first by nationalisations in the 1960s and then by the expulsion of the Asian community in the early 1970s. Although only a small share of the total population, they were the mainstay of commerce and industry. In terms of investment attraction, Uganda is also hindered by its own geography: a landlocked country with few easily exploitable natural resources and located within an unstable region.

In spite of these drawbacks, Uganda has been one of the fastest growing economies in sub-Saharan Africa and also one of the most successful at attracting inward investment relative to its economic size. Investment promotion has been a crucial element in the country's development strategy but would probably by itself have yielded little extra investment had it not been part of a broad and consistent pattern of liberalisation which has assured investors about the direction the economy is heading. The Uganda Investment Authority has also enjoyed strong political support at the highest levels.

Uganda has managed to attract investment even though the 1991 Investment Code is "a restrictive and control-oriented regime for FDI, and if implemented to the letter or in an unsympathetic spirit, it could seriously deter FDI".* Under the Code, the government has the authority to restrict any investment it deems contrary to the interests of Uganda. That Uganda has managed to entice investors in spite of this potential for restrictiveness speaks to the importance of a track record of liberal implementation of existing laws. Nothing assures investors as much as consistency.

Not everything is perfect in the eyes of investors. In addition to weak physical infrastructure, firms complain of delays and corruption in customs and tax administration and a poor record in the courts of adjudicating fairly and promptly on commercial disputes. The lower echelons of government have resisted attempts to reduce their regulatory role as a result of liberalisation. But with a government committed to reform, investors are more willing to abide by these shortcomings.

* UNCTAD (2000), p. 22.

Source: UNCTAD 2000.

---

investors. This is particularly important for countries with little track record in attracting foreign investment, those undergoing rapid political or economic reform or emerging from a period of civil unrest, and those countries which are too small to attract the attention of home country media and hence are not even on the map for multinational investors. In this context, regional promotion can play an important complimentary role to country-level promotion since many prospective investors think in regional terms (*e.g.* "should we invest in South East Europe or in the Baltic?"). The recognition of this fact has motivated the growing interest in regional promotion networks.

While neighbouring countries often see themselves as competitors for FDI, it is more likely that successful promotion in one country will enhance the prospects for investment in neighbouring countries, especially in those regions which are less well known by investors. For this reason, there are often economies of scale to be had by undertaking certain promotion missions jointly at the image-building stage.

The evidence suggests that such image building can be expensive but that, with a good deal of persistence, host countries can succeed in overcoming negative perceptions (Box 2.2 on Uganda). At the same time, image building should not detract from broader efforts to improve the investment climate or divert scarce resources away from other functions of the IPA. Furthermore, image building does not only involve "grand plans" but can also involve addressing more basic "quality of life" issues, such as the quality of services offered by immigration authorities and agencies responsible for granting visas. The UNIDO survey mentioned earlier found that "IPAs in the region play only minor role in the process of awareness creation".[13] Morriset (2003), in a survey of 58 IPAs from various regions, found that image building does yield results in terms of attracting investment, but less than policy advocacy.

2.3.4. Policy advocacy

> **To what extent does the IPA promote and maintain dialogue mechanisms with investors? Does the government consult with the IPA on matters having an impact on investment?**

Most countries now accept that FDI can play a key role in economic development and consequently actively seek foreign investors. Support for such a policy among local consumers and workers or within the lower echelons of government is not always guaranteed. Foreign investment is often associated with more general market-opening policies and the private provision of infrastructure, both of which can prove unpopular within host countries. Allied to more general discontent, government ministries, regional governments and lower level civil servants have often resisted relinquishing their regulatory powers over foreign investors.

An IPA or a one-stop shop is not a substitute for regulatory reform. It can nevertheless serve as a useful exercise by indicating to the host government the extent to which business licensing requirements are cumbersome or redundant. It can also send valuable signals to foreign and domestic investors that the government is serious about reform and promoting investment.[14] A more direct approach to simplifying procedures would be to improve the efficiency of each individual ministry responsible for particular aspects of investment approval. In Tanzania, for example, a "no objection" provision in the Investment Code means that unless a ministry objects within 14 days, the Tanzania Investment Centre is entitled to approve the application.[15]

Investment promotion agencies can play an important role facilitating effective communication between investors and the government. As the interlocutor between the government and the foreign investor, the IPA is often the main source of feedback to government policymakers on the concerns of investors. Conversely, through its regular contact with government and the relevant government agencies, the IPA can be an effective communication channel for investors on government activities having an impact on the investment environment.

Morriset (2003) finds that IPAs which spent more time on policy advocacy were more successful in attracting investors, possibly because of the role of such advocacy in leading to improvements in the investment climate.

2.3.5. *Investment promotion through specific incentives*

> **What mechanisms has the government established for the evaluation of the costs and benefits of investment incentives, their appropriate duration, their transparency, and their impact on the economic interests of other countries?**

The use of financial and other incentives to attract foreign investors (also see the chapter on Tax Policy) is not a substitute for pursuing policy measures that create a sound investment environment, for domestic and foreign investors alike. In the absence of a solid investment environment, competition among countries for FDI may lead to no overall increase in investment and divert public resources away from more productive uses. In some circumstances, however, incentives may complement an already attractive enabling environment for investment or serve as a partial rectification for market imperfections that cannot be addressed by direct policy reforms. Nonetheless, authorities engaging in incentive-based strategies to attract investment must periodically evaluate their relevance, appropriateness and economic benefits against their budgetary and other costs, including long-term impacts on resource allocation. In doing so, authorities also need to consider their commitments under international agreements, since investment incentives can have effects beyond the countries that offer them, including bidding contests leading to a waste of resources. Many governments, including all OECD member countries, consider that it is inappropriate to encourage investment by lowering health, safety or environmental standards or relaxing core labour standards.

It is for these reasons that the OECD Investment Committee developed a Checklist for Assessing FDI Incentive Policies (see Box 2.3). The Checklist serves as a tool to assess the costs and benefits of using incentives to attract FDI; to provide operational criteria for avoiding wasteful effects and to identify the potential pitfalls and risks of excessive reliance on incentive-based strategies. The Checklist and its application to considerations of investment incentives can have a positive effect in minimising potential harmful effects of incentives both for those that employ them and for other governments seeking to attract foreign investment.

Box 2.3. **The OECD Checklist for FDI Incentive Policies**

The desirability and appropriateness of offering FDI incentives:

- Are FDI incentives an appropriate tool in the situation under consideration?
- Are the linkages between the enabling environment and incentives sufficiently well understood?

Frameworks for policy design and implementation:

- What are the clear objectives and criteria for offering FDI incentives?
- At what level of government are these objectives and criteria established, and who is responsible for their implementation?
- In countries with multiple jurisdictions, how does one prevent local incentives from cancelling each other out?

The appropriateness of strategies and tools:

- Are the linkages between FDI attraction and other policy objectives sufficiently clear?
- Are effects on local business of offering preferential treatment to foreign-owned enterprises sufficiently well understood?
- Are FDI incentives offered that do not reflect the degree of selectiveness of the policy goals they are intended to support?
- Is sufficient attention given to maximising effectiveness and minimising overall long-term costs?

The design and implementation of programmes:

- Are programmes being put in place in the absence of a realistic assessment of the resources needed to manage and monitor them?
- Is the time profile of incentives right? Is it suited to the investment in question, but not open to abuse?
- Does the imposition of spending limits on the implementing bodies provide adequate safeguards against wastefulness?
- What procedures are in place to deal with large projects that exceed the normal competences of the implementing bodies?
- What should be the maximum duration of an incentives programme?

Transparency and evaluation:

- Have sound and comprehensive principles of cost-benefit analysis been established?
- Is cost-benefit analysis performed with sufficient regularity?
- Is additional analysis undertaken to demonstrate the non-quantifiable benefits from investment projects?
- Is the process of offering FDI incentives open to scrutiny by policymakers, appropriate parliamentary bodies and civil society?

Extra-jurisdictional consequences:

- Have authorities ensured that their incentive measures are consistent with international commitments that their country may have undertaken?
- Have authorities sufficiently assessed the responses that their incentive policies are likely to trigger in other jurisdictions?

2.3.6. Facilitating linkages

> **What steps has the government taken to promote investment linkages between businesses, especially between foreign affiliates and local enterprises? What measures has the government put in place to address the specific investment obstacles faced by SMEs?**

Countries benefit from FDI in part because the intangible assets (proprietary technology, management and marketing skills) transferred between the parent and its foreign affiliates spill over into the local economy. These spillovers arise largely through linkages between foreign investors and local firms, whether as suppliers, customers, partners or competitors.

At the broadest level, the benefits from inward investment depend on the enabling environment. Open trade and investment regimes combined with an active competition policy generally provide a fertile environment for the transfer of technology. The underlying assumption is that the more a firm is forced to compete, the more technology it will have to transfer to the affiliate in order for it to be competitive in that market. At the same time, the host government can undertake measures to improve the absorptive capacity of the local economy in order to enhance technology transfers, such as through education and training and investments in human capital. "Countries that succeed in continuously fulfilling the evolving skills needs of industry will have a very strong competitive advantage in attracting new investment and moving up the skill and value chain in the type of industry attracted."[16]

In the past, governments have tried to mandate linkages through local content, local equity or joint venture requirements and sometimes even direct technology transfer obligations. However, increasingly policy makers are seeking to promote more "natural" linkages as, for example, through electronic databases aimed at facilitating business partnerships. One reason for this change in approach pertains to the generally poor results associated with enforced linkage policies. For example, when foreign investors are given a protected market as a *quid pro quo* for performance requirements, they have little incentive to transfer the latest technology to their affiliates, and local firms are often happy to partake in the economic rents created by protection rather than enhancing their own competitiveness through linkages with foreign firms. The same result of weak technology transfers can arise when the investor is forced into a joint venture with a local firm. When Kodak invested in China, for example, it was allowed only one wholly-owned subsidiary, while the rest of its affiliates had to form joint ventures. The result was that Kodak invested six times more in its wholly-owned affiliate than in the joint ventures, and the former ended up producing its most advanced film and camera technologies.[17]

Performance requirements have largely been supplanted by a more flexible system in which incentives are offered to the investor in return for the fulfilment of certain obligations relating to linkages. Investors are in theory free to refuse such obligations, although when they include exemptions from import duties, the export oriented investor might find its options limited. Nevertheless, some host country governments have successfully promoted linkages by offering positive inducements for firms to comply.

The countries most frequently cited in this regard are Singapore, Ireland and Malaysia. Under Singapore's Local Industry Upgrading Programme (LIUP), the Economic Development Board provides financial and organisational support for an engineer or manager from a foreign affiliate to assist local suppliers over two to three years. As of 1999, the LIUP resulted in linkages between 670 local business and 30 foreign affiliates and 11 large local enterprises, government-linked companies and government agencies. The general consensus concerning the LIUP is that "Singapore's approach, combining a targeted FDI promotion strategy with a linkage programme, has had positive effects on economic deepening".[18]

The approach taken by countries like Singapore and Ireland reflect the growing recognition of the vital role that small- and medium-sized enterprises play in any economy. These usually account for over 95 per cent of the business population, driving innovation, and underpinning sustainable economic growth and job creation. Conversely, they also tend to suffer most when the policy framework for investment is weak, they have more difficulties gaining access to credit, and they often lack the capacities required to develop relevant linkages with customers and suppliers. For these reasons, policy makers increasingly formulate policies that take into account the needs of SMEs and that promote SME development. Indeed, an OECD Ministerial Conference held in Istanbul, Turkey, in June 2004, focussed specifically on policy priorities for supporting SMEs. These are summarised in the Annex.

If Ireland and Singapore are generally considered as success stories, there are nevertheless certain key facts which need to be kept in mind by any government wishing to follow in their footsteps. Firstly, linkage programmes are expensive: the two countries spend over $40 million each annually, for a population of under four million in each case.[19] This compares with an annual average budget of only $450 000 among the 58 IPAs surveyed by Morriset (2003). Secondly, the Economic Development Board of Singapore and the Irish Development Agency have strong powers within the government to shape and implement policy in this area. Thirdly, both countries have a large pool of skilled workers and of small firms with the capacity to become suppliers to foreign affiliates. The success of these programmes depends in large part on the active and willing collaboration of existing investors. By providing financing and organisational support, the relevant government bodies reduce the perceived risks to foreign investors from engaging in capacity building among suppliers.

2.4. International co-operation for investment promotion and facilitation

In the long run, support for improvements in host country business climates and technical assistance to develop local human capital and supply capacity in local firms will have the greatest impact on investment flows to developing countries. Development assistance by bilateral and multilateral donors provided over $20 billion each year towards business climate improvements in developing countries between 1998 and 2002. Much of this went towards infrastructure (54 per cent), followed by policy-based support (33 per cent) and technical assistance (13 per cent).[20] But such improvements often take time to bear fruit. In the interim, there are many measures which can expand both global investment and linkages with local firms.[21] Such measures have proliferated in recent years.

2.4.1. IPA capacity building

> **Has the government made use of international and regional initiatives aimed at building investment promotion expertise, such as those offered by the World Bank and other intergovernmental organisations? Has the IPA joined regional and international networks?**

Various international organisations participate in capacity building with regional IPAs (see Box 2.4 for the example of MIGA). In addition, the World Association of Investment Promotion Agencies (WAIPA) provides networking opportunities among IPAs and facilitates the exchange of best practice. WAIPA also assists IPAs in advising their respective governments on the formulation of appropriate investment promotion strategies.

The Foreign Investment Advisory Service within the World Bank Group provides investment climate diagnostic studies at the request of host governments. These studies look generally at the legal and regulatory environment in the country concerned, as well as competition policy, market structure and privatisation. They also examine investment promotion policies and institutions and direct and indirect taxation regimes, including investment incentives. In addition, FIAS investment promotion assistance consists of recommendations for a combination of policy, regulatory and procedural reform; institutional frameworks for investment promotion; and methods for monitoring effectiveness. FIAS projects include advice in the following areas:

- developing strategic approaches to attract FDI;
- designing the legal foundation for investment promotion;
- designing the organisational framework for national and sub-national IPAs;
- conducting surveys to help client governments better understand how prospective and lost investors perceive the country.[22]

Box 2.4. **MIGA's Investment Promotion Toolkit**

Recognising the many challenges faced by IPAs in their outreach efforts to investors, the World Bank Group's Multilateral Investment Guarantee Agency (MIGA) developed the Investment Promotion Toolkit. The toolkit is designed to support investment promotion intermediaries in achieving their objectives for attracting and retaining FDI. It serves as a handbook on investment promotion that can be used by IPAs, investment consultancies, sector ministries, international development organisations, national, state and local economic development agencies, and privatisation agencies, among others.

The Toolkit consists of nine modules: understanding trends and drivers behind FDI; developing an IPA; creating an investment promotion strategy based on the locations strengths and weaknesses; building effective partnerships with other organisations; strengthening the location's image; targeting and generating investment opportunities, including maintaining a lead tracking database; servicing investors, including visits, follow-up and aftercare; monitoring and evaluating activities and results; and utilising information technology.

Source: OECD (2002a, p. 41), based on MIGA.

UNCTAD publishes both Investment Policy Reviews and Investment Guides (jointly with the International Chamber of Commerce) in order to improve the policy environment for investment in the host country and to call attention to investment opportunities in that market. UNCTAD's Advisory Services on Investment and Training (ASIT) has 30 years of experience in providing training aimed at increasing the capacity of developing and transition economies to attract and benefit from FDI. ASIT services cover investment policies, enabling legal and regulatory frameworks for investment, and investment promotion strategies.

UNIDO has an active technical assistance programme with sub-Saharan IPAs. The UNIDO-Africa Investment Promotion Agency Network comprises sub-Saharan IPAs, UNIDO offices and an advisory panel from the private sector. The Network is a working group which explores practical, low cost schemes to improve the effectiveness of its member agencies in mobilising domestic and foreign investment. It is also a permanent platform for training, capacity building and continuous linkage to UNIDO's worldwide network of Investment and Technology Promotion Offices.

Other examples of regional initiatives working with IPAs are the South East Europe Compact for Reform, Investment, Integrity and Growth ("The Investment Compact") and the MENA-OECD Investment Programme. The MENA-OECD Investment Programme is working with MENA IPAs as key actors to improve the investment framework and promote a more positive image of the region. Apart from their concrete project oriented work, key challenges for IPAs in the MENA region remain the provision of effective policy advocacy in areas such as changes in regulatory frameworks, enactment of investment-friendly policies, building competitive sectoral strategies, effective investor targeting, the provision of post-investment services, and promoting linkages between international and domestic investors.

In addition to the various programmes mentioned above, many other initiatives are bilateral. For example, the Japan International Cooperation Agency (JICA) regularly sends experts to ASEAN and Eastern European countries' IPAs to provide technical assistance. As part of the MEDA co-operation programme between the European Union and ten partner states in the south and east Mediterranean, the European Commission supports the ANIMA project, which aims at developing a Euro-Mediterranean network of IPAs.[23] The ultimate goal of the project is to increase foreign direct investment in the Mediterranean region from either the EU or other Mediterranean countries through a reinforcement of the capabilities of the MEDA IPAs.

Faced with this plethora of training programmes, IPAs are not lacking advice on how to adopt best practices elsewhere. But resources are often limited and choices have to be made, and it is not necessarily clear that all countries can pursue the same strategies. More empirical work is needed to help IPAs choose among the tools available to promote investment. In addition, Morriset (2003) demonstrates that IPA effectiveness in investment generation is partly a function of external factors: the local business climate, the degree of political support and the resources available. IPA promotion can doubtless be made more efficient and focused, but such training and advice should not divert attention from the broader policy environment in which the IPA operates.

2.4.2. Promoting linkages

> **To what extent has the government taken advantage of information exchange networks for promoting investment?**

International agreements promoting technology transfer

International agreements can be used to foster greater linkages. In the area of intellectual property, the TRIPs Agreement contains specific provisions for technology transfer. Article 66(2) requires developed country members to "provide incentives to enterprises and institutions in their territories for the purpose of promoting and encouraging technology transfer to least developed country members in order to enable them to create a sound and viable technological base".

The OECD Guidelines for Multinational Enterprises represent a political commitment on the part of adhering governments to promote observance of their recommendations for MNEs based in any signatory country and operating anywhere in the world. They provide government-backed voluntary principles of good corporate conduct and include procedures for implementation and follow-up. Under the Guidelines, enterprises should: 1) encourage local capacity building through close co-operation with the local community, including business interests, as well as developing the enterprise's activities in domestic and foreign markets, consistent with the need for sound commercial practice; 2) encourage human capital formation, in particular by creating employment opportunities and facilitating training opportunities for employees; and 3) adopt, where practicable in the course of their business activities, practices that permit the transfer and rapid diffusion of technologies and know-how, with due regard to the protection of intellectual property rights.

Matching suppliers with foreign investors

UNIDO Subcontracting and Partnership Exchanges (SPXs) act as technical information, promotion and matchmaking centres for industrial subcontracting, OEM and partnerships between main contractors, suppliers and subcontractors. The SPX Network provides detailed, standardised, updated and certified data on approximately 20 000 manufacturing companies worldwide. To date, more than 60 SPXs have been set up with UNIDO's assistance in more than 30 countries. SPXs also organise "Supply Development and Upgrading Programmes" for clusters of small-scale suppliers and subcontractors to assist them in meeting the higher resolution quality requirements of major international contractors and buyers.[24] The OECD also provides South Eastern European countries with these sorts of matching opportunities to promote investor-local enterprise linkages.

Forum based activities such as the Tokyo International Conference on African Development (TICAD) process have also been contributing in this effort. The Asia-Africa Investment Technology Promotion Center (AAITPC) was established by TICAD in 2003. The activities of the Center are funded by the Japanese Government and implemented through UNIDO in order to promote Asian investment in Africa by providing opportunities between businesses in the two regions. Recently, the TICAD process established a network to facilitate exchanges of business-related information via information technologies (the

TICAD Exchange Web site) and interaction in both public and private sectors for the promotion of trade and investment between Asia and Africa.

2.5. Conclusion

Investment promotion and facilitation measures can make a difference. Multinational enterprises are sometimes slow to spot profitable investment opportunities and often hesitate before using local suppliers. But successful promotion is expensive and resources need to be used wisely. Some IPA roles are more useful than others, depending on the stage of development of the host economy and the existing stock of FDI in that country.

Investment promotion should complement, not compensate, for a poor investment climate. Without a suitable enabling environment, promotion might even be counterproductive. Similarly, under funded IPAs might also make matters worse since an ineffectual IPA reflects badly on the overall investment climate in the eyes of investors. Successful IPAs are characterised by private sector involvement in its activities and strong political support. One-stop shops are not effective, if they do not help to simplify regulations and mandate a rapid response to investor requests from each relevant ministry.

The positive impact of an IPA may be indirect: through its role in helping to shape policy. The IPA is often the government interlocutor with investors and through its function as a one-stop shop is intimately aware of the complexity of local regulations. There is evidence that the more resources devoted to policy advocacy, the greater the inflows of investment. Agencies in poorer countries should consider also concentrating their efforts on addressing problems encountered by existing investors than on spending money on expensive advertising campaigns and missions to potential home countries. An existing investor's recommendation is often the best promotional tool.

Targeting of investors or industries is often a strategy born of necessity. Such targeting should be based on an assessment of those MNEs most likely to invest and with an industrial profile that best fits with the existing industrial structure in the host economy. It should also be based upon sound analysis of the advantages and opportunities in the country concerned.

Linkages depend first and foremost on the quality of local human capital and on the domestic policy environment. Investors can nevertheless often benefit from the matchmaking services of the local IPA, but such services demand strong institutional capabilities. Successful linkage promotion programmes rely heavily on the foreign investors for training and capacity building. They can only function in an environment of trust.

Notes

1. Morriset (2003), p. 19.

2. Based on OECD (2002a), p. 12.

3. Governments do not always establish a separate agency but sometimes set up a division or a directorate within the existing bureaucracy to promote and facilitate investment. All references to investment promotion agencies assume such alternative arrangements.

4. WAIPA itself was only formed in 1995.

5. UNCTAD (1999), p. 17.

6. OECD (2002a), p. 29.

7. UNCTAD (2004), p. 34.

8. Morriset (2003), p. 14.

9. OECD (2002a), p. 43.

10. *Ibid.*, p. 67.

11. UNIDO (2003), p. 66.

12. Commission for Africa (2005), p. 223.

13. UNIDO (2003), p. 50.

14. OECD (2002b), p. 136.

15. *Ibid.*, p. 101.

16. OECD (2002a), p. 34.

17. World Bank (2004), p. 172.

18. UNCTAD (2001), p. 177.

19. World Bank (2004), p. 171.

20. World Bank (2004), p. 191.

21. Within this context, trade preferences, such as the African Growth and Opportunity Act (AGOA) in the United States, and the European Everything But Arms initiative can play an important promotional role by expanding the markets to which countries benefiting from such schemes can export (which, in turn, can encourage investment). This topic is dealt with in the trade chapter of the PFI.

22. FIAS (2004), p. 20.

23. The Euromed countries include Algeria, Egypt, Israel, Jordan, Lebanon, Morocco, Palestinian Authority, Syria, Tunisia, and Turkey.

24. Liang Dan (2003), p. 83.

References and Further Policy Resources

Asia Africa Investment and Technology Promotion Centre (The Hippalos Centre) (*www.unido-aaitpc.org*).

Commission for Africa (2005), Our Common Interest, London.

Dan, Liang (2003), "Creating efficient networking and effective linkages in investment promotion", in Attracting International Investment for Development, OECD Global Forum on International Investment, Paris.

FIAS (2004), Annual Report, Washington.

FIAS, Private Sector Toolkits (*http://rru.worldbank.org/Toolkits/*).

International Finance Corporation (IFC) (*www.ifc.org*).

Morriset, Jacques (2003), "Does a country need a promotion agency to attract foreign direct investment? A small analytical model applied to 58 countries", Policy Research Working Paper, World Bank – FIAS, Washington.

Multilateral Investment Guarantee Agency (MIGA): Investment Promotion Toolkit (*www.fdipromotion.com/toolkit/user/index.cfm*).

OECD (2004), Istanbul Ministerial Declaration on Fostering the Growth of Innovative and Internationally Competitive SMEs.

OECD (2003a), Assessing FDI Incentive Policies: A Checklist, Paris.

OECD (2003b), Attracting International Investment for Development, Global Forum on International Investment, Paris.

OECD (2003c), "From red tape to smart tape: administrative simplification in OECD countries", Policy Brief, June, Paris.

OECD (2002a), "Strategic Investment Promotion: Successful Practice in Building Competitive Strategies", South East Europe Compact for Reform, Investment, Integrity and Growth, Paris.

OECD (2002b), New Horizons for Foreign Direct Investment, Global Forum on International Investment, Paris.

OECD (2002), SEE Investment Compact, Strategic Investment Promotion: Successful Practice in Building Competitive Strategies (Paris).

OECD (2000), The Bologna Charter on SME Policies (Paris).

OECD (2000), Declaration on Investment and Multinational Enterprises (*www.oecd.org/daf/investment/ instruments*).

OECD LEED Programme (Local Economic and Employment Development).

Thomsen, Stephen (2004), "Investment incentives and FDI in selected ASEAN countries", International Investment Perspectives, OECD, Paris.

TICAD (Tokyo International Conference on African Development) (*www.ticad.net*).

TICAD Exchange Network (*www.ticadexchange.org*).

UNCTAD (1999), Foreign Direct Investment in Africa: Performance and Potential, New York and Geneva.

UNCTAD (2000), Uganda: Investment Policy Review, New York and Geneva.

UNCTAD (2001), World Investment Report: Promoting Linkages, New York and Geneva.

UNCTAD (2004), World Investment Report: The Shift towards Services, New York and Geneva.

UNIDO (2003), Africa Foreign Investment Survey: Motivations, Operations, Perceptions and Future Plans – Implications for Investment Promotion, Vienna.

Us, Melek (2002), "Removing administrative barriers to FDI: particular case of Turkey", in New Horizons for Foreign Direct Investment, OECD Global Forum on International Investment, Paris.

Wells, Louis and N. Allen (2001), "Tax holidays to attract foreign direct investment: lessons from two experiments", in FIAS, Using Tax Incentives to Compete for Foreign Direct Investment, Occasional Paper 15, Washington.

Wells, Louis and Alvin Wint (1991), "Facilitating foreign investment: government institutions to screen, monitor, and service investment from abroad", FIAS Occasional Paper 2, Washington.

World Associating of Investment Promotion Agencies (WAIPA) (*www.waipa.org*).

World Bank (2004), World Development Report 2005: A Better Investment Climate for Everyone (World Bank Group: Washington, DC).

World Bank Private Sector Network (2004), Doing Business in 2005 Sub-Saharan Africa: Regional Profile, Asia-Africa Trade and Investment Conference, November.

ANNEX 2.A1

The Istanbul Ministerial Declaration on Fostering the Growth of Innovative and Internationally Competitive SMEs – Excerpts

Ministers and representatives reaffirm the need to support the development of the best set of public policies that will foster the creation and rapid growth of innovative SMEs. This requires:

a) Policies and an institutional framework that contribute to a business environment that is conducive to entrepreneurship and facilitates entry, growth, transfer of ownership and smooth exit of enterprises. These should be coherent at international, national, regional and local levels and should include:

- Stable macroeconomic policies and well-designed structural policies in areas that impinge on SMEs, such as competition, international trade and investment, financial markets, labour markets and education; and, as regards developing economies, embedding private sector SME strategies in broader development strategies and poverty reduction programmes.

- Enabling regulatory frameworks, which are developed taking into account the needs of SMEs and facilitating their integration into the formal sector; tax systems that entail low compliance costs; the transparent and equitable application of rules and legislation; simple and transparent licence and permit systems; efficient bankruptcy laws and procedures; understandable and coherent product standards in world markets; clearly defined property rights; fair and reasonably priced dispute settlement procedures; and light, predictable administrative procedures.

- Laws and systems of governance that support the development and diffusion of new technologies in ways that enable and encourage SMEs to take full advantage of them, notably by strengthening the science-innovation interface; ensuring the intellectual property rights systems are coherent, easy to understand and used effectively; and promoting access to and use of quality information and communication infrastructure and promoting the enhanced security and trust in the digital economy.

b) SME assistance and development programmes which are clear in terms of their rationale, objectives and beneficiaries. These policies and programmes should be:

- Based on sound research, empirical evidence, public-private dialogue and partnerships, and evaluated regularly for effectiveness and efficiency.

- Cost-effective and designed to encourage activity that would otherwise not have taken place and help SMEs overcome the effects of market failures, without unduly distorting market structures or creating barriers to competition.

- Designed to provide support to large groups of SMEs, including micro-enterprises, for example by helping them to: improve their management skills; obtain finance on reasonable terms; increase their capacity to compete for government procurement; have access to timely advice and information; enhance their ability to take full advantage of information and communication technologies; and improve linkages with other SMEs and large firms to encourage the emergence and development of innovative clusters.

c) **Policies that contribute to mobilising human resources** in order to promote entrepreneurship. This involves, *inter alia*:

- Developing a culture that encourages entrepreneurship and recognises entrepreneurial success. The integration of entrepreneurship at all levels of the formal education system can facilitate this. Formal education should be complemented by learning-by-doing activities and other practical workshops. This objective requires paying close attention to teacher training programmes.

- Promoting the diffusion of training programmes and lifelong learning opportunities by stimulating market provision of such services and, where the need exists, providing hands-on focused courses funded by the private sector.

ISBN 92-64-02586-3
Policy Framework for Investment
A Review of Good Practices
© OECD 2006

Chapter 3

Trade Policy*

* This background document was prepared by Jonathan Gage and Sébastien Miroudot, OECD Trade Directorate, under the supervision of Dale Andrew, Head of the Trade Policy Linkages Division. An earlier version has been published as OECD Trade Policy Working Paper No. 19.

3.1. Introduction

A country's trade policy influences both domestic and foreign investment and is important for any development strategy. Investment has long been recognised as a key ingredient to economic growth and development. This chapter explores how trade policy can:

- Encourage investment – both domestic and foreign. When appropriate, foreign direct investment (FDI) is the focus. The positive role of FDI for development has been recently stressed by the Monterrey Consensus. Trade policy is one of the main determinants of foreign firms in their investment decisions.

- Maximise the contribution of investment to development growth, in particular in the context of trade policy by encouraging technology transfers and other linkages that induce growth.

Section 3.2 discusses the changing interrelationship of investment (domestic and particularly FDI) to trade. Section 3.3 gives an overview of how trade policies can promote an attractive environment for investment (domestic and foreign) and the considerations of when this could lead to economic growth. This section uses a two-by-two framework analysing export and import policies for host and home countries. Section 3.4 concludes by outlining issues that policy makers may consider in formulating trade policy. Because the PFI is to be "an operational, practical guide for policymakers", an annex also details a trade policy framework focused on measures and techniques available to trade policy makers which may be used to assess whether national trade policies may reflect "good practice".

3.2. The changing interrelationships of trade, domestic investment and FDI

The relationship between international trade, domestic investment and FDI is complex and intrinsically interlinked. To begin, trade can either substitute for or complement FDI. Market-seeking firms[1] can serve foreign markets through export sales or through foreign subsidiaries. The latter effectively substitutes FDI for trade. But affiliates of foreign firms in turn create new trade flows with their parent companies or foreign suppliers and can also export to third countries or back to the home country, thus increasing trade. Trade can also draw attention to resources and markets that can highlight investment opportunities. Hence unsurprisingly, greater trade correlates with greater investment flows (Figure 3.1).

Domestic investment can also either substitute for or complement FDI. For a given opportunity, domestic investment may: become non-competitive with FDI; in the case of joint ventures, be used alongside FDI; or in the case of domestic debt, leverage FDI. The tendency when it is complementary (joint ventures or leveraging) is to increase economic activity and induce more trade for a given amount of FDI. Also to the extent that investment (domestic or FDI) positively impacts a host's economic growth, this can also have a trade-enhancing effect.

Figure 3.1. **FDI and trade correlate**

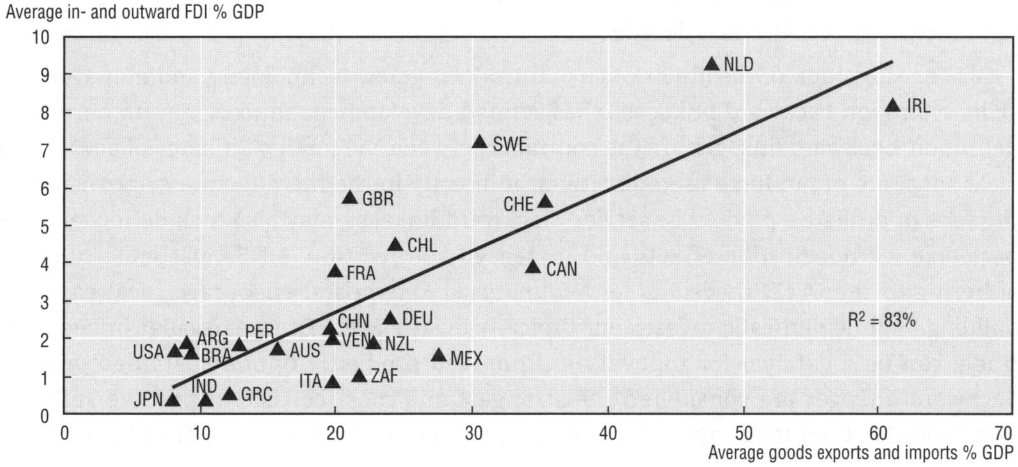

Average in- and outward FDI % GDP

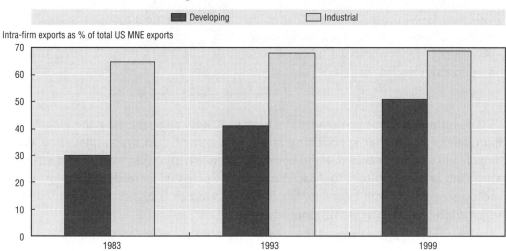

Source: Updated OECD 2002a.

FDI (and to a lesser extent domestic investment) can induce imports in the short term. An investing firm for instance building a new plant may require capital items only available (or cheaper) from foreign sources. Credit rating agencies evaluating emerging sovereign debt are aware of the impact on the current account and will at times discern between types of imports – pure consumption or non-performing investment *versus* capital imports for an investment that will earn its cost.

Increasing intra-firm trade between developed and developing countries highlights the trend towards more trade-intensive foreign investment. For instance, US MNE affiliates located in developing countries have increased their exports to other affiliates rather than to the parent (Figure 3.2). This reflects the new multinational enterprise (MNE) strategies of outsourcing and globalised production with a network of subsidiaries in various countries creating a "global value chain" (UNCTAD, 2002) and mirrors a change in the determinants

Figure 3.2. **Rising intra-firm exports of US affiliates in developing countries implies trade-intensive FDI**

Intra-firm exports as % of total US MNE exports

Source: World Bank, 2003b.

of FDI. Although market-seeking or resource-seeking investments still account for the majority of FDI between developed and developing countries, efficiency-seeking motives have increased over the past decade.

The recognition of the importance of introducing new technologies and management skills – through backward linkages – has refined development thinking. In its narrowest definition, backward linkages are the contracts between the foreign affiliates of a MNE and local suppliers of products used directly or indirectly in the manufacture or provision by the foreign affiliate's product or service. Backward linkages may also include movements of people, demonstration effects and increased competition. MNEs, particularly those adhering to the OECD *Guidelines for Multinational Enterprises*, encourage local capacity building.[2] While domestic investment typically dwarfs FDI, FDI in particular linked with trade, can be a catalyst for innovation, improved productivity and sustained growth. Backward linkages are considered the strongest and most consistent positive spillover (OECD, 2002a). Countries have introduced programmes to facilitate such links (Box 3.1).

Box 3.1. **Ireland's National Linkage Programme succeeded at a critical time**

Since the mid 1980s, Enterprise Ireland (EI) has been operating various linkage programmes to integrate foreign enterprises into the Irish economy. It pursues two tasks: first, to support Irish enterprises to build capacity, innovate and create new partnerships; and second, to assist international investors to source key suppliers in Ireland. EI collaborates closely with foreign affiliates, their parent MNEs, and the various government agencies involved with local suppliers.

Between 1985 and 1987, an estimated 250 foreign affiliates were actively involved in the linkage programme. During that period, affiliates operating in Ireland increased their local purchases of raw materials fourfold, from Irish £438 million to I£1 831 million, and more than doubled their purchases of services from I£980 million to over I£2 billion. In the electronics industry alone, the value of inputs sourced locally rose from 12% to 20%. On average, suppliers saw their sales increase by 83%, productivity by 36% and employment by 33%.

EI's matchmaking worked closely with foreign affiliates to ensure suppliers were *capable* of achieving the demand and quality requirements. One of EI's key criteria used for selecting local suppliers was their management team's attitude and potential to grow. Also noteworthy is that EI's matchmaking is no longer seen as so critical. The need diminished over time as the composition of affiliates, their motivations for locating in Ireland, and their local knowledge, changed. Ireland's competitive advantages in the global value chain became generally recognised.

Source: UNCTAD, 2001.

The influence of e-Business-to-Business (e-B2B) is also changing the global value chain. MNEs are further specialising and establishing e-B2B marketplaces to source components and services in order to benefit from substantial cost savings and efficiency gains.[3] This is an opportunity for host countries. The potential for technology transfer from "backward linkages" with local suppliers in host countries is higher and more worthy to pursue if MNEs start outsourcing more with e-B2B.[4]

With such expanding use of trade-intensive FDI and changing nature of the global value chain, host and home countries may need to be ever more diligent to renew policies to ensure that best practices are in place to capture value for their constituents.

3.3. The investment impact of trade policies

> **What recent efforts has the government undertaken to reduce the compliance costs of customs, regulatory and administrative procedures at the border?**

To analyse which trade policies could help a country foster investment and growth, policies affecting imports and exports in both the host and home countries are considered. A two-by-two approach has been used: the rows distinguish the export and import policies; and in the columns, whether the policies are being used by the host country (host of the investment project) or the "home" country. Home traditionally means the source of the FDI funds but where applicable, this definition is broadened to also generally include the recipient of the final product or source of capital or intermediary goods. This is assumed so as to explore the impact of FDI – or *domestically*-financed projects. The host and home countries are not necessarily assumed to be developed or developing countries.[5] Generally the issues are the same in developed or developing countries although sometimes emphasised differently.[6] Where appropriate, trade policies targeting developing countries are the special focus in this chapter because they are the host countries most in need of economic growth and the PFI is an initiative for development.

Table 3.1. **Two-by-two taxonomy of trade policies**

	Host country	Home country
Affecting Imports	Tariff and non-tariff barriers Barriers on importing capital and intermediate goods Restrictions on services Regional trade agreements[1] Customs administration, technical regulations and trade facilitation	Market access for host products Trade remedies Trade preferences Access to service markets
Affecting Exports	Export restrictions Export promotion strategies Export of services Custom procedures for exports	Export subsidies Export controls

1. Occasionally policies can be mentioned in more than one quadrant. Regional Trade Agreements (RTAs) can for instance be mentioned in all four quadrants. To avoid duplication, RTAs have been placed only in the first quadrant.

3.3.1. Trade policy in the host country affecting imports

> **What steps has the government taken to reduce trade policy uncertainty and to increase trade policy predictability for investors? Are investors and other interested parties consulted on planned changes to trade policy?**

Tariffs and non-tariff barriers (NTBs) on imports might attract, but will typically discourage, investment

High barriers to imports can induce tariff-jumping FDI – FDI as an alternative to trade. There is evidence that firms tend to substitute FDI sales for exports when tariffs are high.

However, empirical studies show that while tariffs were positively correlated with FDI in the past, they are now negatively correlated. This change is in line with the new organisation of international production where MNEs choose to locate their activities in different countries to take advantage of cost differences and scale economies. Tariffs and NTBs can negate the competitive advantages offered by a host economy and negatively affect investors' choice of location.

As suggested by the growth experience in some East Asian countries, strategic trade policies using barriers can also encourage (largely domestic) investment by compensating the firm for its adaptation costs and risk (especially when starting a new activity). The externality faced by pioneering firms is corrected by a temporary market power in the host economy. But nurturing such "infant industries" has problems: i) host governments must predict their *future* comparative advantage – a difficult task; ii) the industry must become internationally competitive otherwise resources are misused. Infant industries have difficulty growing up. Free entry helps rationalise the market and keep only efficient firms producing at world prices. Even the East Asian countries which adopted strategic trade policies and proactive industrial policies have resorted to open-oriented strategies; and, iii) host governments must have identified a market failure where investors do not see an opportunity – an uncertain practice. Other policy instruments are available to correct this externality faced by pioneering firms without resorting to trade policies which create distortions.

Restrictive trade policies also will weaken the positive effects of investment on the host economy. Barriers to imports, like other barriers to entry, can encourage the exercise of market power by firms (foreign or domestic) in the domestic market, which in turn is generally associated with lower efficiency, higher consumer prices and sometimes the use of "second-generation" technology. Therefore those FDI-induced backward linkages with domestic firms and technological spillovers will be less if there are restrictive trade policies. Moreover, small domestic markets with high barriers to imports hinder realisation of scale economies even further limiting the potential gains from trade and its interaction with investment.

Trade openness positively correlates with investment in most empirical studies. Sensitivity analyses of cross-country regressions indicate that trade openness is more likely to be correlated with FDI than any other explanatory variable.[7] Trade liberalisation encourages investment based on comparative advantage with efficiency gains through greater specialisation and dynamic gains through scale economies. Once impediments to trade (and FDI) have been removed, economic factors can become the main determinants of an investor's choice of location (UNCTAD, 2003). A commitment to free trade ensured by bindings under regional and multilateral agreements increases the foreign (and domestic) firms' confidence to invest in the host economy.

Barriers on imports of capital and intermediate goods can be particularly damaging

One important issue regarding market access concerns capital and intermediate goods. Export competitiveness of companies – particularly foreign affiliates – requires state-of-the-art capital and intermediate goods available at world prices. By providing relatively cheaper capital goods, international trade increases the efficiency of capital accumulation. It is acknowledged that high tariffs on inputs may prompt companies to increase local sourcing but at a cost. Domestic firms may not be competitive internationally and foreign firms may be dissuaded from establishing locally. This explains

Box 3.2. **Chile's tariffs: uniform and signalling with scheduled reductions**

Many developed and developing countries escalate tariffs – higher tariff rates for processed and higher-value-added products but with low rates for raw inputs, see Figure 3.4. They also frequently apply tariff peaks to specific products. Such is intended to encourage domestic production in these higher valued products and thereby support greater productivity and wages. Broadly, Chile does not use tariff escalation or peaking. Chile has a uniform applied MFN rate for nearly all products. This tariff rate has been ratcheting down from 11% in 1996 to today's 6% rate effective since January 2003, in clearly scheduled reductions.

The uniform tariff has several benefits:

- Distortions are created not only by the level of the tariffs but the dispersion. If Chile had a 20% tariff on beef but no tariffs of wines, then resources would tend to be reallocated from wine production – perhaps their comparative advantage – to beef which may be neighbouring Argentina's comparative advantage. Chileans may not have looked for, and diversified into, other competitive industries like say farmed fish. The reallocation and oversight could be averted if there was a flat 10% tariff. Disparate tariffs penalise efficient activities (often exports), foster inefficiencies and increase costs within the economy thereby reducing the country's overall competitiveness. Tariffs on imports can in essence be taxes on exports because of the inefficiencies and increased costs. A uniform nominal tariff will usually improve resource allocation and thereby raise economic welfare.[*]

- The uniform tariff is easier to administer. Customs officials need not worry about the tariff rates of different products.

- The administration is less prone to lobbying or rent-seeking activities of questionable (if not negative) value to the economy. It is easier for the Chilean government to reject pleas for special treatment.

- The process is less prone to potential corruption. Custom officials make fewer judgments of tariff classification which will affect the amount of tariff paid; the incentives for corruption are less.

- Disparate tariffs lead to local consumer prices which are distorted – i.e. that do not reflect the true relative costs of production in a free market. A uniform tariff levels the relative pricing amongst imported goods leaving conceptually only distortions between the domestic and foreign products collectively. Depending upon how much imported products constitute of all consumption, it could be a precursor for eventually adopting a flat-rate broadly-based consumption tax. Such a tax approach is usually deemed more beneficial by economists and may be the subject of other policy areas covered by the PFI.

The importance of a uniform tariff schedule has been recognised by some rating agencies. For instance, the Fraser Institute includes a measure for the standard deviation of the tariff rates, see Box 13.

By pre-announcing their schedule of reductions, the Chileans also were able to lock in a schedule which would allow their domestic industries (and foreign companies) to adapt. Such "signalling" allows the Chilean economy to adjust gradually.

[*] Some theoreticians argue to optimise welfare may require tariffs to reflect the demand elasticities of the products but this is more hypothetical than practical.

Source: World Bank (2003b).

why these import-substitution strategies have generally failed and been abandoned. To soften the impact on tariffs on capital and intermediate goods while maintaining some protection, duty drawbacks or tariff exemptions can be offered to exporters. These mechanisms can promote export-oriented investments but only if the system is administered efficiently without additional costs for exporters.

Particularly advantageous backward and forward linkages between foreign and domestic firms are more probable when barriers to trade in intermediate goods are low and local affiliates of MNEs are fully integrated in a global chain of production which uses cutting-edge technology. This is because advanced technologies are regularly embodied in the intermediate product imports. Hence local firms may see more opportunities to supply such advanced intermediates and frequently the MNE affiliates seeking to diversify their sources, will help domestic firms and their employees acquire knowledge and capability required for their manufacture and use (hence increasing the "absorptive capacity" of the host economy). This in turn will reduce the cost of learning other applications of this new technology and lower the start-up costs for other new investments. These backward and forward linkages can channel technological spillovers throughout the host economy.

Services are important for the rest of the economy

FDI in services now exceeds FDI in manufacturing (Figure 3.3). Many services are best transferred through FDI (mode 3 in GATS terminology, see Box 3.3). The rapid growth of FDI in services is also explained by technological progress and the globalisation of production which has led to an important increase in intra-firm trade in services (World Bank, 2003b).

On average, developing countries have higher barriers to trade and investment in services than developed countries, especially in telecommunications, banking and financial sectors (OECD, 2004a). Some empirical studies suggest that for developing countries, services trade liberalisation could yield benefits up to four times greater than liberalising trade in goods because its benefits go beyond the services sectors. Liberalising services trade can also help to promote trade in goods and facilitate the diffusion of knowledge in key sectors such as financing techniques (World Bank, 2003b).

Figure 3.3. **Trade in services and in particular intra-firm services trade is becoming more important**

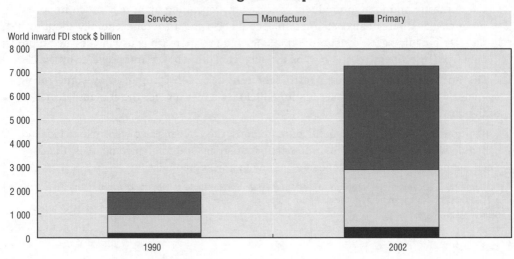

Source: UNCTAD, 2004c; World Bank, 2003b.

> **Box 3.3. The relationship between trade and investment as reflected in the GATS**
>
> The General Agreement on Trade in Services (GATS) is the WTO Agreement which defines the relationship of investment and trade in services. GATS defines four modes through which services can be traded:
>
> **Mode 1 – Cross-border supply:** the supply of a service "from the territory of one member into the territory of any other member". The service crosses the border but both the provider and the consumer stay home.
>
> **Mode 2 – Consumption abroad:** the supply of a service "in the territory of one member to the service consumer of any other member". The consumer physically travels to another country to obtain the service.
>
> **Mode 3 – Commercial presence:** the supply of a service "by a service supplier of one member, through commercial presence in the territory of any other member" (*i.e.* investment through the establishment of a branch, agency, or wholly-owned subsidiary).
>
> **Mode 4 – Presence of natural persons:** the supply of a service "by a service supplier of one member, through presence of natural persons of a member in the territory of any other member". Private persons temporarily enter another country to provide services.
>
> GATS mode 3 thus encompasses FDI as a mode of supplying services. Though mode 3 does not necessarily imply the presence of foreigners working in affiliated companies, mode 4 often accompanies mode 3 as the foreign firm may need to employ non nationals in the host country (for example persons from the parent company entering as "intra-corporate transferees"). Mode 1 and 2 can also be complementary to mode 3 when subsidiaries of foreign companies in developing countries are exporters of services to the parent company (*e.g.* business process outsourcing: a firm creates a subsidiary in a developing country to undertake database services and outsources the management of its databases to the affiliate, an illustration of developed country mode 3 exports leading to developing country exports under mode 1 and 2). Any effort to liberalise foreign investment in services (mode 3) may need to take into consideration barriers to trade in services through modes 1, 2 and 4.
>
> *Source:* OECD (2002c).

Among these key sectors, infrastructure services are of particular interest for developing countries. The low FDI in developing countries is partially explained by the inadequate infrastructure such as transport services, telecommunications, utilities or legal systems. Imports of infrastructure services (which are often FDI themselves) can compensate for the lack of local infrastructure and facilitate FDI.

The GATS schedules provide a useful framework for committing to liberalising trade in services. The positive list approach allows a host country to specify progressive, scheduled ownership and competition liberalisation commitments by sector. Some Latin American countries used this flexibility in their in telecoms commitments (Box 3.4). As noted before, bindings under regional and multilateral agreements can increase the foreign (and domestic) firms' confidence to invest in the host economy.

Having noted the *positive list* approach allows flexibility and degree of comfort to make such international commitments, it is not the only approach. A *negative list* approach – where the country identifies sectors and measures to explicitly carve out – holds out the prospect of achieving greater clarity about what is "in" or "out". For services exporters, it

---

Box 3.4. **Latin telecom GATS commitments "signal" liberalisation**

In the 1997 GATS Agreement on Basic Telecommunications, four Latin American nations committed to phased-in broad liberalisation in the telecoms sector doing away with exclusivity for fixed local and long distance services: Peru (by 1999), Argentina (2000), Venezuela (2000) and Bolivia (November 2001).

An example: Bolivia commits effective November 2001

Sample sector	Market access commitment
Local, domestic long-distance and international voice, data, message or video services for non-public use (services provided to closed groups of users distinct from the service provider): a) Voice telephony; b) Packet-switched data transmission services; c) Circuit-switched data transmission services; d) Telex services.	1) Until 27 November 2001, domestic long-distance and international service only using the ENTEL their local monopoly infrastructure. Commercial presence required for local services. 2) None i.e. not allowed/not meaningful. 3) Until 27 November 2001, domestic long-distance and international service only using the ENTEL infrastructure. Commercial presence required for local services. 4) Unbound, except as indicated in Section 1 the general limitations on immigration.

Modes: 1) Cross-border supply; 2) Consumption abroad; 3) Commercial presence; 4) Presence of natural persons.
Source: www.wto.org.

Amongst developing country regions, Latin America has the highest mainline penetrations, a measure of telephone availability, and that penetration has been growing at one of the fastest rates. In three of the four countries undertaking phased-in liberalisation, penetration per capita grew an average 9.1% per annum from 1993 to 2001 which contrasts with the lower 6.5% average of for instance Paraguay, Uruguay, Suriname and Guyana which made fewer commitments under the 1997 Agreement.

Signalling allows segments of the economy to adapt. Recent research looking into the sequencing of reforms: privatisation, regulation and competition, emphasises avoiding long periods of non-competition but circumstances might justify some "signalling".

Source: WTO; World Bank (1998, 2002b, 2004d); Secretarial calculations on World Bank WDI database.

---

may provide more transparency and certainty about the rules for doing their business. The negative list also offers scope to clearly and unambiguously carve out sectors such as public education, health, and drinking water. The preparation of the list also requires the government to carefully assess all their regulations for consistency with disciplines of national treatment, MFN, etc. which in itself may be useful.[8]

Regional trade agreements create larger markets

> **How actively is the government increasing investment opportunities through market-expanding international trade agreements and through the implementation of its WTO commitments?**

WTO-consistent regional trade agreements (RTAs) can help smaller economies attract domestic and foreign investment by creating larger markets and enhancing dynamic gains from trade. Depending upon the industry, such larger markets combined with economies-of-scale can make investment more profitable. In the context of global value chains (with MNEs producing in different locations), market size is no longer defined by national boundaries. Market size will also depend on the network of trade agreements signed by a country which no longer depends upon geography.[9] RTAs can generate both market-seeking and efficiency-seeking domestic and foreign investment (seeking scale economies for investors both inside and outside the RTA).

Tariff-jumping FDI can occur in free trade areas with high external tariffs but this type of investment is not necessarily welfare-enhancing if local costs of production exceed the cost of imports (World Bank, 2000). However, evidence on recent preferential trade agreements suggests that, in addition to their market enlarging effects through trade liberalisation, these agreements include provisions on other issues, such as investment, services, intellectual property or competition policy, which also significantly impact investment and trade. These modern RTAs show little evidence of generating tariff-jumping FDI.

Facilitating trade can concurrently promote investment and trade

Efficiency-seeking investment involves large volumes of imports of intermediate products and intra-firm trade between local affiliates and their parent companies. Average customs clearances for imports into India and Ecuador of 10 to 14 days respectively compare unfavourably with the average of only about 2 days for high-income countries. The costs incurred to satisfy customs procedures and technical regulations are sometimes higher than tariffs (World Bank, 2004b). Estimates of border procedure-related trade transaction costs (TTCs) for international commerce vary widely from 1% to 15% of the traded goods' value. Poor border procedures particularly which increase waiting times, can reduce the number and value of profitable projects dependent on international trade and hinder FDI and investment in general. Even before considering the dynamic gains of inducing such investment, the income gains from reducing TTCs are substantial and particularly for non-OECD countries. Using the minimum estimate of 1% reduction in TTCs on only the goods trade, gross domestic product may gain up to 0.47% on average in non-OECD countries which is seven times higher than in OECD countries because of the former's generally less efficient procedures and composition of their trade (OECD 2003c).

Improving the efficiency of customs administrations can favourably impact on investment decisions by domestic and particularly foreign firms. Transaction costs can be reduced by more transparent and predictable procedures, impartial and uniform administrative border requirements, simplified clearance systems, harmonisation of administrative requirements, the suppression and streamlining of unduly burdensome procedures, co-ordination, risk management and by introducing electronic customs clearance systems. Customs administrations in some developing countries have recently undertaken important reforms with some success in several instances (OECD, 2003a). Also the WTO is currently exploring trade facilitation rules centred on commitments for border and border-related procedures to expedite the movement, release and clearance of goods as well as the development and implementation of a comprehensive technical assistance program.

Trade facilitation is critical to attract investment (in particular FDI) and beyond just customs procedures and technical regulations. Better infrastructure for sea, land and air transport are associated with higher volumes of trade. Importantly, efficient ports explain bilateral trade patterns better than preferential margins. With regards to telecommunications, the supply response to reducing import tariffs on goods is larger the higher the penetration rate of telecommunications. Just-in-time supply chain management may require good infrastructure combined with procedure and regulation improvements (WTO, 2004). For investment in projects depending upon trade, such trade facilitation can be crucial as evident in Costa Rican's relationships with Intel (Box 3.5).

Box 3.5. **Costa Rica and Intel – Using trade promotion and facilitation**

The US computer industry giant Intel Corp. constructed a $300 million plant that began operation in 1998 in Costa Rica. A small country of only 3.5 million inhabitants with an industry-specific promotion and export orientation was able to lure a major player and build a world-class high technology "cluster".

Many lessons can be learned from this success but as far as trade policy is concerned, noteworthy is that the Costa Rican investment promotion agency (CINDE) used trade and investment promotion along with trade facilitation to persuade Intel. While Costa Rica listened attentively for infrastructure and operational needs and showered Intel with attention and information, many observers felt that it did not offer excessive concessions to Intel and when concessions were offered, they were applied to all other firms as well. These included waiving a 1% tax on assets (extended to all firms in the Export Processing Zones), upgrading road access, increasing the number of foreign air carriers allowed to fly to Costa Rica so that imports and exports could meet just-in-time requirements, tweaking the electricity pricing and power arrangements, and expanding the training in electronics and English. Such was to address "legitimate concerns" of Intel.

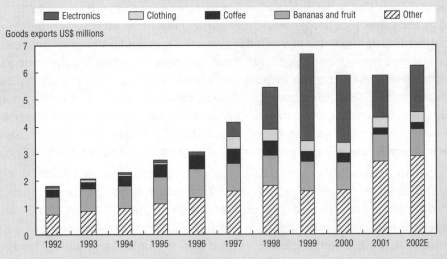

Source: Statistics Canada World Trade Analyser; 2002 OECD Estimates.

Although Intel was not the first electronic foreign investor, it has been the catalyst: Intel's arrival dramatically reduced the perceived risk for new investors. With Intel, numerous other companies such as ACER, ALCATEL, Baxter Healthcare, Panasonic, Lucent, Conair, Siemens, and Hitachi, have diversified Costa Rica's economy away from its bananas and coffee dependence. Even though chip prices declined rapidly in 2000 and Intel retooled in 2001, revenues have been coming back. Electronics represent about one-third of Costa Rica's exports in 2002.

Source: World Bank FIAS 1998 Occasional Paper 11.

In building infrastructure, a host country may consider public-private partnerships (PPPs). PPPs have been used successfully for clearly defined projects with (or arranged) attributable and delineated revenue. PPPs can be particularly attractive for public entities under tight fiscal constraints and additionally if the private partner brings expertise to the project. Risks, costs and profits can be shared between the public and private entities. Such FDI can foster competition but with the host's influence on ownership control. In particular, PPPs can promote trade in services in sectors where public authorities want to remain in charge of the sector opened to private participation. They have been used as an effective tool to promote private investment in sectors of public interest. When competition is opened to foreign companies, PPPs encourage new trade flows through contracts between public and governmental entities and foreign companies.

3.3.2. Trade policy in host country affecting exports

Anti-export bias can discourage investment

Although using quantitative restrictions is generally prohibited by WTO Agreements, some export restrictions such as licensing or export permits still exist in countries for some products (OECD, 2003c). These policies create an anti-export bias that discourages investment, especially export-oriented FDI which is potentially the most beneficial for the host economy.[10]

Export promotion strategies can help attract investment

Export orientation attracts FDI and FDI contributes to export competitiveness. Costa Rica (Box 3.5) combined trade facilitation and export promotion to what many acknowledge as a beneficial outcome. Because developing countries can have difficulties launching new exports where they have a comparative advantage, export promotion policies are often proactive. Care is needed to ensure concessions (if any) are not excessive. An appropriate export promotion strategy may need to be "trade neutral" or "bias free" and does not necessarily imply government support measures. Trade neutral policies which remove anti-export bias may be sufficient to attract export-oriented investment.

Some countries have policies to target export-oriented FDI in sectors with potentially high productivity gains and backward/forward linkages with domestic firms. This strategy could be justified on the grounds of trade theory once scale economies and dynamic gains of trade are accounted for. However:

- Trade policy is generally not regarded as a first best instrument to target investors because it can induce costly trade distortions.
- WTO's Agreement on Trade-Related Investment Measures (TRIMs) prohibits members from using local content or trade balancing requirements to enforce backward linkages.
- WTO members are also subject to the Agreement on Subsidies and Countervailing Measures (SCM) which prohibits linking subsidies to export requirements.
- Several regional trade and bilateral investment agreements prohibit mandatory export or technology transfer requirements.[11]
- Empirical evidence on the effectiveness of export and technology transfer requirements is mixed. Several studies have concluded local content requirements can be costly and inefficient in terms of resource allocation and growth (UNCTAD, 2004b).

Box 3.6. **Banning log exports is unlikely to induce FDI**

Timber-producing nations have enacted bans on export of logs arguing that this will expand downstream wood processing, improve the scale efficiency of domestic processing, create jobs, retain more value-added nationally and reduce deforestation.

The evidence has not been good for the industrialisation strategy. Cambodia's forest product output fell 40% in one year after imposing a log export ban in 1995 and has shrunk since. Bans on log exports at various times in Malaysia have increased wood-based manufacturing but some observers note there has been little evidence that most of these industries are ever going to become internationally competitive, meaning that they constitute a welfare loss. One estimate of the impact of eliminating the Costa Rican log ban, suggests it would be pareto improving and could generate $14 million per year in economic gains.

The domestic value added of sawmilling is frequently negative at world prices in economies with log export bans. Sawmilling $100 of logs locally in Indonesia has been estimated to net $85 of lumber after the expenses of milling. Such will not induce FDI. Either the domestic mills are inefficient behind protectionist barriers and/or they may be cutting species or grades ill-suited for their mills. The latter problem disappears if mills can trade for logs.

Such log bans also lowers the value of standing timber due to the market constraint imposed by the log export ban. There is a pool of pension investment capital well suited for the long term capital appreciation dynamics of owning timberlands. Institutional investment in timberland increased from about $1 billion in 1989 to about $14.4 billion in 2002.[*] This potential source of FDI will generally view log export bans unfavourably.

Empirical evidence also has not been encouraging for the impact of log export bans on forest conservation. For trade liberalisation to increase resource overexploitation and be damaging to welfare may require that the resources are a common pool subject to open access. As integrated forest management schemes are increasingly strengthened in recognition of the problem of the commons, such a scenario is becoming rarer. At best, a log export ban is a second-best policy tool for reducing deforestation and addressing the associated environmental externalities.

[*]   Timberland investment management organisations based in the USA currently manage over 18 million acres of land valued at over $14.4 billion, including international holdings (*http://research.yale.edu*).

Source: FAO database; Kishor *et al.*, "Economic and Environmental Benefits of Eliminating Log Export Bans – The Case of Costa Rica" The World Economy, Apr. 2004; Pearce, *Ready for a Change – Crisis and Opportunity in the Coastal Forest Industry*, Nov. 2001; Ferreira, "Trade Policy and Natural Resource Use: The Case for a Quantitative Restriction", University College Dublin; Sundaram and Rock, "Resource Exports And Resource Processing For Export In Southeast Asia", UNU, Tokyo.

Export processing zones (EPZs) enable a country to liberalise trade in a limited area and to grant specific advantages to exporting firms (such as tax and administrative regulations). EPZs have been created in many developing countries to attract FDI with mixed results for the host economy.[12] Besides EPZs there are other forms of selective liberalisation to try to attract foreign investors while continuing to protect domestic producers from foreign competition. Some countries have succeeded by following this type of strategy but others have not.

How are trade policies that favour investment in some industries and discourage it in others reviewed with a view to reducing the costs associated with these distortions?

Exports of services can be particularly beneficial for developing countries

Developing countries have important export potential in services (UNCTAD, 2002). Besides tourism, some developing countries have been particularly successful in sectors such as port and shipping services, audiovisual services, construction services and health services (OECD, 2004a). As exemplified by India's software industry, computer and related services (Box 3.7 and other highly-skilled activities can also be of export interest to developing countries.)These service exports often build on FDI. Many of the firms in

---

Box 3.7. **International business service outsourcing to India has created value**

India's $1.5 billion outsourcing business illustrates how foreign investment and trade have benefited the country. Along with IT and software, business-process outsourcing is perhaps the most open sector. In 2002, it attracted 15 per cent of total foreign direct investment and accounted for 10 per cent of all exports. By 2008, it is expected to attract one-third of all foreign direct investment and to generate $60 billion a year in exports, creating nearly a million new jobs in the process.

Being a liberalised sector combined with some investments by a few key MNEs, the outsourcing industry took off. Pioneers such as British Airways, GE and Citigroup were among the first to move IT and other back-office operations to India (entered 1996, 1997 and 1998 respectively). The success of these companies demonstrated that the country was a credible outsourcing destination. The MNEs trained thousands of local workers, many of whom transferred their skills to Indian companies that began in response. For instance, Tata Consultancy Services, recently went public in India valuing the company at $8.8 billion with $1.2 billion in total revenues (growing at 30% per annum since 1997 and of which more than 90% are exports) and 28 000 employees (growing at 17% p.a.). Now Indian outsourcing firms control over half of the intensely competitive global IT and back-office outsourcing market. Many of the leading ones started as joint ventures or subsidiaries of MNEs or were founded by managers who had worked for them.

Liberalised sectors have grown faster and business process outsourcing has taken off

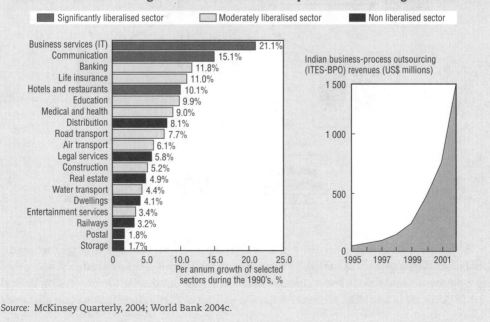

Source: McKinsey Quarterly, 2004; World Bank 2004c.

Box 3.8. **Singapore's trade and documentation logistics is becoming even more integrated**

Exporting using traditional shipping documentation is a complex and lengthy process and can involve as many as 25 different parties and 30-40 different trade documents including bookings, shipping instructions, bills of lading, letters of credit, government permits, etc. One UN study reports up to 60-70% of the data used in one form is re-keyed into another form.

The current logistics documentation

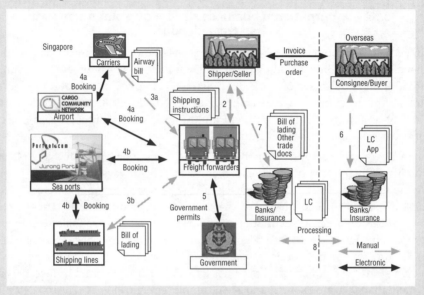

The future

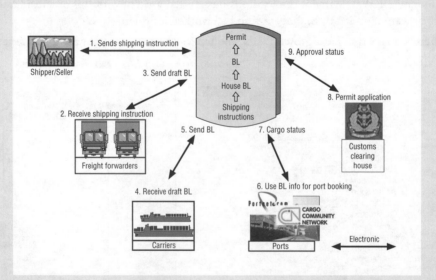

Singapore developed in 1989 the world's first nationwide electronic trade documentation system TradeNet to receive permits from Singapore Customs and other government authorities almost instantaneously. Turnaround time for processing typical trade documents was reduced from 2-4 days to as little as 15 minutes. This system efficiency

> ### Box 3.8. **Singapore's trade and documentation logistics is becoming even more integrated** (cont.)
>
> and lowered business costs for the trading community as well as provided benefits to the Customs administrators. In June 2004, a new integrated trade and logistics information and technology platform was announced to centralise all information for shipping in, to and from Singapore. Companies will no longer need to access multiple systems to enter the same or similar information. Singapore anticipates saving potentially US$400 million over 20 years. In addition new logistics value-added services like multi-country consolidation may generate five times that savings in new revenue. Companies operating in Singapore's export platform should benefit.
>
> *Source:* OECD, 2003a; Harvard Business CAER Paper 72, April 2000; Singapore IDA Media Portal.

developing countries undertaking work outsourced from developed countries are themselves subsidiaries of developed country companies (OECD, 2004a). The subsidiary can then not only provide services to the parent company but also to other markets.

Export-oriented FDI in services has increased considerably. While developed countries dominate services trade overall, developing countries have been particularly successful in some sectors such as audiovisual, port and shipping, construction and health services. They would benefit from considering such strategic sectors in their export promotion policies. A strong domestic market and substantial intra-regional trade helps develop export capacity in services (OECD, 2004a).

> **To what extent do trade policies raise the cost of inputs of goods and services, thereby discouraging investment in industries that depend upon sourcing at competitive world prices?**

Customs procedures and informal export barriers may be burdensome

As noted earlier with regards to imports, efficient customs procedures help a country to offer a business-friendly environment for companies. Export procedures and clearance systems which are not too burdensome facilitate export-orientated projects. In one estimate for Moldova, halving the informal export barriers like cumbersome customs practices, costly regulations and bribes would lift 100 000 to 180 000 individuals out of poverty (World Bank, 2004e). Efficient export procedures (Box 3.8) are crucial to the success of EPZs.

3.3.3. Trade policy in the home country affecting imports

> **If a country's trade policy has a negative effect on developing country exports, what alternative means of accomplishing public policy objectives has the government considered, taking into account the dampening effect that such a restrictive trade policy also has on investment?**

Market access for developing country products can create new opportunities

Export-oriented domestic and foreign investment in developing countries depends upon market access in developed countries or other countries with large markets. If host country firms face high trade barriers to their main markets, there will be less investment – domestic or foreign into the host country. Even developing countries' traditional advantages of low labour costs and abundance of natural resources can be negated.

High home country barriers can be detrimental to the home's own MNE's integration and global production strategies. That can jeopardise their ability to compete internationally. More generally, any slowdown in the multilateral liberalisation process hinders the opportunities of efficiency-seeking investment.

Box 3.9. The elimination of MFA quotas could dramatically alter "competitive advantages"

Multi-Fibre Arrangement quotas in the textile and clothing industry illustrate how protectionist policies in industrialised countries affect FDI location in developing countries. Countries with under-utilised quotas have benefited from higher FDI flows and dynamic gains from new activities that otherwise might have been located in more competitive countries. Binding quotas on the most competitive exporters have reduced their welfare gains from specialisation and economies of scale. Besides being dependent upon picking "winners and losers", these policies introduced trade distortions that lead to an overall loss for the world economy.

There was also a risk that countries have specialised in sectors where they had no true comparative advantage or sectors with potentially less dynamic gains. The scheduled elimination of quantitative restrictions at the end of 2004 could dramatically alter the economics of textile and clothing production. Many expect that the current international fragmentation between the textile and clothing phases of the supply chain will integrate and the attraction of outward processing programmes will fade. The planning for the post 2004 market has already encouraged a reordering of investment and production plans towards the most competitive and integrated suppliers, especially in China.

Source: OECD 2004b; World Bank 2002.

Two market access policy techniques are worthwhile emphasising: *i) tariff peaks* are often used by countries to protect domestic producers from new competitors and tend to be concentrated on products such as[13] certain types of tobacco, nuts and fruits, grains, prepared meats and leather and footwear – products that developing countries export or could export (World Bank, 2002); and *ii) tariff escalation* occurs when tariffs on processed goods are higher than tariffs on related raw materials. Figure 3.4 demonstrates tariff escalation for representative wood products, cotton textiles and passenger cars. As value is added, tariffs tend to be higher. Such escalation can threaten the diversification and upgrading of exports in developing countries and discourage export-oriented FDI.

Barriers applied to imports entering developing countries are on average higher than in developed countries. They include high tariffs, quantitative restrictions, import controls, import bans, etc. These barriers between developing countries can be particularly damaging. More than half of the additional welfare for developing countries created by removing the remaining post-Uruguay Round trade barriers may come from liberalising

Figure 3.4. **Tariff escalation: higher tariffs for higher valued products in the same value chain**

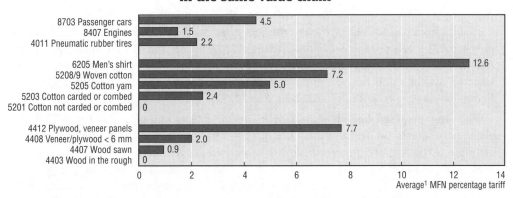

1. Mean of USA, EU, Japan and Canada for sub-headings under this HSC heading in 2000.

Source: Data from UNCTAD TRAINS; Secretariat calculations.

trade with other developing countries (*i.e.* South-South trade) rather than developed countries (*i.e.* North-South trade).[14] Barriers between developing countries reduce intra-regional trade which can prevent the creation of larger markets. This will discourage foreign investors but also discourage even the formation of developing country efficiency-seeking MNEs. Possibly more than one-third of FDI into developing countries comes from other developing countries and such South-South FDI may have grown faster than developed country sources and also have remained relatively more resilient in the post-Asian-crisis period (UNCTAD 2004c).

Trade remedies cause investor concerns

Anti-dumping procedures, safeguards and countervailing measures are trade remedies used to protect an industry threatened or injured by foreign competition. In some cases, they may have an economic value.[15] They are legal measures accepted in WTO agreements but can be a major concern for exporters. These measures tend to be assessed against higher valued products and designed to offer relief to industries which are facing increased competition. Hence they can have the effect of preventing developing countries from advancing up the value chain.

Anti-dumping procedures, along with safeguards and countervailing measures, are sometimes described as having a "chill effect" on investment as they introduce uncertainty concerning market access for products exported from host countries. Even the threat of such measures can redirect FDI from a possible host to the home country, a case known as "quid pro quo" investment.[16] Investors seek predictability.

Trade preferences may benefit developing countries

Trade preferences encourage investment by giving developing countries better market access. Preferences can influence investor's choice of location by increasing the profitability of investment in selected countries.

Sometimes trade preferences may not be effective. As noted with the MFA quota elimination (Box 3.9) if the preferences do not reinforce a comparative advantage then there is a risk that if these preferences are eroded, the investment will be uncompetitive. Investment will be particularly sensitive to this risk if its payback period exceeds the term of the granted preference.

Box 3.10. **African exports under AGOA are increasing, and some evidence of FDI too**

Imports from sub-Saharan Africa to the USA have risen dramatically. The price of oil is only part of the reason. Since its inauguration in 2000, the African Growth and Opportunity Act[*] (AGOA) provides duty- and quota-free access into the USA to various exports from selected African countries. US imports under AGOA could exceed $20 billion in 2004, a figure that has grown from under $9 billion in 2002.

While the increased trade is reasonably clear, the link to more FDI entering Africa has been more anecdotal. In their 2004 Comprehensive report, the USTR identified seven example textile/apparel projects that are in various stages of start-up requiring about $500 million in FDI from various international sources. Also tabled was the $350 million Chad-Cameroon oil pipeline. AGOA has also been identified in the past as a contributor to create 38 000 South African jobs (many in the auto industry). Mauritius did well from textiles and tourism before AGOA was launched, but many of its textile companies are investing in other parts of Africa including a cotton thread factory in Mali. Mauritius also plans a factory to spin yarn, to take advantage of AGOA III.

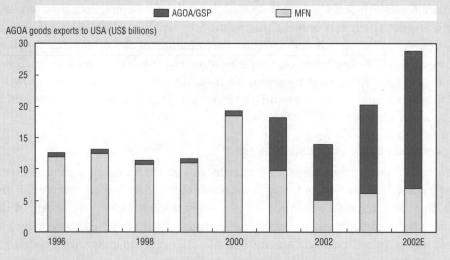

AGOA goods exports to USA (US$ billions)

Source: USITC trade database; OECD.

AGORA III, the latest enactment signed July 2004, extends preferential access for imports until 2015 and allows more third country fabric sources for three years. With the longer time frame, investment may make more sense. With the ability to source fabric from more non-USA sources, losing the cost disadvantage of shipping fabric from the USA may make the African textile/ clothing industry more competitive.

* AGOA is not the only such opportunity for sub-Saharan Africa. Many developed countries offer preferential treatment including the EU under GSP and Economic Partnership Agreements.

Source: The Economist; AGOA Web site, USITC May 2004 Comprehensive Report; OECD (2004b).

Rules of origin in relation to preferences and RTAs also affect investment decisions of companies. When they prevent a company from importing inputs from the most efficient countries, rules of origin discourage efficiency-seeking FDI (UNCTAD, 2002). Preferences granted to developing countries may be undermined by the rules of origin as most products exported from these countries will be excluded from the preferential treatment if they incorporate inputs from third country suppliers (OECD, 2004b).

Box 3.11. **Chinese Taipei's Hsinchu Science-based Industrial Park entrepreneurs return home**

Two thirds of all notebook computers are made in Chinese Taipei. Chinese Taipei owes much of its export success in electronics to two factors: *i)* its close links with the US, particularly through the thousands of young people that go each year to study at American universities and end up working in Silicon Valley; and, *ii)* the commoditisation of the PC in the early 1980s such that the likes of Dell and Hewlett Packard sell their brand name equipment from Original Equipment Manufacturers (OEMs) like those in Chinese Taipei. It was the Chinese Taipei citizens in Silicon Valley who spotted this commoditisation first, and recognised that their home country was a good place for all those no-name companies.

Government officials travelled regularly to America in the 1970s and early 1980s, seeking the advice of Chinese Taipei-Americans in industry and academia and luring back some of the best. Chinese Taipei had already gone through the usual development phases of attracting export-oriented foreign firms and developing its own export industries. But as its labour was no longer cheap, it needed higher valued exports. With ex-Silicon Valley entrepreneurs, the government built the beginnings of Hsinchu; helping companies settle by offering tax incentives, shared factory space and a location beside a national laboratory from which many of Chinese Taipei's most successful high-tech firms have been spun off. They further encouraged a venture-capital industry, convincing a Chinese Taipei executive from Hambrecht and Quist, one of Silicon Valley's top investment banks, to set up a venture fund in Chinese Taipei which spurred many imitators.

Since Hsinchu began in 1980, the park has become home to 369 companies exporting integrated circuits, personal computers and other electronics for total of US$25 billion per year. Paid-in-capital has grown to US$29 billion of which now only 8% is foreign sourced, down from 21% in 1990.Hs

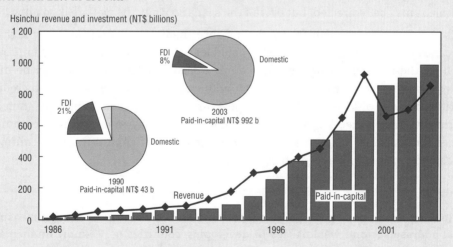

Hsinchu revenue and investment (NT$ billions)

Source: Hsinchu Web site; 1 US$ = 34 NT$ as at 19 August 2004.

The mode 4 workers were crucial to the success of Hsinchu but the Chinese Taipei host country has not been the only beneficiary. Home country consumers have benefited with lower cost laptops while Dell and Hewlett Packard – Home MNEs – concentrate on their competitive advantages of design, marketing and distribution.

Source: The Economist; Market Intelligence Center; Hsinchu Web site.

Access to services markets can be critical

Access to services markets also matters to encourage export-oriented FDI in developing countries. To provide services via mode 1 or 2 and take advantage of outsourcing opportunities, developing countries need market access in sectors where they have a strong potential.

Liberalisation of mode 4 in home countries can also contribute to increase investment and to create linkages in host countries. Temporary workers of developing countries working in developed countries can return home and help foreign or domestic companies start new activities, Box 3.11.

The temporary movement of natural persons as service suppliers can also make businesses in the home country aware of the pool of skilled labour in the host country and lead to the cost effective outsourcing of work and create value. The Indian business processing outsourcing (Box 3.7) exemplifies how value can be created in developing countries in services which allow the MNEs in the developed countries to become more efficient, globally competitive and assuming their business is competitive, pass the benefit largely to consumers potentially worldwide.

3.3.4. Trade policies in the home country affecting exports

Home export subsidies may discourage host investment

Export subsidies (as well as domestic supports) in the home country for goods that could otherwise be imported from developing countries discourage export-oriented investment in these countries. Subsidised products sold on third-country markets also harm developing countries producers and reduce incentives for firms to invest in their industries. This may be a rare example where more trade may occur, some may benefit, investment may be redirected, but overall the scenario would be welfare damaging.

Export subsidies on capital goods and intermediate inputs (the latter if there is confidence the subsidies will be ongoing) could lead to investment. Such may improve the return on the investment in the host country. Also, potentially there may be market failures in financing which might be better addressed in the more established credit and securities markets of a home rather than host jurisdiction. If such is the case, then home government export credit, insurance or trade finance may make sense if commercial sources are unavailable. Such a case is becoming rarer if capital markets continue to deepen and broaden in the credit they will finance.

> **To what extent does trade policy support and attract investment through measures that address sectoral weaknesses in developing countries (*e.g.* export finance and import insurance)?**

Export controls and restrictions while often required can impede technology transfers to hosts

There are international obligations which require countries to apply export restrictions.[17] Some export controls[18] are designed to avoid disseminating sensitive technologies that may have repercussions for national and international security. In implementing these controls, balance between security and trade is required to be in line with international obligations. This balance is needed between legitimate security concerns at home and the host countries' trade interests.

It is also possible that an export control or restriction may induce an investment in a host country that would have otherwise made sense in the home country. This would be the counterpart of "tariff-jumping" FDI in the context of export restrictions rather than import tariffs.[19]

As capital and trade move more freely, what home governments do with their export policies and how it impacts development in host countries becomes less critical – the host country's policies tend to be more crucial. Hence it may not be surprising that very little work has been done on the impact of home country trade export policies on investment patterns.

Notes

1. FDI is often classified into four types according to the investing firm's motives: market-seeking (to get access to new foreign markets), resource-seeking (to get access to resources not available at home), efficiency-seeking (to take advantage of cost differences/scale economies and rationalise production), and strategic asset seeking (to acquire strategic assets or prevent competitors from obtaining them). Dunning, J. (2002), "Determinants of Foreign Direct Investment: Globalisation Induced Changes and the Role of FDI Policies", paper presented at the ABCDE-Europe Conference, Oslo, June 24, 2002.

2. Under the Guidelines, MNEs should "encourage through close co-operation with the local community, including business interests" (General policies #3) and encourage transfer and rapid diffusion of technologies and know-how (Science and Technology #1 to #5) (OECD, 2000).

3. After some high profile failures in 2002, e-B2B statistics have been increasing. Of firms surveyed spending $100 million or more on goods, 11.7% of *intermediary inputs* were purchased online in 2003 and surpassed the figure for indirect materials, such as office supplies for the first time. Online sourcing can bring year-on-year cost savings of 5%. (Financial Times/Forester Research, October 2003.)

4. Some technologies may benefit small firms in poor countries more. For example, credit available to small firms in poor countries increases more than average when credit information sharing technology is applied (World Bank, forthcoming). As costs fall for many new technologies, benefits may accrue more to smaller and poorer participants.

5. While FDI inflows to developing countries come primarily from developed countries, there is a significant share from other developing countries. South-south investment is estimated at about 36% of total FDI inflows to developing countries in 2000 and is growing faster than North-South FDI (World Bank, 2003a).

6. In Figure 6 of the Annex, trade impediments considered serious or very serious by firms are similar for developed or developing countries but predictably for instance, the "impediments to mobility of business people" is more an issue for firms of developing countries, and "foreign investment restrictions" is more an issue for firms of developed countries.

7. Chakrabarti, A. (2001), "The Determinants of Foreign Direct Investment: Sensitivity Analyses of Cross-Country Regressions", Kyklos, Vol. 54, 1, pp. 89-114.

8. For a discussion of the potential benefits, New Zealand outlines the reasons for adopting the negative list approach in their Chile and Singapore *Closer Economic Partnership* agreements. *www.mfat.govt.nz/foreign/tnd/ceps/cepchilenzsing/infobulletinjuly04.html*. OECD, *Regionalism and the Multilateral Trading System*, 2003, pages 33-37 also discusses the negative vs positive list approaches.

9. There is a trend to more cross-regional RTAs. As at October 2003, 40% of the proposed RTAs notified to the WTO were cross-regional (WTO Regionalism workshop, 2003).

10. Some theoreticians argue if the host country is a "large" exporting country which can affect the terms of trade for the product exported, then an export tax can be welfare enhancing. This is largely hypothetical because few countries can influence their exports' long-term world market prices.

11. For instance NAFTA 1106(1) states that host countries can not oblige a company of a partner to export a given level or percentage of goods or services or to transfer technology, a production process or other proprietary knowledge (subject to competition issues).

12. The competition in incentives can cause a "prisoner's dilemma" for any individual state. Such has been an argument for a multilateral agreement to limit the proliferation and escalation of location incentives. In addition, local labour legislation may not be fully enforced in the EPZs.

13. Listing is of products whose tariff rate exceeds 50% in any 8-digit subheading in any of USA, EU, Japan or Canada. Many other goods exceed 15% – a frequently-used criterion to identify peaks.

14. 57% estimated by Anderson, K., "Agriculture, Developing Countries and the WTO Millennium Round", CEPR/CIES, December 1999.

15. Some argue that such measures are *ex ante* instruments that allow countries to commit to international agreements they would otherwise be unable to sign without such "escape" clauses.

16. Blonigen, B.A. and R.C. Feenstra (1996), "Protectionist Threat and Foreign Direct Investment", NBER Working Papers No. 5475, March. See also Bhagwati *et al.*, "Quid Pro Quo Investment", American Economic Review, 82(2), May 1992.

17. Including for example CITES, Montreal Protocol on the Ozone Layer, Nuclear Non-Proliferation. For an illustrative list of restrictions adhering to such obligations, see Table 3, OECD TD/TC/WP(2003)7/FINAL.

18. Such as the export controls of "dual use" items as recommended by UNSC Resolution 1540 of 28 April 2004.

19. As an example, in May 1981, the Japanese (home) voluntary export restraint of automobiles into the USA (host) may have induced Honda, Nissan and Toyota to invest in plants in the USA.

References and Further Policy Resources

APEC-OECD Integrated Checklist on Regulatory Reform (*www.oecd.org/gov*).

OECD (2000), The OECD Guidelines for Multinational Enterprises, (Paris: OECD).

OECD (2002a), Foreign Direct Investment for Development. Maximising Benefits, Minimising Costs, (Paris: OECD).

OECD (2002b), "The Relationship between Trade and Foreign Direct Investment: A Survey", TD/TC/WP(2002)14/FINAL.

OECD (2002c), GATS: The Case for Open Services Markets, (Paris: OECD).

OECD (2003a), "Trade Facilitation Reforms in the Service of Development", TD/TC/WP(2003)11/FINAL.

OECD (2003b), "Analysis of Non-Tariff Measures: The Case of Export Restrictions", TD/TC/WP(2003)7/FINAL.

OECD (2003c), "Quantitative Assessment of the Benefits of Trade Facilitation", TD/TC/WP(2003)31/FINAL.

OECD (2004a), "Services Trade Liberalisation: Identifying Opportunities and Gains", TD/TC/WP(2003)23/FINAL.

OECD (2004b), "Structural Adjustment in Textiles and Clothing in the Post-ATC Trading Environment", TD/TC/WP(2004)23/FINAL.

OECD Working Party on Export Credits and Credit Guarantees (*www.oecd.org/trade*).

UNCTAD (2001), World Investment Report 2001: Promoting Linkages (New York and Geneva: United Nations).

UNCTAD (2002), World Investment Report 2002: Transnational Corporations and Export Competitiveness (New York and Geneva: United Nations).

UNCTAD (2003), World Investment Report 2003: FDI Policies for Development: National and International Perspectives, (New York and Geneva: United Nations).

UNCTAD (2004a), "Transnational Corporations: Are incentives a good investment for the host country? An empirical evaluation of the Czech National Incentive Scheme", UNCTAD/ITE/IIT/2004/3.

UNCTAD (2004b), Foreign Direct Investment and Performance Requirements, (New York and Geneva: United Nations).

UNCTAD (2004c), World Investment Report 2004: The Shift towards Services, (New York and Geneva: United Nations).

World Bank (1998), Privatization and Emerging Equity Markets, Flemings and The World Bank.

World Bank (2000), Trade Blocs, Oxford University Press.

World Bank (2002a), Global Economic Prospects and the Developing Countries – 2002, The World Bank.

World Bank (2002b), "An Assessment of Telecommunications Reform in Developing Countries", Working paper, The World Bank.

World Bank (2003a), Global Development Finance 2003 – Striving for Stability in Development Finance, The World Bank.

World Bank (2003b), Global Economic Prospects and the Developing Countries – 2003, The World Bank.

World Bank (2004a), "Trade Facilitation: Using WTO Disciplines to Promote Development", Trade Note May 10, 2004, The World Bank.

World Bank (2004b), Doing Business in 2004, The World Bank.

World Bank (2004c), Sustaining India's Services Revolution, The World Bank.

World Bank (2004d), Reforming Infrastructure, The World Bank.

World Bank (2004e), "Informal Export Barriers and Poverty", Working paper June 2004, The World Bank.

World Trade Organisation (1997), "The Relationship between Trade and Foreign Direct Investment", Note by the Secretariat, Working Group on the Relationship between Trade and Investment, WT/WGTI/W/7 www.wto.org.

World Trade Organisation (2002), "Key Issues Concerning Foreign Direct Investment and the Transfer and Diffusion of Technology to Developing Countries", Note by the Secretariat, Working Group on the Relationship between Trade and Investment, WT/WGTI/W/136 www.wto.org.

World Trade Organisation (2004), World Trade Report 2004, www.wto.org/.

ANNEX 3.A1

Framework Considerations for Measuring the Effectiveness of Trade Policies and "Good Practices"

A.1. Foreword

The Policy Framework for Investment is to be a non-prescriptive, flexible, operational and practical guide for policymakers. The body of this chapter identifies and explores specific trade policies and their impact on investment and growth. This annex is a possible framework for a flexible, operational guide to *trade* policy making.[1]

Box 3.A1.1 introduces the underlying participants of a project and reiterates the importance of trade policy. The next section provides a trade policy framework addressing appropriate tools and measures. The final section focuses on the role of governments in trade policy and how some of the examples discussed in the text may illustrate "good practices".

A.2. The trade policy framework

Trade policy making is iterative, interactive and evolving

Almost all the good practices documented in this chapter were iterative and interactive; governments, entrepreneurs, investors and other concerned parties co-operating and negotiating to provide the right environment for successful projects. There is a loop at work. Throughout the loop, the trade policy makers need to consider "have circumstances changed?" and if so, what such changes imply for the country's attributes, opportunities and appropriate policies.

Good trade policies will not necessarily be identical for all countries. This is particularly true for smaller, less-endowed countries that may need to target their resources most effectively. Small countries in particular can benefit from trade and investment. No developing country is "too small" or "too poor" to attract FDI (OECD, 2004e), but they may need to plan. Especially for small countries, the host country may need to realistically assess their comparative advantage. What are the country's attributes and what opportunities should the host government emphasise? When possible, host governments may let market forces identify the successful businesses and not preclude sectors by "picking winners and losers". A level playing field for trade policies is often best even for small economies.

While not necessarily being the same for all countries, trade policies need to be coherent with the rest of the policies of the country.[2] Liberal trade is no panacea. Trade

Box 3.A1.1. **The confluence of an entrepreneur with FDI opportunity will involve trade**

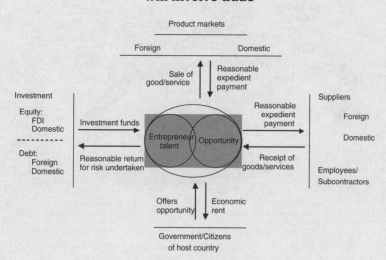

A project is the confluence of an opportunity (be it a market, resource, efficiency, or M&A opportunity) and entrepreneurial talent. The "knowledge-capital MNE model" recognises that *MNEs transfer entrepreneurial talent rather than financial resources.* But entrepreneurial talent is not necessarily supplied solely by the foreigner or a domestic participant, it can arise from a joint venture or franchise whereby the talent is supplied by both domestic and foreign participants; as for example the entrepreneurs of Chinese Taipei's Hsinchu Park (Box 3.11).

With very few exceptions, a project will require investment capital. The entrepreneur must promote the opportunity to the financiers and choose the most cost effective instruments offered so as to minimize the cost of capital for the project. The entrepreneur must market the merits of the project – minimising the perceived risk. Not only may the project's viability and initiation depend upon that "selling" but also the return to the entrepreneur/opportunity.[1]

The entrepreneur will "sell" the merits of the project using a business plan. All business plans must – and usually it is the first item – describe the product market. *For a FDI-financed project today, that product market will be international* with rare exceptions.[2] Therefore trade is involved and a liberal trade policy is likely to be essential for the project to be viable.

The project will typically require supplies of raw materials, goods and services usually during all phases of the project (building, start-up and operating). *For FDI-financed projects, some supplies must be foreign* except for the rare occasion.[3] Therefore again trade is involved and a liberal trade policy is once again integral for the project.

1. Note that the host government's interests and the entrepreneur's can be largely considered the same. Negotiation between the two can frequently assume a positive-sum game. This was one of the lessons of Costa Rica (Box 3.5). There will be negotiation to split the economic rent from the entrepreneur's reasonable return but that should be secondary to the value that can be achieved through a successful project.
2. The product market will be international recognising the arguments in the text of this chapter. Resource-seeking FDI and the ever more present efficiency-seeking FDI both by definition involve international product markets. Only market-seeking FDI may be focused solely on domestic product markets but more frequently now, scale economics require serving a regional trade area, *i.e.* international product markets.
3. For efficiency-seeking or market-seeking FDI, this international component/product supply is self-evident. For resource-seeking FDI, some foreign-source equipment is likely to give the foreign company the credibility to do the project otherwise investors will question what advantage the foreign company brings to the project. Note that these considerations taken with those in Note 2 above imply that almost every FDI-financed project must have some trade-related aspect.

Figure 3.A1.1 **The trade policymaking loop; measuring up and sensing change**

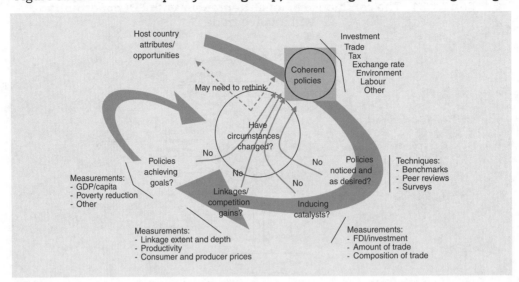

policy alone will not achieve higher GDP/capita, poverty reduction and those other ultimate goals without coherence with investment, tax and other policies.

Nonetheless there are some interim steps and measurements that can guide trade policy makers in assessing whether the economy is moving toward those ultimate goals. Are the trade policies: i) getting noticed and will the reactions to those policies attract investment, trade and growth? ii) inducing the catalysts, in particular those entrepreneurs and financiers referred to in the prior section to invest in the economy? and iii) contributing to growth in the domestic economy through linkages and a more competitive atmosphere? These are interim considerations, each having their own measurements, but often interlinked. Inducing potential catalysts may depend upon sourcing those domestic suppliers and competitively priced component parts. The following three sections focus on these interim steps.

Are the trade policies getting noticed and appreciated?

To be effective, trade policy reforms need to be seen. Small countries in particular may have to be proactive to get noticed. There are three techniques whereby trade policy makers can get noticed and at the same time make sure that the message is the one they want.

Trade policy reforms will influence benchmarks

Annex 3.A2 lists twelve benchmark indices that are influenced by trade policy.[3] Such ratings are used comparatively across countries as well as over time to reflect improving or deteriorating investment conditions, of which one contributor will be trade policy. An improving and comparatively good relative index would assist a country to attract domestic and foreign investment. They have been used by entrepreneurs in business plans to reassure investors. An improvement and comparison in these measures can also tell trade policy makers if a country's efforts to improve policy are working.

Frequently the benchmark indices will use proprietary statistical techniques. Also qualitative judgment is sometimes used as in the case of Standard and Poor's sovereign

POLICY FRAMEWORK FOR INVESTMENT: A REVIEW OF GOOD PRACTICES – ISBN 92-64-02586-3 – © OECD 2006

Box 3.A1.2. **An illustration: how trade policy affects the economic freedom of the world index**

As an example of how trade policy impacts such indices, the Fraser Institute's Economic Freedom of the World index includes five "Freedom to Trade Internationally" measures (one of 5 areas scored):

Measure	Converted to a score of 0 to 10 with	
	0 if	10 if
1) **Taxes on international trade**		
a) Revenue from taxes on internal trade as a percentage of exports plus imports	No taxes	Taxes ≥ 15% of total trade
b) Mean tariff rate	No tariffs	Average ≥ 50%
c) Standard deviation (SD) of tariff rates	Uniform tariffs	SD ≥ 25%
2) **Regulatory trade barriers**		
a) Hidden import barriers	Uses GCR*	
b) Costs of importing including tariffs, license fees, bank fees, and time required for administrative red tape of importing equipment using GCR*	Cost ≤ 10% of equipment cost	Cost ≥ 50%
3) **Actual trade compared to expected** using regression	Actual trade twice predicted	Actual trade half predicted
4) **Official versus black-market exchange rates**	No-black market	Black market ≥ 50% premium to official
5) **International capital market controls**		
a) Access of citizens to foreign capital and foreign access to domestic capital markets	Uses a survey within the GCR*	
b) Restrictions on engaging in capital market exchange with foreigners	Uses the IMF report on 13 types of capital controls	

*   GCR: Global Competitiveness Report.
Source: www.freetheworld.com.

ratings. Hence it is commonly impossible to be definitive on how trade policies eventually flow into the rating score. This underscores the importance of trade policy makers being proactive and marketing their country's attributes and policies to the rating agencies themselves.

Some of these benchmarks have been statistically analysed by the OECD and provide mixed but potentially useful predictions of inward FDI. Overall indices themselves may predict poorly but the sub-indices – in particular the indicators of regulatory quality and restrictiveness, government intervention, macroeconomic stability and technological advancement – correlate more closely with FDI inflows (OECD, 2004e). Hence trade policy which in some cases impacts these sub-indices more may be more influential in attracting FDI than implied by trade policy's effect on the overall index itself.

The benchmarks tend to explain different economic characteristics and differ in the level of generalisation (OECD, 2004e). It is also probable within the set of benchmarks provided in Annex 3.A2, that some benchmarks are more sensitive to the type of investment instrument and circumstance. Noteworthy, the rating agencies are particularly influential for large projects involving "investment-grade" debt financing but probably less influential in more risky circumstances. Hence, countries may need to focus on different benchmarks depending upon their particular circumstance and the type of projects they are trying to attract.

For the practical aspects of a trade policymaker, they may wish to track the benchmark scores of particular interest over time and relative to their neighbouring countries in terms of geography and income. They may also consider defining which policy changes could make the most impact for the least effort. These could often be simplifications to regulations (World Bank, 2004b). They may also wish to contact the agency or group responsible for the index to discuss the particulars of their circumstance. This is a two-way communication – the policy maker may understand what drives the rating (and investors) at the same time the agency understands how motivated the country is to modify and improve the trade and investment environment. It can be a virtuous circle.

Most benchmark indices overlook the importance of *services* trade. Noticeably absent in the *Freedom to Trade Internationally* is any measure of the restrictiveness for trade in the service sectors, particularly for the banking and telecommunications sectors. As such, trade policy makers (also rating agencies and investors) may seek other indices being developed, including those in the OECD Trade Directorate.[4]

Peer reviews can guide effective policy making

Peer review is a process whereby the quality and efficiency of a country's policies, laws, regulations, processes and institutions are examined and assessed *vis-à-vis* those of their peers, in a non-adversarial context. Effectiveness of peer reviews derives from the influence of the peers during the process: i) mix of recommendations and dialogue with the peer countries; ii) public scrutiny, comparisons, and ranking among countries; and iii) the impact of the above on domestic public opinion, national administrations and policy makers. The ultimate goal of peer reviews is to help or encourage the reviewed country to: improve its policy making; adopt best practices; and comply with established standards and principles.[5]

The most directly applicable peer review for trade policy is the WTO's Trade Policy Review Mechanism. Peer reviews carried out by other international organisations which cover elements of trade policy include: OECD EDRC Economic Surveys; APEC Individual Action Plan (IAP); IMF Country Surveillance Mechanism; IMF/World Bank Financial Sector Assessment Program (FSAP), and; the UNCTAD Investment Policy Reviews.

Surveying businesses can give insights

Several benchmarks above assess policies in part by surveying businesses. Trade policy makers may also survey businesses and other parties themselves. APEC surveyed 461 firms in 21 countries (Figure 3.A1.2):[6]

- Trade impediments were consistently considered higher in developing countries (*vis-à-vis* developed countries) except for foreign investment regulations – 26% of the respondents of developing *versus* 32% of developed-country firms identified foreign investment regulations as a serious or very serious trade impediment.

- Developing country firms (*vis-à-vis* developed) were impacted visibly more by customs procedures, the impediments to mobility of business people, quantitative restrictions and restrictive business practices.

- The highest scoring impediment for developed country firms was restrictive administrative regulations.

Figure 3.A1.2. **Trade impediments considered serious or very serious**

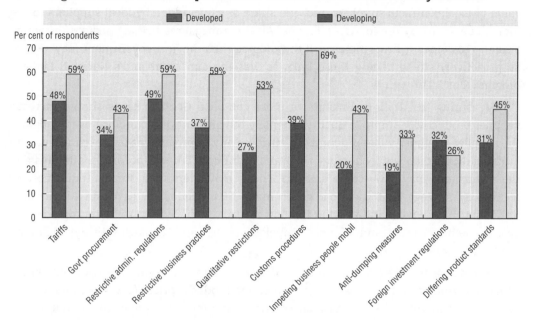

Source: APEC Business Facilitation Survey; Sept. 2000.

Are the trade policies inducing the potential catalysts?

Surveying businesses can lead to insights. It hopefully can also lead to those entrepreneurs that can bring together the elements for successful projects. Success in inducing catalysts will increase two key statistics: the inflow of FDI and trade. As explained in Section 1 of the main text, sometimes FDI can lead to current account deficits. Hence the composition of the imports can also be important. If the imports are capital items that will earn a return rather than simply be consumed, then the trade policy maker and the benchmark rating agencies may be less concerned.

Some trade policy reforms have negligible costs; others are suited to cost-benefit analysis

Some trade policy reforms need not be fiscally costly. Applying uniform tariffs (as per Chile, Box 3.2), can be fiscally neutral. Listening attentively (as per Costa Rica, Box 3.5) is cheap and yet a host government may find infrastructure opportunities beneficial to both MNEs and themselves. For Costa Rica, some improvements such as the increased frequency of international air carriers benefited more than just Intel. Also some of the infrastructure improvements were jointly-financed by Intel and the Costa Rican government to the benefit of both Intel and the residents of Costa Rica.

But if concessions are given or expenses are incurred for trade facilitation or trade promotion, then care is appropriate. One tool available to the trade policy maker is a traditional cost-benefit analysis. As an example of the potential difficulties, estimates of expanding the Czech investment and trade promotion suggest that the social price may exceed $40 000 per job created (UNCTAD, 2004a).

Are we getting the backward linkages and competition gains?

There are two concepts when measuring the effectiveness of linkages (UNCTAD, 2001). For measuring the *extent* of linkages, three measures (or variations thereof) have been studied: a simple count of the number of domestic firms that supply a foreign affiliate; the value of local contracts supplied; and, the share of value-added by local suppliers to the total value added by the foreign affiliates. All three measures rise as linkages to foreign affiliates to domestic firms increase. If they do not, then the host government may need to be proactively strengthening these links as was the aim of Ireland's National Linkage program (Box 3.1).

Measuring the *depth* of linkages is more complex. Good linkages should increase supplier productivity, improve quality, intensify the amount of technology used and shift the supplier to higher-value products. To attribute any improvement in these measures to linkages rather than say technology advances is difficult. Surveys of foreign affiliates and their suppliers may give some insight. These may identify a further education or technology strategy that the host government may need such as Costa Rica's trade promotion and facilitation co-ordination with Intel (Box 3.5). Listening to the entrepreneurs in India and Chinese Taipei (Boxes 3.7 and 3.11 respectively) identified productivity gains.

Another factor in assessing whether the economy is achieving the competitiveness gains of liberalisation is to measure consumer and producer prices (over time and relative to neighbouring countries). Lower relative prices can indicate improving competitiveness for local industries – since local industries also consume – as well as being beneficial to final consumers in the economy. Increased consumer surplus can be a general benefit of the trade induced by the foreign investment.

A.3. The governments play an essential role

The host government (typically acting on behalf of the citizens) offers the opportunity for which they would receive benefits in the form of taxes (income, resource or other). The entrepreneur needs fair compensation but to the extent that there is excessive profit (economic rent), conceptually *a good practice would pass these excessive returns to the host government/citizens*. It is easier said than done.

In an ideal world, policies and agreements between the host government, entrepreneurs and others, are well defined and determined preferably before major

Figure 3.A1.3. **Policy uncertainty matters**

Concerns identified by firms operating in developing countries

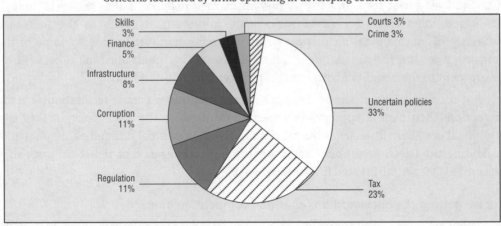

Source: World Bank; WDR 2005 (forthcoming).

Table 3.A1.1. **Examples of "Good Practices" in the context of this Trade Policy Framework**[*]

Examples of "Good Practice"	Why it is important in a trade and investment context	Examples highlighting this "Good Practice" as provided in the text
Eliminating inefficient practices	Cut red-tape costs as they will deter entrepreneurs and foreign financiers and will discourage projects in the host jurisdiction.	The average customs clearances for imports into India and Ecuador of 10 to 14 days respectively compare unfavourably with the average of only about 2 days in high-income countries. New technologies can automate much of the traditional paperwork as per Singapore's integrated logistics documentation, Box 3.8.
Encouraging trade neutral policies	Allow the entrepreneurs to choose projects compatible with comparative advantages for the host country.	Chilean's uniform tariff schedule (Box 3.2) is potentially ideal for all countries. Policies should not encourage projects built upon superficial competitive advantages as per the MFA quotas (Box 3.9) or log export bans (Box 3.6).
Improving market access for host products	Give the entrepreneurial talent a market to sell into.	AGOA (Box 3.10) makes a special effort to open access for African developing countries.
Allowing competitive sourcing	Let the entrepreneur source capital and intermediary products at internationally competitive prices and quality.	The elimination of MFA quotas will require some clothing manufacturers to consolidate with their textile source (Box 3.9).
Promoting linkages	Provide the circumstances that foster domestic suppliers to supply intermediary goods and services to the project and potentially from that base become an international supplier. This will increase a host's and MNE's productivity.	New technologies may promote such backward linkages in the new framework of e-B2B marketplaces. Matchmaking was particularly successful by Ireland in the initial phases of development (Box 3.1).
Appreciating the value in services specialisation	Recognise the value of services for an entrepreneur to create value for the host country and make the home's MNEs globally competitive.	India's software services (Box 3.7).
Improving labour mobility for entrepreneurial talent	Allow the entrepreneurial talent to apply their talent in foreign jurisdictions. It can create a win-win for both host and home country.	Chinese Taipei's Hsinchu Park (Box 3.11).
Avoiding policy uncertainty	Reduce policy uncertainty so that the required rates of return to investors decrease. Policy uncertainty will lower the returns to the entrepreneur/opportunity, if not cancel the project entirely.	Such should encourage practises like Chilean's scheduled reductions in their uniform tariffs (Box 3.3) and Latin America's telecom GATS pre-commitments (Box 3.4).
Helping market the project(s)	Support the entrepreneur to "sell" the project to financiers. It may improve the returns to the entrepreneur and opportunity.	Listening to legitimate concerns of entrepreneurs and investors was a highlight in Costa Rica's success in attracting Intel (Box 3.5).
Avoiding excessive concessions	Promotion may be necessary for a small host country to become noticed but expenditures may need to be analysed against benefits. It would be typically inappropriate for the host government to guarantee a project's commercial outcome.[1]	The Costa Rican example (Box 3.5) suggests concessions do not need to be excessive.
Identifying market failures	Recognise the limitations of some host countries. For instance, some projects may need the financing of more established securities markets of home rather than host markets. Such a case is becoming rarer if capital markets continue to deepen and broaden in the credit they will finance.	Such may be the case for African states in which AGOA, Box 3.10 has links to US Export-Import Bank.
Facilitating trade	When appropriate, allow the entrepreneurial talent to use local resources for pre-shipment approvals for entry into a home jurisdiction. This can help integrate global value chains.	Costa Rica has improved their logistical infrastructure to accommodate Intel's just-in-time requirements (Box 3.5).

[*] An illustrative list, not necessarily applicable to all circumstances.

1. It is a general principle in finance that the party that is best able to judge, manage and accept a particular risk is the party that assumes that risk. It usually would not be in a host's best interest to guarantee a commercial outcome and could lead to problems of moral hazard.

expenses are incurred by the entrepreneur. Few dispute a host's right to regulate, but many consider it inappropriate to change the rules or have conflicting rules. This requires a balanced assessment.

Just the perception of policy uncertainty can be detrimental. Uncertainty will increase the return on investment required by investors if not cancel the investment altogether. Policy – including trade policy – uncertainty can be a major concern in developing countries, Figure 3.A1.3.

Good trade policy practices as they relate to investment

In developing this policy framework, what then may constitute "good practices" for trade policy? In the following table, each row identifies: an illustrative list of examples of "good practices"; why such a practice might be considered important in the context of trade and investment, and; examples that were used in the body of the text.

Notes

1. By focusing on trade policies, this document does not attempt to address *general* good policy-making practices like having clearly defined objectives, measures against objectives, and participant buy-in as will be found cited in for instance the World Bank's Poverty Reduction Strategy Papers (PRSPs).

2. Not precluding the possibility that coherent policies may also require international co-operation such as defined in multi, regional or bilateral trade agreements.

3. This listing was created by inspecting the internet descriptions of fifteen indices analysing the environment for doing business identified by the World Bank (2004b), adding one about to be introduced and two investment-related indices. Of those, the twelve that explicitly refer to trade policy are listed in Annex 3.B. The other six indices are also likely to be influenced by trade policy.

4. Description of the OECD banking and telecommunications restrictiveness indices can be found at TD/TC/WP(2004)32/REV1.

5. For a paper considering the practical options for implementing a peer review mechanism, see OECD, "Practical Modalities of Peer Review in a Multilateral Framework on Competition", CCNM/GF/COMP/TR(2003)10.

6. A limitation of this survey was that responses from foreign affiliates (if any) were not separated from domestic companies. Also, it was not explicitly asked whether the impediments were caused by the host or home countries although some impediments may be considered self-evident. Another useful source of European business attitudes to international investment rules (some with trade policy implications) was published in 2000, *http://europa.eu.int/comm/trade/issues/sectoral/invesment/index_en.htm*.

ANNEX 3.A2

Benchmark Indices for Evaluating Trade Policy

Table 3.A2.1. Benchmark indices which explicitly mention "trade policy" in their Web description

Index	Source	Measurement for	Trade policy implication to the index
World competitiveness yearbook	Institute for Management Development; *www.imd.ch*	Competitiveness of 49 countries using hard data and perception surveys.	Besides various measures of trade (gross, balance, % of GDP), several trade policy measures are found in business survey questions including whether: customs' authorities help facilitate the efficient transit of goods; protectionism affects business conduct; immigration laws prevent businesses from employing foreign labour; cross-border transactions are freely negotiated with foreign partners; and, foreign investors can acquire control in domestic companies.
Global competitiveness report	World Economic Forum; *www.weforum.org*	Competitiveness of 80 countries using hard data and perception surveys.	This index has several aspects of trade policy which contribute to an overall score. One of the more interesting aspects is the "technology transfer-in-trade" subindex. The technique varies depending upon whether the country has a core competence or not. Countries with a higher technology-based export sector are deemed to have a greater propensity to absorb technologies from abroad. Regression is used to make this estimate.
Index of economic freedom	Heritage Foundation and Wall St Journal; *www.heritage.org*	Assessment by in-house experts drawing on many sources for 161 countries.	The index measures how well countries score on a list of 50 independent variables divided into 10 broad factors of economic freedom. One such factor is "trade policy".
Economic freedom of the world	Fraser Institute; *www.freetheworld.com*	Assessment by in-house experts drawing on many sources for 123 countries.	See Box A.1.
Country risk service	The Economist Intelligence Unit; *www.eiu.com*	Investment risk ratings for 100 countries.	The business rankings model examines ten separate categories of which one is "foreign trade and exchange controls" using a 1 (very bad for business) to 5 (very good). In that category, there are four sub-questions. Two involve capital account items. Two involve clear trade policy issues: *i)* Tariff and not tariff protection use average tariff levels (1 ⇔ average tariff > 20%; 5 ⇔ average tariff < 5% with an adjustment to the score of "at least 1 point if licensing and import inspection is significant"); and *ii)* actual trade as a % of GDP *versus* expected by regression (1 ⇔ actual < 0.6 expected; 5 ⇔ actual > 1.5 expected).
Business environment and enterprise performance	EBRD and World Bank; *www.info.worldbank.org/ governance/beeps2002*	Government effectiveness, regulatory quality, rule of law, and corruption in 27 transition economies.	The regulation quality index combines three aspects with equal weights. One of them is customs and trade regulations.

Table 3.A2.1. **Benchmark indices which explicitly mention "trade policy" in their Web description** (*cont.*)

Index	Source	Measurement for	Trade policy implication to the index
International country risk guide	Political Risk Services; *www.prsgroup.com*	Investment risk ratings for 140 countries.	PRS Country Reports forecast the risk of doing business and include *Tariff Barriers* – the average and range of financial costs imposed on imports; *Other Import Barriers* – formal and informal quotas, licensing provisions, or other restrictions on imports; *Payment Delays* – the punctuality, or otherwise, with which government and private importers pay their foreign creditors, based on government policies, domestic economic conditions, and international financial conditions; *Taxation Discrimination* – the formal and informal tax policies that either lead to bias against, or special advantages favouring international business.
Foreign policy magazine globalisation index	A.T.Kearney; *www.atkearney.com*	Incorporates 16 key indicators of global integration for 62 countries.	The index incorporates 16 key indicators of global integration in four baskets. The economic integration basket includes data on trade and FDI. FDI measures are double-weighted "due to its particular importance in the ebb and flow of globalisation".
FDI confidence index		Attractiveness of 60 countries for FDI based upon company surveys.	The FDI Confidence Index is based on an annual survey of CEOs, CFOs and other top executives of Global 1 000 companies. Country and sector coverage among the participating companies reveals a normal distribution compared to the Global 1 000 population. Although trade policy is not explicitly addressed, trade policy will influence whether a surveyed executive will consider a country for FDI.
2004 Offshore location attractiveness index		Attractiveness of 25 countries for offshore services.	Besides using both the above indices, it weighs extent of bureaucracy and some trade facilitation measures.
Sovereign credit ratings	Standard and Poors; Moody's; Fitch; and others *www.standardandpoors.com; www.fitchratings.com ; www.moodys.com*	About 100 countries have been rated for the ability and willingness to service debt. Notable is the S&P/UNDP initiative in rating seven HIPC African countries.	This description is from the Fitch guide to sovereign ratings. Specific measures of "trade and foreign investment policy" include: the principal measures taken to control imports (quotas, tariffs, non-tariff barriers) by sector; average tariff applied to manufactures weighted by category and an estimate of the overall degree of effective protection; description of the agricultural import regime, including variable levies etc; export subsidies including loans available at below market rates and any other export promotional measures; policy towards trade liberalisation with a timetable for removal of any measures. There are other measures which focus on investment.
Doing business in 2006	World Bank; *http://rru.worldbank.org/DoingBusiness/*	The 2005 index considered 145 countries on (largely regulatory) obstacles to growth.	One of the new topics to be featured in the upcoming *Doing Business in 2006* index is trade logistics assessing the procedures, time and cost for an exporter to bring goods from factory to the ship, train or truck and across the border, and also to import a good: customs, pre-shipment inspections and technical and quality certification.

Source: World Bank 2004b which identified 12 indices; this listing was pared down to those that most clearly integrated "trade policy" in their description.

POLICY FRAMEWORK FOR INVESTMENT: A REVIEW OF GOOD PRACTICES – ISBN 92-64-02586-3 – © OECD 2006

ISBN 92-64-02586-3
Policy Framework for Investment
A Review of Good Practices
© OECD 2006

Chapter 4

Competition Policy*

---

* This background document was prepared by Michael Gestrin, Investment Division, OECD Directorate
  for Financial and Enterprise Affairs, with inputs from Patricia Heriard-Dubreuil, Jeremy West, and
  Michael Wise from the OECD Competition Division.

4.1. Introduction

Competition policy has come to play an increasingly important role within the context of the global development agenda. For example, the Monterrey Consensus, the values and objectives of which underpin the *Policy Framework for Investment*, emphasised "the promotion of a competitive environment" in order to allow "businesses, both domestic and international, to operate efficiently and profitably and with maximum development impact" (paragraph 21). The Monterrey Consensus also called on members of the WTO to implement the commitments made in the Doha Development Declaration, which recognised "the needs of developing and least-developed countries for enhanced support for technical assistance and capacity building in [the area of competition policy], including policy analysis and development" (paragraphs 23-25).[1] Work undertaken at the OECD, UNCTAD, the World Bank and the WTO, among others, has underscored the relevance of competition policy from a development perspective. Furthermore, developing countries have been adopting competition laws and policies in ever-increasing numbers, pointing to benefits that these would seem to associate with doing so. While approximately 27 developing countries adopted some form of competition law during the 1990s,[2] an additional 35 were in the process of implementing competition laws as of February 2004.

The primary objective of competition policy is to enhance consumer welfare by promoting competition. Economic efficiency is generally enhanced by encouraging competition, and thus one of the key links between competition policy and development has been the role that competition policy plays in increasing economic efficiency. The efficient use of resources is especially important in the development context where resources are particularly scarce, an issue emphasised in the Monterrey Consensus. The economics literature generally distinguishes between static and dynamic economic efficiency. Competition policy has variously been ascribed a role in promoting both. The main static effects of competition are to reduce the ability of firms to raise price above marginal cost and to ensure that firms produce at the lowest possible costs. The dynamic consequences of competition can include incentives to innovate, to imitate, and to invest in the development of new technologies and know-how. Competition policy reinforces economic efficiency by preventing or providing remedies for market structures and business practices that weaken the degree of inter-firm rivalry in markets.

In addition to the potential benefits of the implementation and enforcement of competition law and policy in terms of static and dynamic efficiencies, competition authorities have also been ascribed a more general advocacy role. Although the advocacy role of competition authorities defies a precise definition, it has been associated with public education and awareness activities, development of a competition culture, research documenting the need for market-opening measures, and involvement in policy formulation and implementation beyond competition law itself. It has been suggested that these activities "may be among the most useful and high payoff activities undertaken by [competition authorities]", especially insofar as the removal or reduction of regulatory impediments to market entry across a range of policy areas (*e.g.* trade policy, investment policy, regulated industries, etc.) "can be central to the establishment of healthy market economies in developing and transition economies" (Anderson and Jenny, 2002, p. 7, cited in WTO, 2003, p. 14).

In addition to these overarching links between competition policy and development, a number of more specific contributions of competition policy to development have been identified in work undertaken by the OECD, UNCTAD, the World Bank and at the WTO, among others. These include:

- the promotion of consumer welfare;
- preventing excessive concentration levels and resulting structural rigidities;
- addressing anti-competitive practices of enterprises (including MNEs) that can negatively affect the trade performance and competitiveness, on both the import and export sides, of developing countries;
- reinforcing the benefits of privatisation and regulatory reform/deregulation initiatives;
- establishing an institutional focal point for the advocacy of pro-competitive policy reforms and a culture of competition; and
- increasing an economy's ability to attract and maximise the benefits of investment.[3]

It is this last issue that this chapter addresses, including issues that are particularly relevant with respect to the relationship between competition policy and the creation of an attractive environment for FDI in the development context.

4.2. The relationship between competition policy and an attractive environment for investment

> Are the competition laws and their application clear, transparent, and non-discriminatory? What measures do the competition authorities use (*e.g.* publishing decisions and explanations on the approach used to enforce the laws) to help investors understand and comply with the competition laws and to communicate changes in the laws and regulations?

4.2.1. Competition policy within the broader governance framework

For competition policy to be effective, businesses and other stakeholders need to understand the "rules of the game". This requires that competition laws and policies be transparent and their implementation predictable. It also requires that rulings on competition cases be made based on non-discriminatory criteria and consistently. In other words, while no two situations are the same, under reasonably similar circumstances decisions ought to be consistent with each other. Transparency can be promoted by, for instance, ensuring that businesses and other interested parties have access to all necessary information, by offering guidance on the interpretation of the competition laws and by publishing reasons for judiciary and regulatory agency decisions. Transparency and predictability help to improve the investment environment, because they reduce the risk of inconsistent application of laws and regulations and lower uncertainty faced by investors and others. (Also see the chapter on Investment Policy.) In addition, transparency reduces firms' costs of compliance and promotes confidence by reassuring investors that they are being treated fairly and that government is exercising its powers responsibly.

> **Do the competition authorities have adequate resources, political support and independence to implement effectively competition laws?**

The distinction between adopting a new law or policy and effectively implementing it can represent the difference between success and failure. Effective policy implementation requires that the competition authority have the resources and political support to do the job properly. Competition authorities must often challenge vested interests, such as private firms with monopolistic positions in the market or state-owned firms that fall under the regulatory authority of other parts of government. In the absence of a strong political commitment, efforts to promote competition, and hence investment, are in such cases likely to fail. Furthermore, a strong commitment to policy implementation and oversight at the political level can help to protect competition authorities themselves from regulatory capture. Political support for competition policy, which includes supplying sufficient resources for effective enforcement, is an important determinant of the potential contribution of competition policy to an attractive investment environment. Institutional settings vary widely, complicating the assessment of the degree of political support for competition policy, or of its vulnerability to special-interest intervention. Criteria that might be considered could include the status of the competition authorities within the government structure and the institutional arrangements for insulating enforcement decision-makers from political direction or influence.

4.2.2. Anti-competitive practices that inhibit investment

> **To what extent, and how, have the competition authorities addressed anti-competitive practices by incumbent enterprises, including state-owned enterprises, that inhibit investment?**

Incumbent enterprises can sometimes discourage investment by abusing their market power. For example, if an incumbent maintains exclusive distribution arrangements with its retailers or wholesalers, and the cost of establishing an alternative network is prohibitive, new entry and new investment may be impeded. Likewise, if a producer sells a product below cost (appropriately defined) with a view to recouping losses incurred after rivals have exited the industry, or would-be new entrants have been deterred. A credible threat of predatory pricing behaviour discourages prospective investors and can discourage investment in upstream and downstream industries. The demonstrated willingness of competition authorities to prevent, correct and sanction anticompetitive practices can thus have a significant positive bearing on the investment climate.

One type of barrier to entry consists in what is usually referred to as structural barriers. Structural barriers to entry pertain primarily to the various sunk costs (*i.e.* costs that can not be recovered by the firm in the event of exit from the industry) that firms must bear upon entry. In other words, sunk costs represent the investment that is put at risk by the investor.[4] Generally speaking, sunk costs act as a barrier to entry when these push the total cost of the project (variable costs, plus sunk and non-sunk fixed costs) above the expected net present value of the investment in question.[5] Other structural barriers to entry can include absolute cost advantages enjoyed by competitors (*e.g.* if the competitor has an inimitable technological advantage), economies of scale, and large capital requirements, including those associated with network industries (*e.g.* telecommunications).

Another type of barrier to entry is generally referred to as behavioural in nature. Behavioural barriers to entry consist of the various ways in which incumbent firms (domestic, foreign or state-owned) can impede market access by abusing their market power. For example, if a firm maintains exclusionary arrangements with retail or wholesale distributors in a given market (reciprocal exclusivity), and access to this distribution network is essential for serving the market in question, this effectively acts as a barrier to entry (assuming that the cost of establishing a second distribution network is prohibitive). Another type of behavioural barrier concerns predatory behaviour, which involves undercutting rivals with a view to eliminating these from the market in question (or "foreclosing" the market to new entrants). This can and usually does involve selling products below their cost of production with a view to recouping losses once weaker rivals (or new entrants) have been eliminated and monopoly pricing can be implemented or resumed. Predatory behaviour can have both an immediate and a more long-term impact on new investment insofar as the threat of predatory behaviour by a powerful incumbent (*e.g.* based upon precedent and reputation) could act to discourage prospective investors.

In practice, the distinction between structural and behavioural barriers to entry is not clear cut, with behavioural barriers usually being facilitated by structural barriers (and both often underpinned by aspects of the regulatory or policy environment). In the absence of structural barriers to entry, new firms will normally respond to any abnormal profits being earned by incumbents by entering the market, thus bringing prices back down to competitive levels. One of the challenges faced by governments has been to sort out, between various structural and behavioural market barriers, those that do not unduly harm competition and those that can and should be eliminated.

> **Do the competition authorities have the capacity to evaluate the impact of other policies on the ability of investors to enter the market? What channels of communication and co-operation have been established between competition authorities and other relevant government agencies?**

Some government policies and regulations directly discourage investment, for example, through prohibitions or restrictions on investment in certain sectors. Other policies and regulations are less direct, but can also discourage investment. Trade restrictions, for instance, can make a national market too small for those investments where economies of scale need to be reaped to be viable. One of the key challenges to establishing a sound investment environment is to identify and remove the unnecessary impediments to new investment. In this context, and without prejudice to the authority of government to regulate and the authority of other agencies in the conduct of their responsibilities, it is desirable to involve the competition policy authorities. This would help when laws and regulations are being developed to better appreciate competition policy perspectives, which through inter linkages bear on the investment environment.

More generally, ensuring coherence across policy areas is a principle of the Policy Framework for Investment. But it can present difficult trade-offs, notably in the domain of competition policy. For example, intellectual property rights (IPR) reward investments in creative and innovative activities with exclusive rights, limiting direct competition for a period. In the absence of IPR, such investment would be smaller, or non-existent. The difficulty for policy lies in balancing the considerations of competition policy and ensuring an incentive to create and innovate through, for instance, investments in research and development. There are also cross border considerations, including issues associated with the impact of licensing in home countries on competition in host countries, an area which has been identified as requiring further consideration.

4.2.3. Open trade and investment regimes can significantly reduce barriers to entry…

It has been argued that one of the best ways of ensuring that structural and behavioural barriers to entry do not impede investment is to simply maintain open trade and investment policies.[6] The reasoning behind this line of argumentation is that competition from potential foreign investors or from imports will naturally act to discipline firms that would seek to exercise some form of market power. In effect, by maintaining open trade and investment regimes the relevant market is no longer limited to the national market. For example, a firm that enjoys a monopoly position in a given country (in the sense that it is the sole producer located in the country) will nevertheless not be able to behave like a monopolist if monopoly pricing and above normal rents attract international competition which, in turn, drives prices back down. Alternatively, restrictive investment (and trade) policies are probably one of the "best" ways of establishing impediments to entry that enable incumbents to exercise market power.

However, experience suggests that open trade and investment regimes are not sufficient for ensuring the maintenance of contestability in national markets (i.e. the threat of new entrants in response to signals indicating abnormally high rents). Structural characteristics in any given economy can act to "buffer" incumbent firms from competition, even in the context of liberal trade and investment regimes. These can include, inter alia, the inherently local nature of some markets, the non-tradability of certain products and services, and regulations that are not per se restrictive from a trade or investment perspective (e.g. standards and licensing requirements). Furthermore, private restrictive practices, such as collusion in an adjacent (upstream or downstream) market, may inhibit trade and investment. Indeed, a number of countries with relatively open trade and investment regimes have reported on the need to complement open trade and investment regimes with active enforcement of competition laws (see Box 4.1 on the experience of Argentina).

4.2.4. Barriers to entry associated with FDI

One source of investment that has become increasingly important for developing countries consists of FDI. Although many of the barriers to entry identified above are

> ### Box 4.1. **The experience of Argentina with competition law and policy in the context of trade and investment liberalisation**
>
> In 1989, the Government of Argentina launched a radical reform of the economic system, involving, among other reforms, the lowering of trade barriers, the privatisation of the majority of state enterprises, the elimination of many industrial regulations, and the complete deregulation of foreign direct investment. During the early stages of this reform process, competition law and policy played a minor role in the expectation that the deregulation of markets and the liberalisation of trade and investment would be sufficient to provide competitive discipline and to achieve economic efficiency. However, over time, competition policy came to play a more important role as it became clear that, although the liberalisation of trade and investment did serve to encourage competition and economic efficiency in many sectors, this was not the case in all sectors. Examples of structural constraints and private business practices that served to constrain competition despite trade and investment liberalisation, and for which investigation by the Argentine National Commission for the Defence of Competition was deemed necessary, included:
>
> - Concentration in the liquefied petroleum gas industry, including control over key parts of the value chain (port facilities in particular), was associated with domestic prices remaining abnormally high.
>
> - Suspected collusion among incumbents within MERCOSUR in certain industries aimed to keeping out new entrants.
>
> - Apparent "stickiness" of response by potential new (especially foreign) entrants into the market in response to liberalisation due to structural barriers, including extremely strong brand dominance in one industry and the small size of the domestic market in another.
>
> - Suspected differential pricing by a quasi-monopolistic supplier, according to which a key customer was offered the international (competitive) price and smaller customers, for whom international sourcing would have been more difficult, were offered a much higher price.
>
> - Suspected discriminatory pricing by the subsidiary of an MNE with a dominant position globally for the product in question.
>
> *Source:* UNCTAD (1997). See also OECD (2004) for similar examples from Russia.

"neutral" insofar as they do not "discriminate" between foreign and domestic investors (*i.e.* they will discourage both), some barriers to entry are more specifically relevant with respect to their potential negative impact on FDI. In some cases this is because foreign and domestic investors are provided different levels of treatment. In other instances barriers to entry are *de facto* pertinent to FDI because the latter is a major, if not the main, source of the type of prospective investment in question. An important policy implication of this observation is that competition authorities, in their capacity as advocates of a culture of competition, including competition from foreign investors, need to cast their nets wide in order to identify potential policy impediments to the entry of foreign investment, even where these are not labelled as such or directed at foreign investors.

Exclusivity as a form of FDI incentive

As mentioned above, structural and behavioural barriers to entry often complement each other. In many instances, government regulation underpins this relationship. For example, one unusual issue at the inter-face of competition policy and FDI that has emerged in recent years concerns the granting of exclusivity to foreign investors as a form of FDI incentive. From the perspective of the firm offered this type of concession, the advantage lies in being able to exercise market power in the market in question (i.e. the firm enjoys some control over pricing and can therefore charge above marginal cost). From the perspective of government, the appeal of this type of incentive is that, at least on the surface, there is no immediately obvious financial cost and a firm that is granted some form of exclusivity is likely to be willing to pay more for the assets in question than would otherwise be the case. Indeed, the ultimate costs of this type of incentive are difficult if not impossible to calculate since these are borne by the customers of the supplier in the form of the above-normal prices the latter is able to charge and by the economy more generally in the form of the forgone benefits of subsequent investment, including FDI (i.e. subsequent investment that is barred as part of the exclusivity contract granted to the original investor).

For example, in 1995, the Sri Lankan government privatised the Colombo Gas Company through the sale of 51 per cent of the company to a foreign investor. As part of this deal, the foreign investor was given a five year monopoly for natural gas in the Sri Lankan market, protected from both import and foreign investment competition. As in most cases involving exclusivity as an incentive to attract FDI, the foreign investor was immune from the Sri Lankan competition authority and competition law until the end of the term of the agreement (UNCTAD, 1997).

Setting aside the question whether the granting of exclusivity to attract FDI is a good idea or not, competition authorities should be involved in decisions such as these since they bear directly upon the competitive structure of an economy. Competition authorities have come to play an increasingly important advocacy role such that their mandate extends beyond merely enforcing competition law, and in the case of incentives for FDI based upon exclusivity this advocacy role should involve, at a minimum, an evaluation of the (largely hidden) costs associated with such arrangements.[7]

"National champions"

Does the competition authority periodically evaluate the costs and benefits of industrial policies and take into consideration their impact on the investment environment?

Within the context of their development strategies, some governments have sought to promote "national champions", which, by definition, involves granting preferential treatment to some firms over others on the basis of nationality.[8] Although not SOEs, *per se*, national champions often do involve significant state involvement (both financial and with respect to management), and are usually granted some form of exclusivity (i.e. protection from trade and investment-based competition) in the national market. The arguments for national champions usually rely on considerations of dynamic (versus static) efficiency. They include arguments to the effect that economies of scale cannot be attained without restrictions on competition, these economies of scale allow for more spending on research and development, and, by extension, only once such economies of scale have been reached can firms realistically expect to be able to compete on international markets. The issue of national champions has been contentious and underlies one of the key difficulties in incorporating dynamic efficiency objectives into competition policy – how to find the right balance between static and dynamic efficiencies without reducing competition to such levels that any potential dynamic gains are completely eroded through "slack" – the inefficient use of resources within firms resulting from a lack of external market discipline, i.e. competition.

As in the case of "exclusive contracts" and regulated industries, efforts to promote national champions generally entail specific provisions aimed at limiting FDI. This is usually done on the grounds that the costs to the economy associated with limits placed on competition are outweighed by some other, either dynamic (e.g. promoting innovation) or social (e.g. provision of essential services) benefits. However, it remains that any policies specifically aimed at limiting competition in particular sectors run the risk of creating inefficiencies, reducing welfare in parts of the economy due to the exercise of monopolistic or monopsonistic market power, reducing investment in sectors of the economy that depend on protected firms due to the knock-on effects of higher costs, and creating powerful vested interests opposed to any reduction in protectionism. As such, there is a strong case to be made for the on-going involvement of competition authorities in the formulation and implementation of policies that would limit competition, especially with a view to ensuring that the costs of such limits (as difficult as these are to evaluate) do not outweigh any hoped-for benefits.

Granting privileged market positions to SOEs or other regulated firms

What is the role of the competition authorities in case of privatizations? Have competition considerations having a bearing on investment opportunities, such as not permitting market exclusivity clauses, been adequately addressed?

One of the most important areas of government regulation that can impact negatively on the ability of MNEs to enter a national market through FDI concerns regulated industries, including industries dominated by state owned enterprises (SOEs). Regulated sectors occasionally fall outside the reach of competition law. Indeed, certain types of firm behaviour and industry structures that would normally be considered anti-competitive (or potentially anti-competitive) in the private sector are sometimes permitted in the public sector. The most obvious instance of SOEs or otherwise highly regulated firms acting as impediments to FDI is when these have a mandate to act as the sole supplier in a particular industry (i.e. private firms, either foreign or domestic, are simply not allowed to enter this market). This has been the case, for example, in the energy and telecommunications sectors in a number of countries. However, regulated firms can also serve to impede entry to the extent that they are able to engage, through their linkages to the private sector either as buyers or suppliers, in many of the restrictive business practices associated with private firms (see Box 4.1). While recognising that legitimate differences exist between countries with respect to the relative roles ascribed to the private and public sectors,[9] it remains that competition authorities can play an important role in shedding light on the costs and benefits of policies that limit competition, thus contributing to more transparent, and informed policy formulation.

Competition authorities have sometimes found themselves at the margins of policy formulation and oversight of regulated industries,[10] including with respect to the wave of privatisations that swept through many regulated sectors during the 1990s. The motivation for many privatisations has been the recognition that many activities can be run more effectively and efficiently by the private sector. However, a concern of governments and competition authorities has been to avoid replacing public with private monopolies. This challenge has sometimes been complicated by conflicting objectives associated with privatisations, namely the desire to create more efficient industry structures, on the one hand, and the desire to sell state owned assets at the highest possible prices, on the other. Bidders for publicly owned companies, including MNEs, will be willing to pay more if they believe that they are buying a monopoly position in a particular market. However, as with the provision of exclusivity as a form of incentive to attract FDI, the primary consideration of competition authorities should be the long-term competitive benefits that FDI can bring to an economy rather than possible short-term budgetary windfalls.

> **To what extent are competition authorities working with their counterparts in other countries to co-operate on international competition issues, such as cross-border mergers and acquisitions, bearing on the investment environment?**

To this point, the discussion of the relationship between competition policy and the attractiveness of an economy for investors has focused on various barriers to entry that can impede domestic and foreign investment. In the second half of the discussion, several barriers to entry that are particularly relevant from an FDI perspective, such as "exclusive contracts", regulated industries, and efforts to promote national champions, were highlighted. However, once FDI takes place, a number of additional issues can come into play. The main reason for this relates to the fact that many MNEs have considerable financial resources at their disposal, they operate in industries that are often dominated globally by a handful of large firms, and they are able to establish dominant positions in many national markets through their foreign investments (even when this dominant position is not offered by the government as an incentive). Within the development context, the two main concerns of governments and competition authorities with respect to MNEs have been; 1) that MNEs expressly seek to exploit particular national markets, and 2) that the activities of MNEs can have structural implications with potentially negative effects on competition in some national markets.

With respect to the possibility that MNEs expressly seek to exploit their positions in particular national markets through FDI, this issue has received increasing attention in recent years as competition authorities have become more active in prosecuting various anti-competitive practices, and as evidence that MNEs are able to engage in market sharing arrangements at the global level has come to light. Many examples of successful prosecution in competition cases have involved competition authorities in developing countries, indicating that the implementation *and enforcement* of competition laws is not limited to developed economies (see, for example, WTO, 2003). Furthermore, empirical studies indicate that countries that have implemented competition laws have generally experienced less egregious price gouging at the hands of international cartels than countries without competition laws, indicating that these can serve as an important deterrent to abuse of market power (see, for example, WTO, 2003, section III).

With respect to structural issues, one of the key links between competition policy and FDI pertains to the involvement of competition authorities in reviewing proposed mergers and acquisitions. The potential importance of this issue is highlighted by the fact that mergers and acquisitions constitute the predominant mode of MNE expansion into foreign markets, accounting for 57 per cent of FDI inflows in 2002 (UNCTAD, 2003). Mergers and acquisitions are routinely reviewed by competition authorities with a view to determining whether particular combinations might give rise to levels of concentration that could be inimical to competition and, hence, efficiency.

Although the role of competition authorities in reviewing cross-border mergers and acquisitions has been limited predominantly to developed countries, in some cases competition authorities in developing countries have intervened where a merger between firms based outside the country has had implications for industry structure and competition in the host economy. For example, the proposed acquisition of one United States multinational by another in 1996 would have given their Mexican affiliates up to 67 per cent combined market share for certain products. The Mexican Federal Competition Commission therefore ordered the acquiring multinational to divest five major brands, thus reducing the combined company's market shares to around 50 per cent or less.

In another case of an international merger having implications for levels of concentration between existing foreign affiliates, two leading tea suppliers to Pakistan fell under common control of a major multinational. The Pakistan Monopoly Control Authority found that the prices paid by the companies for tea imported from related suppliers were higher than prices paid to unrelated international suppliers and therefore required that the multinational withdraw one of its brands and reduce its shareholding in one of the affiliates to 40 per cent.

Apart from a few fairly specific issues raised in the context of mergers and acquisitions involving MNEs and the possible implications of such transactions for market structures in countries in which the firms involved previously competed, generally FDI does not present challenges for competition authorities that require these to distinguish between foreign and domestic investors.[11] Indeed, competition law in most countries implicitly embodies the national treatment principle insofar as no distinction is made between domestic and foreign firms. As argued above, one of the overarching links between competition policy and an attractive environment for investment consists in ensuring that structural and behavioural impediments to market access do not discourage investment, irrespective of whether the investment is domestic or foreign. However, it remains that MNEs, by definition, operate across borders and thus create cross-border policy issues. Consequently, international co-operation among competition authorities has become more common with a view to addressing competition issues that span jurisdictions.

4.3. Conclusion

Competition authorities can play a positive role with respect to creating a healthy investment climate in developing countries. While competition policy should and usually does stay neutral insofar as it does not distinguish between foreign and domestic firms, this chapter has highlighted a number of issues that competition authorities should take into consideration within the context of creating an attractive environment for both domestic and foreign investment. While recognising that different countries at different levels of development will have different priorities, both between competition policy and other policy objectives and with respect to the internal objectives of competition policy itself, and also recognising that significant differences exist with respect to the role ascribed to competition and the private sector by different governments, this chapter has identified certain issues and questions that policy makers should take into consideration with a view to ensuring that regulatory and other impediments to competition do not run counter to efforts to improve the investment environment in pursuit of development objectives.

Notes

1. A number of existing WTO agreements already contain provisions that are relevant from a competition and investment perspective. For example, the TRIPS agreement (the Agreement on Trade-Related Intellectual Property Rights) stipulates that members of the WTO may take "appropriate measures … to prevent the abuse of intellectual property rights by right-holders or the resort to practices which unreasonably restrain trade or adversely affect the international transfer of technology" (article 40). A number of regional agreements that deal with trade and investment issues have also incorporated provisions dealing with competition issues. For example, the North American Free Trade Agreement (NAFTA) contains provisions that address competition issues related to SOEs and also has provisions on co-operation between competition authorities (chapter 15). See Trade and Competition Policies for Tomorrow, Ch. 4, "Competition Elements in International Trade Agreements: A Post-Uruguay Round Overview of WTO Agreements" and Ch. 5, "Implications of the WTO Agreements on Basic Telecommunications", OECD (1999).

2. By 2001, approximately 80 countries in the world had some form of competition law, WTO (2003).

3. One of the dynamic benefits associated with competition concerns the continuous investment in newer, more efficient technologies that supplant older products and processes. As such, competition policy is not just associated with the quantity of investment but (perhaps more importantly) the quality of investment that an economy is able to attract.

4. Sometimes regulatory barriers to entry are treated as a distinct type of barrier to entry. However, many regulatory barriers can be seen as a specific type of sunk cost. For example, many performance requirements or requirements that attach conditions to entry, such as testing for product safety, represent sunk costs for firms that must bear them.

5. In other words, an investor will want to at least break even, i.e. the expected returns over the life of the investment need to at least cover sunk plus variable costs.

6. Indeed, it has even been argued that, especially for smaller economies, open trade and investment regimes can effectively substitute for competition law and policy.

7. Including the possibility that a position of market dominance may last much longer than the formal period of exclusivity, unless special measures are taken to encourage new entry when that period ends.

8. Such as protection from competition through restrictions on FDI and trade protection, exemptions from competition law and various fiscal advantages.

9. Indeed, the Policy Framework for Investment recognises a country's sovereign "right to regulate".

10. It should be noted, however, that in a number of economies competition authorities have come to play a greater role in policy-making and formulation concerning regulated industries.

11. See Trade and Competition Policies: Options for a Greater Coherence, Ch. 5, "Merger Review and Market Access", OECD (2001).

References and Further Policy Resources

OECD (1994), Merger Cases in the Real World – A Study of Merger Control Procedures, Paris.

OECD (1995), Antitrust and Market Access, Paris.

OECD (1995), Revised Recommendation of the Council Concerning Co-operation between member Countries on Anti-Competitive Practices Affecting International Trade, Paris.

OECD (1996), Market Access after the Uruguay Round: Investment, Competition and Technology Perspectives, Paris.

OECD (1996), Shaping the 21st Century: The Contribution of Development Co-operation, Paris.

OECD (1998), Competition Policy and Intellectual Property Rights, Paris.

OECD (1998), Open Markets Matter: The Benefits of Trade and Investment Liberalisation, Paris.

OECD (1998), Recommendation of the Council Concerning Effective Action Against Hard Core Cartels. Paris.

OECD (1999), Trade and Competition Policies for Tomorrow, Paris.

OECD (1999), Report on Notification of Transnational Mergers, Paris.

OECD (2000), Hard Core Cartels, Paris.

OECD (2001), New Patterns of Industrial Globalisation: Cross-Border Mergers and Acquisitions and Strategic Alliances, Paris.

OECD (2001), Recommendation of the Council Concerning Structural Separation in Regulated Industries, Paris.

OECD (2001), Trade and Competition Policies: Options for a Greater Coherence, Paris.

OECD (2002), Fighting Hard-Core Cartels: Harm, Effective Sanctions, and Leniency Programmes, Paris. 2002.

OECD (2002), Nature and Impact of Hard Core Cartels and Sanctions against Cartels Under National Competition Law, Paris.

OECD (2002), Synthesis Report on Parallel Imports, Paris.

OECD (2004), OECD Global Forum on Competition: Preventing Market Abuses and Promoting Economic Efficiency, Growth, and Opportunity, Paris.

OECD (2004), Competition Law and Policy in Russia: An OECD Peer Review, Paris.

OECD (2004), "Roundtable on Intellectual Property Rights", Competition Committee Roundtable, Paris.

OECD (2005), Council Recommendation on Merger Review, Paris.

OECD-World Bank (1998), A Framework for the Design and Implementation of Competition Law and Policy, Paris and Washington, DC.

UNCTAD (1997), World Investment Report 1997: Transnational Corporations, Market Structure and Competition Policy (United Nations: Geneva and New York).

UNCTAD (2002), Closer Multilateral Cooperation on Competition Policy: The Development Dimension, Geneva.

UNCTAD (2002), Recent Important Competition Cases in Developing Countries (TB/D/COM.2/CLP/26).

UNCTAD (2002), Experiences Gained so far on International Cooperation on Competition Policy Issues and the Mechanisms Used (United Nations: Geneva and New York).

WTO (1997), "Trade and Competition Policy", in Annual Report of the World Trade Organization, Chapter IV, Geneva.

WTO (1998), Synthesis Paper on The Relationship of Trade and Competition Policy to Development and Economic Growth, WT/WGTCP/W/80.

WTO (2002), Modalities for Voluntary Cooperation, WT/WGTCP/W/192, Geneva.

WTO (2002), Provisions on Hardcore Cartels, WT/WGTCP/W/209, Geneva.

WTO (2002), Support for Progressive Reinforcement of Competition Institutions in Developing Countries Through Capacity Building, WT/WGTCP/W/182, Geneva.

WTO (2003), Study on Issues Relating to a Possible Multilateral Framework on Competition Policy, WT/WGTCP/W/229, Geneva.

ISBN 92-64-02586-3
Policy Framework for Investment
A Review of Good Practices
© OECD 2006

Chapter 5

Tax Policy*

*   This background document was prepared by W. Steven Clark, Head, Horizontal Programmes Unit, OECD Centre for Tax Policy and Administration.

5.1. Introduction

A country's tax regime is a key policy instrument that may negatively or positively influence investment. Imposing a tax burden that is high relative to benefits realised from public programmes in support of business and high relative to tax burdens levied in other competing locations, may discourage investment, particularly where location-specific profit opportunities are limited or profit margins are thin. In addition, the host country tax burden is a function of not only statutory tax provisions but also of compliance costs. A poorly designed tax system (covering laws, regulations and administration) may discourage capital investment where the rules and their application are non-transparent, or overly-complex, or unpredictable, adding to project costs and uncertainty over net profitability. Systems that leave excessive administrative discretion in the hands of officials in assigning tax relief tend to invite corruption and undermine good governance objectives fundamental to securing an attractive investment environment. Policy makers are therefore encouraged to ensure that their tax system is one that imposes an acceptable tax burden that can be accurately determined, keeps tax compliance and tax administration costs in check and addresses rather than contributes to project risk.

A modern, competitive, stable and transparent tax system, one that links host and home country tax systems through a well established tax treaty network to avoid double taxation, can send a strong positive signal to investors, both domestic and foreign. Investors generally prefer a low host country tax rate applied to a broadly defined profit base. At the same time, special incentives may play an important role in certain cases. Where tax incentives are used, care must be taken to ensure that incentive types and design features are chosen that are less likely than others to result in unintended and excessive revenue losses to non-targeted activities.

Balancing revenue losses from tax relief against the possible investment response is an important consideration in the majority of cases where companies can manage a modest host country tax burden. This recognises that tax relief may be too generous, in excess of that necessary to provide a tax environment that is supportive of investment. Where corporations are able to contribute to the financing of infrastructure development (*e.g.* roads, airports, telecommunications networks, and legal frameworks) that they benefit from, and are required to do so under a competitive but not easily manipulated set of tax rules, the tax system can serve to both attract investment and support parallel efforts to build a strong industrial base.

A central challenge for policy makers endeavouring to encourage domestic and foreign direct investment, but with limited financial resources to commit, is a careful weighing of relative advantages and disadvantages of alternative tax policy choices and design options in meeting the twin goals of attracting investment while at the same time raising revenues to support infrastructure development and other pillars of an enabling environment for direct investment.

This chapter explores these issues with the objective of providing background information and a summary "checklist" to guide policy makers when formulating a tax policy strategy that is supportive of investment, taking a "holistic" view of the role of the tax system.

Section 5.2 begins by sketching out various economic decisions influenced by taxation, decisions that impact the path of a country's economic development. Section 5.3 takes focus on the impact of taxation on investment, and highlights not only direct effects on after-tax rates of return (and thus possible effects on investment location and scale decisions), but also "budget effects" linking taxation to non-tax government programs in support of investment financed out of tax revenues. Section 5.4 elaborates tax considerations for policy makers to consider when assessing the possible need for reform towards a tax system better able to support investment.

5.2. Tax policy and development

Tax policy influences economic development through its influence over a number of economic decisions, including employment decisions, decisions over how much to invest in skills (human capital), as well as scale and location decisions involving investment in plant, property and equipment. Taxation also influences the relative attractiveness of purchasing or leasing tangible business property. The tax treatment of research and development (R&D) in different countries, and of payments under licensing agreements, impacts decisions over whether to produce intangibles (and if so, where) or purchase them or license them from others, with special tax-planning considerations arising in the case of intra-group transactions.

Some of the key linkages between tax policy and development may be highlighted as follows:

- *Employment*. Tax policy affects labour supply and labour demand decisions. Labour supply is influenced by the personal income tax (PIT) system (marginal PIT rates, thresholds, non-wastable earned income tax credits), and the social security contribution (SSC) system (employee SSC rates, thresholds). Labour demand is influenced as well by the SSC system (employer SSC rates, thresholds) and by tax effects on investment.

- *Investment in education and training (e.g. post-secondary education, skills upgrading)*. Tax factors in by influencing the benefits of (returns on) investment (with PIT and SSC contributions reducing, or augmenting with employment tax credits, wage income), and influencing the costs of investment incurred by firms (*e.g.* where firms are provided with special tax breaks to help defray the cost of training) and/or individuals (*e.g.* tax relief for education expenses).

- *Investment by firms in tangible and intangible assets*. Taxation alters the after-tax rate of return on investment by influencing after-tax revenues, net acquisition costs of assets and costs of equity and debt finance, leading to direct effects on investment.

- *Access to intangible assets through purchase or license agreements*. Rather than investing in R&D to develop intangible assets, influenced by the availability (or not) of special tax deductions and/or tax credits for R&D, a firm may purchase intangibles from others, or acquire the rights to use such assets. Taxation influences the optimal amount of intangible capital to hold, as well as the relative attraction and reliance on alternative means to acquire such capital (with possible implications for the scale of "spillover" effects on the domestic economy).

Tax policy also plays a role in influencing whether economic development is sustainable:

- *Income distribution effects*: Tax policy influences income distribution (*e.g.* progressive *versus* flat PIT rate structure, basic allowances, non-wastable tax credits). As sustainable economic development places constraints on inequality in income distribution, tax policy may hinder or help underpin support for a growth agenda.

- *Environmental effects*: Tax policy may be used as a market-based instrument to address environmental degradation (*e.g.* so-called "green" taxes). The use of market based instruments (environmental taxes, tradable permits) is now widely recognised as a more efficient means to address certain environmental concerns (*e.g.* global warming), than regulatory approaches.

- *Budget effects*: Tax policy, covering the tax treatment of investment, employment, other economic activities, transactions and assets, has indirect "budget" consequences, by influencing the amount of tax revenue available to fund public expenditures including programmes identified by investors as of critical importance in shaping the investment environment.

5.3. Taxation and investment – what are the linkages?

In examining tax effects on investment, one can distinguish effects on direct investment representing a significant active equity interest, from effects on portfolio investment by those holding a passive equity interest. This article focuses on effects on direct investment, including business expansions, branch investment, investment in subsidiaries, and mergers and acquisitions.

One can also distinguish tax effects in the "pure" domestic case (resident shareholders investing in domestic assets) *versus* cross-border investment, both inbound foreign direct investment (FDI) in domestic assets by non-resident shareholders, and outbound direct investment abroad (DIA) in foreign assets by resident investors. This article does not address special considerations relevant to the influence of home country taxation on outbound direct investment.[1]

A further distinction is between tax effects on direct investment of various types: in physical capital [*e.g.* plant, property and equipment (PP&E)]; investment in intangible assets (*e.g.* patents) through R&D; and investment in human capital (*e.g.* education, training). This article concentrates on tax effects on physical capital, and in particular PP&E scale and location decisions. Special tax considerations relating to the development and use of intangibles are not covered.

In examining the linkages between taxation and direct investment in physical capital, one is confronted with a range of taxes that form part of the tax system of developed (*e.g.* OECD) countries, as well as developing countries on an established transition path. The taxes include corporate income tax, non-resident withholding taxes, customs duties, personal income tax, social security contributions, value added tax, and other (generally less relevant) taxes. Home as well as host country taxes may factor in.

Focusing on domestic and inbound direct investment in physical capital, this article concentrates on primarily host country considerations, and highlights two main linkages between taxation and investment.[2] The first is the direct effect of taxation on the after-tax hurdle rate of return on investment. The second is the "budget effect" which recognises the basic role of tax in funding government programs, and the importance placed by business on adequately funding infra-structure development and skills development programs and public governance initiatives central to creating an enabling environment for investment.

5.3.1. Direct effects of taxation on investment

The taxation of profit derived from investment in a given host country [in the pure domestic case, or in the case of foreign direct investment (FDI)] may directly affect the amount of investment undertaken by influencing after-tax rates of return on investment.[3] In theory, a high (low) effective tax rate on domestic source income could be expected to discourage (encourage) domestic investment by resident investors, as well as inbound foreign direct investment.[4]

However, as in other areas, theory must be resolved with practice. It is clear that in general host country taxation adds to investment costs, particularly in the pure domestic case.[5] However, the predicted direct effect – that investment would fall if host country taxes are increased, and would increase if taxes are reduced – is not always observed.

Most would agree that a host country tax burden that is very high relative to other countries – influenced by statutory/legal provisions and by compliance costs – generally is discouraging to investment and could, in certain cases, be a deciding factor in not investing or reinvesting in a host country.

The more difficult issue is when – that is, under what circumstances and by which means – can a relatively low host country tax burden discourage capital flight, encourage additional investment, and swing location decisions in a country's favour? When, for example, can reduced statutory tax rates or incentives be expected to attract additional investment? As elaborated in section3, by identifying the factors that condition whether host country tax relief or subsidies can be expected to deliver additional investment, policy makers can assess how best to design an overall policy approach, one with mutually reinforcing elements, to provide an environment encouraging to direct investment.

While statutory tax provisions are clearly important, policy makers are also encouraged to consider difficult to measure (yet potentially impeding) business compliance costs associated with the level of transparency of the tax system.

5.3.2. Budget effects of taxation on investment

Host country taxation also impacts investment indirectly by contributing to, or constraining, the financing of the expenditure side of the budget equation. This point recognises that investment may be encouraged or discouraged by the state of infra-structure in a country (e.g. roads, airports, seaports), the skills profile of the workforce, the state of public governance, and other aspects of the investment environment that are supported by tax revenues.

It is often rightly emphasised that non-tax factors are of central importance to investment decisions – however often overlooked is the fact that public infra-structure, education and public governance policies and programmes and other key aspects of an enabling environment for investment require financing. And in many if not most countries, tax revenues are an important if not main source of funds (recognising that printing money to finance projects is inflationary, while borrowing funds is also subject to constraint).

Corporate tax and other taxes derived from investment contribute to general tax revenues used to finance government expenditure. While these taxes may form a relatively small percentage of total tax revenues, the absolute amounts may be large and should be seen as a potential source of revenue that may be used to help address non-tax investment deterrents identified as seriously impeding investment activity.

As noted, a central question facing policy makers is, under what circumstances and conditions can a relatively low host country tax burden operate to discourage capital flight, attract additional investment, and swing location decisions in a country's favour? Behind this question rests a central trade-off – by reducing taxes on host country investment and subsidizing investors, revenues are foregone that could instead be used to build up infrastructure, improve labour skills, strengthen governance, and address what in many country contexts are the real impediments to investment.

Thus the focus in most country contexts should be on the twin goals of designing tax systems and investor packages that are attractive to investment, while at the same time not foregoing funds that could be more usefully applied to fund public expenditures identified by investors as of critical importance.

5.4. Taxation and investment – A review of main considerations

The following provides a list of issues that policy makers are encouraged to consider when assessing whether a given host country tax system, and in particular corporate tax system, is supportive of direct investment in real productive capital, while also adequately addressing other tax policy objectives.

5.4.1. Comparative assessment of the tax burden on business income

> **Has the government evaluated the level of tax burden that would be consistent with its broader development objectives and its investment attraction strategy? Is this level consistent with the actual tax burden?**

How much tax revenue governments raise depends on their broader objectives. In this context, a central issue in gauging what level of tax burden would be consistent with the government's investment attraction strategy is whether the country offers appealing risk/return opportunities, taking into account framework conditions, market characteristics and location-specific profits, independent of tax considerations. Governments are encouraged to give recognition to the reasonable expectations of taxpayers when designing or reforming the tax system. Investors are generally willing to accept a higher tax burden the more attractive are the risk/return opportunities. On the returns side, potential investors examine the level of business costs, such as those attached to complying with regulations and administrative practices (see chapters on Public Governance and on Competition Policy) and pay attention to factors, such as the ability to recruit skilled labour (see chapter on Human Resource Development). On the risks side, potential investors examine the level of non-diversifiable risks associated with securing access to capital and profits (see chapter on Infrastructure and Financial Sector Development). Absolute and comparative assessments with regard to competing tax jurisdictions are also relevant for investor location decisions.

Framework conditions

Important to potential investors are questions over costs and non-diversifiable risks associated with securing access to capital and profits, adjusting to macroeconomic conditions, and complying with laws, regulations and administrative practices, including the following:

● How stable is the political system? How stable and accessible is the legal system protecting property rights including, in the foreign investor case, the right to withdraw capital and repatriate profits? Do capital controls exist?

● How stable is the monetary system and fiscal framework and what is the accumulated public debt? What are expectations over future inflation, interest and exchange rates?

● In what areas is public governance weak and where is corruption a problem?

● How significant are the costs and risks to business associated with the preceding considerations?

Market characteristics

Also centrally important to investors are considerations of output and factor market demand and supply:

● What is the domestic market size? How large is the domestic consumer market (number of households, average level and distribution of per capita income)? How large is the domestic producer market (number of firms, asset size, input requirements)? How large and accessible are markets in other (*e.g.* neighbouring) countries?

● What labour force skills are available in the host country and what employee benefits (*e.g.* social security) are provided by the state? What energy sources and raw materials are available in the host country? Are labour costs (wages plus mandatory employer social security contributions), energy costs, raw material costs high/low relative to competing jurisdictions?

● What is the state of the host country's infra-structure covering transportation services (airports, seaports, rail systems, roads), telecommunications (phone/fax/internet services), other services important to business? Are private costs of using/purchasing infra-structure services high/low relative to competing jurisdictions?

Prevalence of location-specific profits

Assessments by investors of the risk/return on investment in a host country would normally factor in framework conditions and market characteristics of the country (or a region of the country where market characteristics vary by region). Assessments would be made in absolute terms, and relative or comparative terms (to examine risk/return differences when serving a market from one or more alternative locations).[6] In other words, a central question is how location-specific are the potential profits and risk when locating in/operating from a given host country?

For many if not most investments, levels of profit and risk associated with undertaking a given business activity part of a value-added chain, or meeting a particular market demand, may vary significantly across alternative locations, and may in certain cases be "location specific" – that is, may require a physical presence in a particular location. Examples of the latter would include privatizations, the extraction of natural resources, and the provision of restaurant and hotel services. In such cases, if profits can be expected at levels of risk investors are willing to assume, the profits are location-specific – that is, they cannot be realised by locating in another country or jurisdiction. This is not to say there would not be other similarly attractive (or more attractive) projects in other markets. It simply recognises that such investment projects could be expected to be undertaken if profitable, at acceptable levels of risk.

At the other extreme, investment projects to serve particular markets (*e.g.* investments to support the provision of "head office" or intra-group financial services) may be carried out from any one of a large number of alternative locations, at roughly the same profit/risk.

In between these extremes would be projects where there are several locations for a particular investment that offer similar economic profit at the roughly same level of risk (or alternatively, higher/lower profits at higher/lower levels of risk). Examples include R&D facilities and manufacturing plants producing outputs (*e.g.* pharmaceuticals, computer chips) for export markets.

Implications for tax policy

In general, investors are willing to accept a higher host country tax burden the more attractive are pre-tax profits for a given risk when investing in that country, with reference to framework conditions, market characteristics and location-specific profit opportunities. As emphasised in this article, the attractiveness of investment opportunities in a host country depends, in small or large part, on the type of business activity, on past and current public expenditure allocations towards public programs (*e.g.* education) and projects (*e.g.* infrastructure) supportive of framework conditions, and other market characteristics.

Where a profitable investment opportunity is specific to a particular host country, the tax burden may be largely irrelevant to an investment decision. Indeed, in principle, the tax burden on location-specific profit could be increased up to the point where economic profit is exhausted without discouraging investment.[7] Moreover, tax comparisons across locations (states/countries) generally would not factor in (with profit being specific to a particular location). Thus, where an economy offers an abundant set of location-specific rents, policy makers may understandably resist pressures to adjust to a relatively tax burden, to avoid tax revenue losses and windfall gains to investors (and to foreign treasuries in the case of inbound investment). Reducing the effective host country tax rate (*e.g.* to levels observed in competing countries) while possibly attracting capital in elastic supply, would give up tax revenues without impacting investment capital in inelastic supply.

In the context of economic profit that is not location-specific, comparisons with tax burdens imposed in competing locations would be expected to factor in. Where the number of competing locations is many (few), then the number of relevant tax comparisons would be many (few). If a given business activity can be carried out in a competing location that imposes tax on business at a relatively low rate, while offering as attractive a pre-tax risk/return profile as location A (taking account of all benefits, non-tax costs and risks associated with each location choice), then in theory investors would be unwilling to bear a tax burden in location A in excess of that rate.[8] Where a competing location offers a less attractive pre-tax risk/return profile, then investors may be willing to pay a higher tax burden in location A without being encouraged to invest elsewhere. However, where a competing location offers a more attractive pre-tax risk/return opportunity, it does not follow that a relatively low tax burden in A could be expected to compensate for investment impediments and swing investment in location A's favour. This is particularly true where tax incentive relief is low relative to additional costs incurred in investing in A, and/or contributes rather than reduces project costs and risks.

These generalisations, while helpful in considering possible outcomes of different host tax burdens, gloss-over practical assessment difficulties, and must be qualified on several counts. Under the simplified predictions remain difficulties over how to asses the relative significance to business profits of business framework and market considerations in competing locations. Where investment conditions in a given location are on balance more attractive than those elsewhere, the question arises as to how much higher the tax burden at source may be set without significantly impacting investment. And where investment can be expected to decline, at what rate and in what sectors? There also remains the fact that for inbound investors resident in countries operating residence-based tax systems, significant scope may exist for such investors to partially or fully offset host country tax using foreign tax credits provided by the home country. Whether this type of relief applies depends on the relative setting of host and home country tax rates, rules on the pooling or separate treatment of different sources of foreign income, as well as the current needs of the investor for repatriated earnings.

What is the average tax burden on domestic profits, taking into account statutory provisions, tax-planning opportunities and compliance costs?

The statutory tax burden on domestic profits ought to be assessed using quantitative measures and qualitative information, taking into account the main statutory provisions and the effects of tax-planning strategies commonly employed by domestic and foreign-owned businesses (*e.g.* thin capitalisation, non-arm's length transfer prices) to lower the host country tax burden. Compliance costs from excessive complexity, non-transparency and unpredictability should also be factored in.

Assessment of host country tax burden

On the quantitative side, corporate marginal effective tax rates (METRs) and corporate average effective tax rates (AETRs) are commonly used to assess the net effect of (certain) main statutory provisions in determining effective tax rates by type of capital asset (machinery and equipment, buildings, inventories, intangibles) and by investor type (taxable resident, tax-exempt resident, non-resident). Such measures may be finessed by factoring in effects of tax-planning strategies employed in the host country to strip out taxable profits (*e.g.* thin capitalisation, non-arm's length transfer prices) to tax havens.

An attraction of measuring corporate marginal and average effective tax rates is that they can be modelled with reference to statutory tax provisions alone, found in tax legislation and regulations (*i.e.* they do not require information on actual tax revenues collected). However, as such summary measures cannot readily incorporate the effects of all relevant tax provisions bearing on the average host country tax burden, they need to be qualified with regard to such effects (*e.g.* the impact of rules governing the carry-forward of business losses, and capital losses).

Furthermore, where taxpayer-level information is available (*i.e.* taxpayer financial statements, tax returns), a stratified sample of corporations should be chosen and relevant micro-data examined in order to obtain measures of the tax burden on domestic firms, on an aggregate and disaggregate basis (profitable and taxable, profitable and non-taxable, non-profitable; small, medium and large with reference to total assets; main industry sector; region). As examined elsewhere, results based on micro-data provide a much stronger basis to analyze tax burdens across sectors and over time.[9]

Compliance costs should also be factored in, at least on a qualitative basis. Too often, policy makers assess a host country tax burden with reference to only the direct effects of statutory provisions. A *more appropriate measure takes into account tax compliance costs*, which in some cases may be quite significant, depending on the degree and sources of complexity, transparency and predictability.[10]

Tax burden linked to an excessively complex business tax system

In addressing today's complex business structures and transactions, a certain degree of complexity in the tax system is to be expected. However, where investors view a tax system (laws, regulations and/or administration) to be excessively complex relative to other tax systems, the added expense to project costs incurred in understanding and complying with the tax system would tend to discourage investor interest.

Such a review would begin by identifying the various sources of complexity – including those linked directly to tax policy, those relating to mechanisms by which policy is implemented, and those linked to tax administration – and examining whether the degree of complexity is avoidable with consideration given to approaches adopted by other countries.

One area to consider is whether the structure of the depreciation system for tax purposes (number of classes of depreciable capital cost, assignment of depreciation methods) is consistent with international norms. If the depreciation system has been characterised frequently by business as overly complex, then serious consideration should be given to possible simplification.[11]

As an illustration of possible trade-offs when addressing complexity, consider integration of corporate and personal income taxation of equity income to reduce or eliminate double taxation of domestic profits. Where double taxation relief is desirable (*e.g.* creates investment (host country benefits) that more than outweighs tax revenues foregone), it is important for policy makers to recognise the advantages that a simple approach could bring. In this example a relevant trade-off could be between efficiency, calling for a variable imputation tax credit at the personal level that depends on the amount of corporate tax actually paid on distributed income, and simplicity, which may call for partial inclusion of dividend income, or a fixed dividend tax credit based on a notional or assumed level of corporate tax.

Tax burden linked to a non-transparent business tax system

Another important aspect of tax compliance costs concerns transparency. In considering this issue, it must first be recognised that even a relatively simple system may lack transparency, as for example where tax laws and terms are unclear, tax returns and information materials are difficult to obtain, and taxpayer compliance support is weak. As with complexity, a lack of transparency contributes to project costs. It also raises concerns of fairness, and may lead to suspicion that the tax system is tailored to the interests of a subset of taxpayers, including those earning higher incomes, able to afford professional tax advice and possibly benefiting from special tax treatment. Perceptions of unfairness challenge tax systems based on voluntary compliance, as they tend to encourage non-compliance and transition of business activity to the "underground economy", raising revenue concerns and concerns of the weakening of government performance more generally.

Policy makers are therefore encouraged to satisfy themselves that tax laws and regulations are drafted clearly and preferably by those trained in legal drafting of tax provisions. Tax returns, explanatory notes and information circulars should be readily available to taxpayers (*e.g.* electronically), and services should be available to provide advance rulings on the tax treatment of transactions where tax outcomes are unclear.

Another important "transparency" issue is whether business tax liability in certain cases is established at the discretion of tax authorities (*e.g.* through individual rulings, or informal dealings), rather than through uniform application of tax laws and regulations. Where administrative discretion is provided, the policy reason for providing this discretion should be questioned, as a key concern is whether administrative discretion contributes to or invites corrupt practices on the part of tax officials (*e.g.* the taking of bribes). Where it does, administrative discretion may contribute to investor uncertainty over final tax liability and the tax liability of other firms. Where corruption is a problem and administrative discretion contributes to project risk due to uncertainties over tax treatment, the potential benefits of such discretion (*e.g.* tighter control over tax relief) should be weighed against the various costs including those linked to reduced transparency.

Tax burden linked to an unpredictable business tax system

Non-transparency in the tax area contributes to investor difficulty in gauging with some degree of certainty future after-tax returns on host country investment. So too can frequent reforms of tax systems, even where they are relatively simple and transparent. While a certain degree of unpredictability may be associated with all tax systems, a system may be judged to be relatively or excessively unpredictable if the host country has a history of frequent and dramatic changes to important elements of the tax system, that is, elements bearing significantly on investment returns.

Relevant questions on this issue include: what elements of the tax system have contributed to unpredictability and how can these be best avoided? Is responsibility for tax legislation governing the taxation of business income assigned to a single ministry of the central government (*e.g.* Ministry of Finance), recognising difficulties that arise where this is not the case? Are (all) income tax laws/regulations contained in a single body or act of legislation, recognising difficulties that arise where this is not the case? Is a single ministry, department, or agency of central government responsible for the administration of corporate income tax and personal income tax (*e.g.* with local/regional offices)? If income tax legislation and administration are not centralised, what problems of co-ordination have arisen, what has been the impact on taxpayer tax compliance costs (in relation to complexity, predictability, transparency), and what reforms are desirable?

> **Is the tax burden on the business enterprises of investors appropriate with reference to the policy goals and objectives of the tax system?**

In deciding the tax burden to impose on the domestic profits of business enterprises, governments weigh the objectives guiding overall tax policy design, including efficiency and equity concerns, compliance costs and revenue requirements. Where different goals suggest different tax burden levels, an appropriate balancing of competing objectives is desirable, initially taking revenue requirements as given.

Choice over an appropriate host country tax burden on investment, shaped by balancing considerations, may begin with a fixed overall revenue requirement (to fund a given set of public expenditures including transfers to other levels of government, with revisions to overall revenue targets and expenditures possibly required). Given revenue requirements, policymakers would normally rely on a mix of taxes to meet those needs (*e.g.* taxes on income and profits, taxes on property and wealth, consumption taxes, trade taxes, other taxes) for reasons of equity, as some taxes tend to be borne more by some taxpayers compared with others, and efficiency, as various tax bases respond to a greater or lesser extent differently to taxation. In other words, there are limits to reliance on a given tax base, so a variety of taxes are typically included in the "tax mix". In addition to efficiency and equity concerns, other considerations (*e.g.* taxpayer compliance costs, tax administration costs, as well as others) factor in.

Efficiency concerns, based on an assessment of individual utility derived from income, leisure and other factors impacting individual welfare (*e.g.* a clean environment) consider the extent to which the underlying activity of a tax responds to changes in the level of taxation. In general, efficiency is judged to be reduced where a productive activity such as labour or investment, generating returns in excess of opportunity costs, is reduced, for example by a tax on wages or profits. In contrast, efficiency or welfare may be enhanced where pollution is reduced, for example with the introduction of an environmental tax.

Equity concerns generally call for an equal sharing of the tax burden across different taxpayers with roughly the same income or purchasing power (horizontal equity), and a progressive tax burden as income is increased, with those earning more income paying a higher percentage of their income in tax.

A balancing of considerations finds support in most countries for tax on business income at the personal and corporate level – primarily for horizontal equity reasons (between employees earnings wage income, self-employed earning wage and capital income, owners of unincorporated businesses, and shareholders). Given a desire to tax income from capital, a corporate income tax provides a withholding function, taxing income that could otherwise be avoided (by profit retention) or difficult to tax under accrual rules.

Efficiency considerations in policy choices over the appropriate tax burden on business hinge on the sensitivity of the business income tax base to taxation. Where the tax base is sensitive, generally lower levels of taxation would be called for on efficiency grounds. That is to say that in setting the level of the tax burden on domestic business income, policy makers must factor in limits to taxation of business income, with higher taxation tending to encourage capital flight and non-reporting.

> **If framework conditions and market characteristics for investors are weak, has the government evaluated the limitations of using tax policy alone to influence favourably investment decisions?**

Policy-makers are encouraged to reflect on the disappointing experience of economies that have attempted to rely on a low tax burden – typically targeted at foreign investment – to boost investment. Where framework conditions or market characteristics are weak, first consideration should be given to addressing the sources of a weak investment environment. Realistic expectations should be made of how much additional investment a reduced tax burden would bring forth and the scale of tax-planning opportunities created. Where a low tax burden is to be achieved through the use of special tax incentives, evaluations of their potential to attract investment ought to take into consideration the possibility that tax incentives may discourage investment by contributing to project cost and risk and induce a misallocation of resources.

A corollary to this is that a host country with weak framework conditions and following a special tax incentive strategy may be giving up significant tax revenues that could collected without discouraging investment that has been made in the host country for reasons unrelated to tax – revenues that could be used to help strengthen the enabling environment for investment.

A further issue concerns the method by which a low tax burden is achieved, and in particular, whether tax relief applies to returns on marginal or infra-marginal investment. To varying degrees, tax relief will result in windfall gains – that is, tax relief to investors (or increased revenues to foreign treasuries) that does not result in additional investment, but supports investment that would have gone ahead in the absence of that relief – even where such relief is specifically targeted at additional investment.

Consider for example incremental tax credits, where tax relief is tied to some percentage of current investment in excess of average annual investment in prior years. Even in such cases, some fraction of qualifying investment would be expected to occur in the absence of the credit. Windfall gains are more likely where flat credits are used (that provide tax relief equal to some percentage of current investment), chosen for simplicity or to avoid certain distortions with the incremental model. Windfall gains are even more likely for incentives that provide tax relief equal to some percentage of profit derived from new and existing capital. A tax exemption for a certain fraction of profit, or a reduced statutory corporate income tax rate, would be examples of relief in respect of returns on new and existing capital. As existing capital is already in place, relief granted in respect of such capital provides a pure windfall gain.[12]

> **Where the tax burden on business income differs by firm size, age of the business entity, ownership structure, industrial sector or location, can these differences be justified? Is the tax system neutral in its treatment of foreign and domestic investors?**

Tax systems may purposefully impose a non-uniform effective tax rate on businesses, based on criteria such as the size and age of an enterprise, its ownership structure (*e.g.* domestic *versus* foreign-owned), the type of business activity or its location. In other cases, certain firms may be specifically targeted to receive preferential tax treatment. Where tax relief is targeted, policy makers should examine the arguments in favour and against such preferential treatment, be able to weigh up these arguments and be in a position to justify differential tax treatment. (On the issue of fair treatment of investors, see the Chapter on

Investment Policy.) Where justifications are weak, first consideration should be given to a non-targeted approach, so as not to induce a misallocation of resources.

In addressing this issue, the analysis could include an assessment of the average effective tax rate (AETR) on profits of i) small and medium-sized enterprises (SMEs), ii) large enterprises majority-owned by residents, iii) large multinational enterprises (MNEs) controlled by foreign parent companies, taking into account main statutory tax provisions?[13] Such an approach could be used to inform an assessment of whether tax-driven variations in AETRs across businesses of different size, ownership structure, and industrial sector can be justified, taking into account unintended distortions and other costs that they create.[14]

5.4.2. Determination of taxable business income

> Are rules for the determination of corporate taxable income formulated with reference to a benchmark income definition (e.g. comprehensive income), and are the main tax provisions generally consistent with international norms?

With any corporate tax system, investors expect the calculation of corporate taxable income to adequately reflect business costs, via basic tax provisions such as loss carry-forward rules that are not more onerous than those commonly found elsewhere. Investors also view negatively the double taxation of income within the corporate sector, and generally expect zero taxation of or tax relief on, inter-corporate dividends, particularly when these are paid along a corporate chain.

Tax officials of Governments wishing to retain and attract investment should be encouraged to address (and weigh, within the set of overall policy objectives) various concerns of investors with respect to tax base rules. These concerns may be raised by the following set of questions:

- Do tax depreciation methods and rates adequately reflect true economic rates of depreciation of broad classes of depreciable property (serving as benchmark rates) and account for inflation?

- Are possible time limits on the carrying forward (and possibly back) of business losses, to offset taxable income in future (prior) years, sufficiently generous/consistent with international norms? [The case for generous carry-forward is particularly strong where depreciation claims are mandatory, rather than discretionary. Also important to consider is the interaction between depreciation and loss carry-forward rules.]

- Are inter-corporate dividends (paid from one resident company to another) excluded from corporate taxable income to avoid double/multiple taxation? Are domestic dividends paid to resident individuals subject to classical treatment, or is integration relief provided in respect of corporate tax on distributed income (e.g. partial inclusion of dividend income, or imputation or dividend tax credit)? Is there evidence that such relief lowers the cost of funds for firms? Or is such relief intended to encourage domestic savings? Where integration relief is given in respect of distributed profit (dividends), is similar relief provided in respect of retained profit (e.g. partial inclusion of dividends and capital gains)?

- Where capital gains are subject to tax on a realisation basis, are taxpayers allowed a deduction for capital losses (*e.g.* against corresponding taxable capital gains)? Do "recapture" rules apply to draw into taxable income excess tax depreciation claims on depreciable property?

- Is the tax treatment of wage income, as well as interest income, dividends and capital gains (realised at the personal or corporate level) designed to minimize incentives to i) characterise one form of income as another, and ii) choose one organisational form over another (incorporated *versus* unincorporated) for purely tax reasons? In other words, are efforts made to minimize tax arbitrage possibilities?

At the same time as addressing investors' concerns, policy makers should be encouraged to:

- Limit windfall gains (*i.e.* the provision of tax relief that does not achieve desired goals) to investors and, in the case of inbound direct investment, foreign treasuries.

- Minimise scope for the exploitation by business of the tax system (*e.g.* through tax arbitrage).

- Ensure single taxation of income sourced in the host country (*e.g.* through enforcement of domestic tax rules, and negotiation of tax treaties).

- Keep tax administration costs in check.

5.4.3. Prudent use of targeted tax incentives

> **Have targeted tax incentives for investors and others created unintended tax-panning opportunities? Are these opportunities and other problems associated with targeted tax incentives evaluated and taken into account in assessing their cost-effectiveness?**

Unfortunately, tax incentives are all too often viewed as a relatively easy "fix" by those working outside the tax area, and those with limited experience working in it. A tax incentive may be quickly incorporated into a budget announcement, and holds out the apparent advantage of not requiring a cash-equivalent outlay, in contrast with an infrastructure development, manpower training, or other programme introduced to foster investment. The reasoning goes as follows: by targeting tax relief at new investment, a tax incentive will only reduce the amount of tax revenue raised on additional investment – revenue that would not have been raised anyway in the absence of the incentive.

However, this perception misses the fact that tax incentive relief, even when targeted at new investment, will always be sought by businesses outside the target group. Existing firms will attempt to characterize themselves as "new", and other similar tax-planning strategies can be expected that will deplete tax revenues from activities unrelated to any new investment attributable to the tax relief, with lost revenues often many multiples in excess of original projections. In contrast, direct cash grants, while raising possibly greater concerns over inviting corruption (unless significant administrative discretion is also involved in the granting of targeted tax incentives), may offer greater control over various types of abuse.

Tax holidays and partial profit exemptions, typically targeted at "new" companies, offer significant scope for tax relief unintended by the tax authorities. Other forms of targeted tax relief may also create unintended scope for tax planning, and result in revenue losses well in excess of levels originally anticipated (e.g. where the relief spills over to benefit non-targeted taxpayer groups). While notoriously difficult to predict, policy makers are encouraged to consult widely to sharpen estimates of the revenue losses from a given incentive.

Tax holidays and partial profit exemptions are typically targeted at "new" companies. However, it is hard for tax administrators to determine if a newly-established company is actually financed by new capital, or instead by capital already invested in the host country. In other words, much of the "new" capital may in fact be previously existing capital that has been re-characterised as new (e.g. through liquidation of an existing company, with the capital invested temporarily in an offshore holding company, then re-invested in the host country with the appearance of new investment by that offshore company).

Provisions providing for a partial or full profit exemption also open up transfer pricing opportunities to artificially shift taxable income of business entities in the host country that do not qualify for special tax relief to entities that do. Aggressive transfer pricing techniques essentially involve the use of non-arm's length prices on intra-group transactions, and non-arm's length interest rates on intra-group loans, to shift taxable income to low or no-taxed entities. The shifting of tax base in such cases is artificial in the sense that it takes the underlying business structure as given, and simply manipulates prices to shift the taxable income associated with the structure to obtain the most tax efficient outcome. As guarding against such abuse of the tax system is becoming increasingly difficult with increased trade in intangibles (for which an arm's length price is often difficult to fairly establish by tax authorities, due to limited or non-existent second markets to look to), so too is it becoming increasingly difficult to guard against excessive revenue losses stemming from incentives providing for a full or partial profit exemption.

It should also be pointed out that where a tax incentive is in place and previously unforeseen tax-planning opportunities become all too apparent, it is not without cost for the government to withdraw the incentive to protect the domestic tax base from further erosion. While cancelling incentive relief for future investment may be accepted by investors, cancelling relief tied to prior investment decisions – that may have been based on the expectation of tax incentives previously on offer – can carry a significant cost. In particular, policy credibility is seriously undermined, weakening the ability of government to influence investment behaviour in the future through policy adjustment. Given this, where tax incentive relief linked to investment expenditure (e.g. enhanced or accelerated depreciation, investment tax credit) is cancelled, tax relief tied to prior investment generally should be respected (not withdrawn) – unless the costs are so exorbitant that respecting past commitments would be devastating to public finances.

To varying degrees depending partly on the instrument used, reduced host country taxation will provide tax relief in respect of investment that would have been undertaken in the absence of such relief – so-called "windfall gains" to investors and, in the case of FDI, foreign treasuries. Windfall gains arise even where tax relief is targeted at "incremental" investment in excess of some average of past investment. Avoiding windfall gains, however, generally comes at the cost of increased complexity.[15]

Within the context of a general policy goal to avoid windfall gains (and losses), *transitional considerations* related to the introduction and removal of tax incentives should be addressed. Where tax relief is provided, a general aim is to target tax relief to incremental investment, that is, investment that would not have occurred in the absence of the incentive. Conversely, where tax relief is withdrawn, it is important to attempt to ensure that past investments are not penalised.

Targeted tax incentives may create *unintended distortions* to the allocation of productive capital, and to corporate financing and repatriation decisions, implying welfare losses.[16] Accelerated depreciation rates, for example, may create welfare losses where they do not adequately reflect variations in true economic rates of depreciation across capital asset classes (serving as benchmark rates). Similarly, reinvestment allowances providing a tax deduction equal to some percentage of reinvested (pre-tax) profit would tend to discourage investment financed by new equity, and may raise the overall cost of funds, implying welfare losses.[17]

Unintended distortions may also be created where inter-actions between tax incentives and other provisions of the tax code (*e.g.* depreciation treatment, loss treatment) are not adequately addressed. Furthermore, policy-making, if not properly co-ordinated, may result in the "stacking" of multiple tax (and non-tax) incentives on offer by different Ministries, at the same level or by different levels of government (*i.e.* targeted at the same or similar business activities, assets, or regions), creating unintended distortions including possible over-investment in certain cases.

Tax incentives, even those held out as simplifying measures, may also create *additional complexity* and add to compliance and tax administration costs. For example, some argue that tax holidays are a simple incentive to administer, as there is no need for corporations (or government) to worry about maintaining financial records to support tax returns over the holiday period. However, in order for firms to claim tax deductions (*e.g.* business loss carryovers) following the holiday period, a full record of revenues and costs over the holiday period would normally be required. Assembling and verifying this data post-holiday may be more difficult and time consuming than had the required financial records been maintained all along.

Tax incentives may also *encourage corruption* and aggravate concerns raised by poor public governance. When used, targeted tax incentives should be designed to be as automatic as possible in their application, to avoid the involvement of tax officials in the determination of the application of provisions to individual taxpayers. Also to be avoided are situations where tax officials undertaking audits have the power to withdraw tax incentive relief, without special safeguards against corrupt practices. Frameworks should be in place to discourage bribery of tax and customs officials in such cases.

Lastly, targeted tax incentives may be *inconsistent with international obligations* (*e.g.* national treatment obligations, State Aid Rules applicable for member countries of the European Union).

Where strong political pressure is felt for introducing tax incentive relief, despite analysis indicating limited investment response relative to the revenue losses (to existing qualifying and non-qualifying investors) and administrative costs entailed – implying failure to meet a cost-benefit test – policy makers should argue the case for exploring options to address the impediments to investment directly.

Addressing main impediments to investment

When considering the use of targeted tax incentives to support investment, due attention should be paid to scope for addressing investment impediments directly. Attention to tackling real impediments unrelated to tax should be addressed prior to, or at a minimum parallel with, attempting a tax solution.

Where weak framework conditions (poor budget management, poor public governance, corrupt practices on the part of tax and customs officials) and/or high project costs (linked to poor infrastructure, high labour costs or other factor costs) are impeding to investment, certain public officials may be attracted to the option of recourse to tax incentives. In such cases, policy makers should be encouraged to consider what policy and administrative changes may be implemented to address investment impediments directly, beginning with areas where progress can be achieved quickly. Where policy adjustments require additional tax revenues, priority areas should be identified and revenues bases examined.

Broad-based tax relief and non-tax relief

When considering possible tax strategies to attract investment, consideration should be given to non-targeted relief measures to avoid the problems encountered with targeting. Such approaches could include a reduced statutory corporate tax rate applied to a broadly-defined corporate tax base (in order to avoid unintended consequences and revenue losses) as an alternative strategy of narrowing the tax base through a reliance on targeted tax incentives. Consideration should also be given to addressing possible impediments in the tax system owing to restrictive provisions (*e.g.* limited loss carry-forward rules), or provisions contributing to compliance costs.

Finally, it is important for tax officials to recall that financial assistance to business may be delivered outside the tax system. This more transparent mechanism may be more desirable, particularly where the tax administration system is relatively inexperienced or weak and open to corruption.

5.4.4. *Tax expenditure reporting and evaluation*

> **Are tax expenditure accounts reported and sunset clauses used to inform and manage the budget process?**

Tax expenditure analysis measuring revenue foregone by targeted tax incentives and other departures from a benchmark tax system should be a feature of fiscal policy in countries where attracting investors and addressing public governance issues (see chapter 10 on Public Governance) are high on the policy agenda. Such accounts should be subject to public scrutiny and be considered alongside corresponding direct expenditures to inform the budget process.

Tax expenditure assessment requires the Ministry of Finance or Tax Administration Department maintaining a micro-simulation model to estimate tax revenue and income distribution effects of proposed and actual tax reforms, drawing on a representative sample of personal and corporate income tax returns. Assessing foregone revenues should take into account, to the extent predicted, likely tax planning responses. Such analyses should be based on a variety of inputs, including consultations with business and findings of other countries that have tested similar measures (taking into account different host country conditions in shaping outcomes).

For proper management of public finances, tax incentives targeted to boost investment should be assessed in advance and, if introduced, evaluated on a periodic basis to gauge whether such measures continue to pass a cost-benefit test. To enable a proper evaluation and assessment, the specific goals of a given tax incentive need to be made explicit at the outset. Further, if tax incentive legislation is introduced, "sunset clauses" calling for the expiry of the incentive (e.g. 3 years after implementation) should be included to provide an opportunity to assess whether the incentive should be extended or not.

5.4.5. International co-operation

> **Are tax policy and tax administration officials working with their counterparts in other countries to expand their tax treaty network and to counter abusive cross-border tax planning strategies?**

A wide tax treaty network is helpful to countries seeking to raise and attract investment in several ways. First, and perhaps foremost, tax treaties operate to avoid double taxation of cross border returns – with the prospect of double taxation on cross-border returns being a major concern in the cross-border investment context. In the absence of a tax treaty between a host and home country, double taxation of returns will normally arise where the two countries treat a given return differently. For example, countries may take different views on the source or origin of income, and/or the type of income paid (e.g. interest versus dividends), with different characterizations triggering different tax treatment. Tax treaties operate to avoid these different characterizations and thereby minimize the scope for double taxation, thereby reducing project costs (with tax viewed as a business cost).

Tax treaties, by providing greater transparency over the tax treatment of cross-border investment, also help reduce investor uncertainty over tax treatment. Indeed, certain articles of tax treaties are specifically aimed at establishing procedures [e.g. mutual agreement procedures (MAPs)] to help resolve disputes over the allocation of taxing rights between host and home countries. A wide tax treaty network therefore tends to make countries more attractive, in relation to tax considerations, both as locations for business activity, and as places from which to conduct global business operations, by lowering projects costs as well as project risks.

Third, tax treaties generally stipulate lower non-resident withholding tax rates on dividends, interest and royalties. Indeed, treaty negotiated rates are often significantly lower than statutory withholding tax rates that would otherwise apply. This aspect of tax treaties also serves to lower project costs.

At the same time, tax treaties provide a framework to enable exchange of information amongst tax authorities to counter more aggressive forms of tax-planning in relation to foreign source income as well as domestic source income (that may be stripped out to tax havens through the use of special corporate structures and financing and repatriation strategies).

Notes

1. The tax treatment of foreign source income generally would be an important tax consideration when deciding where to locate a corporate base from which to hold foreign assets. However, a discussion of the special tax considerations arising in this context are beyond the scope of this article, which concentrates on investment for production purposes rather than management/co-ordination purposes.

2. The term "host country" is commonly used in the context of cross-border (inbound or outbound) investment to refer to the country in which a productive asset is located (e.g. where a company is located and income is sourced), with the term "home country" used to refer to the country in which the investor (owner of the productive asset) resides. In this article, we also use the term "host country" to refer to the country in which a company is located, and apply this term both in the context of inbound foreign direct investment (non-resident investor in a domestic enterprise) and pure domestic investment (resident investor in a domestic business). Thus use of the term "host country" need not imply FDI.

3. Both the level of the effective tax rate on profit and the method (types of tax, and their design features) by which that effective tax rate is set may be relevant.

4. Similarly, home country taxation of foreign source income may directly impact investment – the higher (lower) the net home country tax rate on foreign profit, generally the lower (higher) the level of direct investment abroad (DIA) by domestic firms in instances where tax impacts investment decisions. Effects on domestic investment of home country taxation of foreign source income are less than clear – whether an effective tax burden on foreign source income that is low relative to that on domestic income discourages or encourages domestic investment depend, in part, on whether DIA is a substitute for or complement of domestic investment.

5. In the cross-border situation, this need not be the case. In particular, private investment costs generally would not be affected where increased (decreased) host country taxation is offset by an increased (decreased) foreign tax credit being allowed by the home country tax system of the investor.

6. Exceptions to this general approach would include certain privatizations where potential pure economic profit is both location and time-specific.

7. An eventual exhaustion of economic profit recognises that not all revenues raised from an increase in host taxation would be allocated to public expenditures that directly support business (e.g. education, infrastructure). In principle, where revenues from taxes on business are allocated to programs that provide direct and immediate support to business, a higher tax burden could be levied without discouraging investment. However, this presumes that relevant program spending is as efficient as private spending, ignores lags between tax collection and the delivery of benefits to business, as well as other uses of public funds.

8. Transaction costs in decoupling business activities should be taken into account in considering alternative location choice.

9. See for example OECD 2003, Using Micro-data to Assess Average Tax Rates, OECD Tax Policy Studies No. 8.

10. In addressing this issue, one can measure for SMEs and MNEs, the average amount of professional time (of tax accountants, tax lawyers, tax administrators) per year required to comply with the tax code. This can be converted to an average annual compliance cost to business, with reference to the average hourly wage of a tax professional, and included in the calculation of total tax liability of a representative sample of firms.

11. A related tax policy issue is whether depreciation rates adequately reflect true economic rates of depreciation of broad classes of depreciable property (serving as benchmark rates) and account for inflation.

12. Where additional investment is constrained by cash flow, tax relief on profit derived from previous investment may encourage current investment by supplying a source of funds. However, where such financing constraints do not exit, tax relief on returns to installed capital (e.g. through a reduction in the statutory corporate tax rate) will provide a pure windfall gain.

13. In modelling effective tax rates on SMEs, consideration should be given to enterprises structured in corporate and unincorporated form (information on the relative (asset) size of the incorporated *versus* unincorporated sector would indicate the relative importance of alternative measures). For incorporated firms (SMEs and possibly large resident-owned firms) with limited access to international capital markets, consideration should be given to average effective corporate tax

income rates inclusive of corporate and personal income taxation to incorporate possible personal tax effects on the cost of funds. In modelling FDI, consideration should be given to inbound investment from several different countries. This could include a non-treaty case where a statutory (non-treaty) dividend withholding tax rate would apply, and where one could assume no home country taxation. In considering treaty cases, the sample should include a major capital exporting country operating a source-based system (dividend exemption), as well as one or more operating a residence-based tax system (dividend gross-up and credit).

14. This bullet concerns differences in effective tax rates that arise from the application of different tax rates and rules to similar transactions (*i.e.* it does not concern differences that arise from the application of similar rules to different transactions). For example, rates of capital depreciation, for tax purposes, typically differ by type of capital asset. This means that effective tax rates will differ across sectors to the extent that capital stocks of firms in one sector differ in composition from stocks of firms in another. Such differences may be viewed as structural, rather than tax driven. An example of the latter would be where the same type of asset is depreciated at a different rate depending on the sector. This bullet concerns tax-driven differences of this sort.

15. For example, avoiding windfall gains on accelerated depreciation requires that the balance of undepreciated capital cost, at the time of introduction of this incentive, be depreciated at pre-reform as opposed to accelerated rates to avoid tax relief in respect of pre-reform capital stocks. Windfall gains are inevitable in certain cases, depending on the mechanism used to deliver tax relief. For example, in general it is not practically possible to target a new reduced corporate tax rate to profits from new investment alone (*i.e.* not practically possible to ring-fence such profits, to the exclusion of profits from prior investment).

16. This paragraph concerns unintended distortions, recognising that tax incentives generally are intended to influence or distort the allocation of capital away from patterns that would be observed in the absence of the incentive. Whether intended distortions created by tax incentive use are welfare improving depends on whether the incentive corrects a true market failure.

17. In contrast, an enhanced investment allowance providing a deduction equal to some percentage of qualifying investment, providing relief regardless of the source of finance, would not raise the same problem.

References and Further Policy Resources

Council of Europe/OECD (2006), Council of Europe/OECD Convention on Mutual Administrative Assistance in Tax.

OECD (1992), Model Agreement for Simultaneous Tax Examinations.

OECD (2001), Recommendation of the Council on the Use of the OECD Model Memorandum of Understanding on Automatic Exchange of Information for Tax Purposes.

OECD (2001), Transfer Pricing Guidelines for Multinational Enterprises and Tax Administrations.

OECD (2002), Agreement on Exchange of Information on Tax Matters.

OECD (2003), Assessing FDI Incentive Policies: a Checklist.

OECD (2005), Model Tax Convention on Income and on Capital.

ISBN 92-64-02586-3
Policy Framework for Investment
A Review of Good Practices
© OECD 2006

Chapter 6

Corporate Governance*

* This background document was prepared by Daniel Blume, Corporate Affairs Division, OECD Directorate for Financial and Enterprise Affairs.

6.1. Introduction

This paper addresses corporate governance[1] as one of the policy areas for inclusion in the *Policy Framework for Investment* (PFI) under the OECD *Initiative on Investment for Development*. It provides background both on the relationship between corporate governance and a sound investment environment, and on some of the key corporate governance issues that policy makers should consider in this context. This document will serve as the basis for one of the ten policy chapters to be developed for inclusion in the *Policy Framework for Investment*, each setting out key questions and issues for policy-makers' consideration in the context of promoting an environment that is attractive to domestic and foreign investors and that enhances the benefits of investment to society.[2] Importantly, the questions presented in this report are not intended and should not be seen as a substitute for the work by the OECD Steering Group on Corporate Governance to develop a methodology for assessing the implementation of the OECD *Principles of Corporate Governance*.

The OECD has actively worked to promote good corporate governance since first adopting the *Principles of Corporate Governance* in 1999, recognising their importance in contributing to financial stability, investment and economic growth. Following their adoption, they have become recognised as an international benchmark for policy-makers, investors, corporations and other stakeholders worldwide. The OECD in co-operation with the World Bank Group has undertaken an extensive programme to increase awareness and understanding of the *Principles* and encourage their use that has involved more than 80 countries (OECD and non-OECD) around the world. The Financial Stability Forum identified the Principles as one of 12 key standards important to achieving sound financial systems. The World Bank also uses the *Principles* as the underlying basis for country corporate governance reviews that have been carried out in more than 40 developing countries over the last four years, known as Reports on Observance of Standards and Codes (ROSCs). The UN's Monterrey Consensus Declaration also cited the importance of corporate governance as a factor in promoting a stable and predictable environment for investment and development. The Declaration suggested that "special efforts are required in such priority areas as economic policy and regulatory frameworks for promoting and protecting investments, including in the areas of human resource development, avoidance of double taxation, corporate governance, accounting standards and the promotion of a competitive environment."[3]

The *OECD Principles* were revised in 2004 based upon an extensive review of experience both within OECD countries and with non-OECD countries through Regional Roundtables on Corporate Governance in Asia, Eurasia, Latin America, Russia and Southeast Europe, as well as through consultations also involving countries from Africa, the Middle East and the Caribbean. The Roundtables have held more than 30 meetings since the *Principles* were first adopted, and each region, using the *Principles* as a reference, has developed consensus-based conclusions, recommendations and priorities summarized in Regional White

Papers, as well as in the 2003 OECD report, *Experiences from the Regional Corporate Governance Roundtables*. This paper draws particularly upon Roundtable experience, as well as the *Survey of Corporate Governance Developments in OECD Countries*, in identifying some of the issues that have emerged as priorities. One of the strongest underlying motivations for adopting these Roundtable recommendations and for continuing to pursue their implementation is that each region has recognised the important link between good corporate governance and investment.

This paper is intended to support discussion of some of the key aspects that policy-makers and others concerned with corporate governance should take into consideration, as one element of a sound environment for investment, but does not aim to be comprehensive and should not be considered as the basis for a review of corporate governance practices in a particular jurisdiction. The *OECD Principles* themselves (available at *www.oecd.org/daf/corporate/principles*) should continue to serve as the main reference for policy dialogue.

In addition, the OECD is currently carrying out much more detailed and comprehensive work, under the responsibility of the Steering Group on Corporate Governance, to develop an overall methodology for review of country experience and corporate governance policy dialogue, based upon the *OECD Principles of Corporate Governance*. The Steering Group requested that this work support efforts to update the methodology for corporate governance Reports on Observance of Standards and Codes (ROSCs) that the World Bank carries out to reflect the 2004 revision of the *Principles*, as well as to serve as a basis for future OECD policy dialogue to strengthen corporate governance in member countries. The draft methodology closely follows the *Principles*, setting out likely practices to be considered, and "essential criteria" to be taken into consideration. In addition, the draft methodology stresses the importance of considering how different elements of the corporate governance framework may be complementary or interdependent in achieving the objectives of the *Principles*, while avoiding a "check-list" approach.

6.2. The role of corporate governance in achieving an attractive investment environment

Corporate governance reform is an important aspect of broader reform programmes aimed at securing an environment attractive to both domestic and foreign investors and that enhances the benefits of investment to society. As the Preamble to the *OECD Principles* states, "The degree to which corporations observe basic principles of good corporate governance is an increasingly important factor for investment decisions. Of particular relevance is the relation between corporate governance practices and the increasingly international character of investment. International flows of capital enable companies to access financing from a much larger pool of investors. If countries are to reap the full benefits of the global capital market, and if they are to attract long-term 'patient' capital, corporate governance arrangements must be credible, well understood across borders and adhere to internationally accepted principles. Even if corporations do not rely primarily on foreign sources of capital, adhering to good corporate governance practices will help improve the confidence of domestic investors, reduce the cost of capital, underpin the good functioning of financial markets, and ultimately induce more stable sources of financing."

The corporation is at the very heart of the investment process, requiring a constant search for the most efficient ways to combine all the different resources needed to produce those goods and services that meet market demand. Of special interest for a discussion on corporate governance is the economy's ability to match commercially viable projects with the financial resources that are required to actually turn an idea into a profitable enterprise. To be sure, capital is only one among several important inputs that are needed to build a competitive company. Skilled labour, managerial talent and intermediary goods and services are also vital. But, while access to capital is not a sufficient condition, it is for all practical purposes a necessary one. This is particularly true for equity financing, which allows companies to increase their exposure to risks that are associated with long term and forward looking undertakings such as the opening up of new business lines, corporate re-structuring, research activities, product development and market expansion.

But it is not only the absolute *amount* of available capital that will determine the ability to increase economic welfare through capital formation. Equally important is the effectiveness with which it is *allocated* among alternative investment opportunities and, not least, how well the corporation's final use of it is actually *monitored*. If household savings and available corporate funds for some reason do not reach their best possible use, society will undoubtedly forego opportunities that would have generated additional economic welfare. Under such circumstances, entrepreneurs will not find appropriate funding for profitable projects; existing companies will not be able to expand their operations; potentially profitable innovations will never be commercialised, etc. Moreover, necessary re-structuring of individual companies and entire industries will be impaired, and productive assets will be locked into underperforming activities.

These three steps in the investment process – to mobilise capital, to allocate capital among alternative ends, and to monitor the use of the invested capital – are among the key functions of the financial system. In market economies, they are carried out by a multitude of individual investors and the overall outcome will to a large extent depend on their individual skills and incentives. But the result will also be highly dependent on the institutional framework of laws, regulations and business practices that shape and affect the interactions between equity investors and the corporation, that is to say, the corporate governance framework.

By specifying the distribution of rights and responsibilities among the different participants to the corporation, the quality of the corporate governance framework influences the outcome at all stages of the investment process. A few examples may help to illuminate this point:

- At the first stage of the investment process, secure methods of ownership registration and the opportunity to obtain legal redress for violation of shareholder rights are just two examples of corporate governance provisions that will facilitate the mobilization of capital. If investors cannot be assured that the assets they invest in are properly recognised and protected, their savings will remain idle, hidden away or instantly consumed, instead of being employed in productive uses.

- At the second stage of the investment process, reliable and transparent accounts of corporate operations and their financial situation are essential to make informed decisions about the allocation of financial resources among alternative uses.

- At the third stage, the procedures for corporate decision-making, the distribution of authority among company organs, the design of incentive schemes and workable lines of accountability are all obvious corporate governance issues that have to be in place in order to ensure that companies actually use their resources effectively.

Looking at these relationships, it is evident that the importance of good corporate governance goes far beyond the interests of shareholders in an individual company. It is a public policy concern. A weak corporate governance framework will severely impede all stages of the investment process and hence the economy's overall prospects to maintain a strong private sector basis for economic growth. Poor corporate governance will damage the capacity to mobilise savings, hinder efficient allocation of financial resources, and prevent proper management of corporate assets.[4]

6.3. Key elements of a corporate governance framework

The following section, drawing extensively from the OECD Principles, the Survey of Corporate Governance Developments in OECD Countries and the OECD report on Experiences from the Regional Corporate Governance Roundtables, highlights a number of key questions for policy-makers to consider as they seek to develop sound national frameworks for good corporate governance. The Principles (not including the Preamble or Part II annotations) are provided for reference as an annex. It also includes questions related to governance of state-owned enterprises, drawing upon the OECD Guidelines on Corporate Governance of State-Owned Enterprises adopted by the OECD Council in April 2005.

What steps have been taken to ensure the basis for a corporate governance framework that promotes overall economic performance and transparent and efficient markets? Has this been translated into a coherent and consistent regulatory framework, backed by effective enforcement?

An effective corporate governance framework requires an effective legal, regulatory and institutional foundation, which all market participants can rely upon when they enter into their multitude of contractual relations. This legal, regulatory and institutional foundation typically comprises elements of legislation, regulation, self-regulatory arrangements, voluntary commitments and business practices that are the result of a country's specific economic circumstances, history and traditions. The desirable mix between legislation, regulation, self-regulation, voluntary standards, etc. will therefore vary from country to country. As new experiences accrue and business circumstances change, the content and structure of this framework might need to be adjusted. In this process, it is essential to assess the quality of the domestic framework in light of international developments and requirements.

The regulatory and legal environment within which corporations operate is of key importance to overall economic outcomes. Policy makers have a responsibility to put in place a framework that is flexible enough to meet the needs of corporations operating in widely different circumstances, facilitating their development of new opportunities to create value and to determine the most efficient deployment of resources. To achieve this goal, it is important that policy makers remain focused on the ultimate economic outcomes from interventions. When considering different policy options, it is also useful to undertake an analysis of the impact on key variables that affect the functioning of markets, such as incentive structures, the efficiency of self-regulatory systems and dealing with systemic conflicts of interest.

Corporate governance requirements and practices are typically influenced by an array of legal domains, such as company law, securities regulation, accounting and auditing standards, insolvency law, contract law, labour law and tax law. Under these circumstances, there is a risk that the variety of legal influences may cause unintentional overlaps and even conflicts, which may frustrate the ability to improve corporate governance. When looking at the legal and regulatory framework, it is therefore important to be aware of this risk and take measures to limit it.

In each of the Regional Corporate Governance Roundtables, the need for effective enforcement and implementation has emerged as a key priority. This reflects a view that a sound legal framework for corporate governance, while important, is not sufficient for ensuring the effective functioning of the capital markets. Laws and regulation but also most private arrangements designed to protect the rights of shareholders and ensure equitable treatment of different shareholders and stakeholders derive their strength from the broader implementation and enforcement environment. If existing institutions are weak, implementing and enforcing private agreements as well as laws and regulation becomes more difficult. A corporate governance framework must therefore include both a set of policies and a regulatory/institutional framework to ensure its implementation.

While enforcement is a general problem of development, it particularly affects firms seeking external financing, as well as impacting on the valuation of shares of existing, listed firms. Financial contracts involve the commitment of the firm to adhere to certain obligations, in particular to share its profits by paying an appropriate rate of return to the providers of external financing. A weak enforcement environment therefore has a negative impact on share value, and makes it more difficult for firms to commit to honour financial contracts and attract new financing as well.

A number of elements of enforcement are addressed in subsequent questions in this paper. Among other things, it should be noted that effective enforcement requires that the allocation of responsibilities for supervision, implementation and enforcement among different authorities is clearly defined so that the competencies of complementary bodies and agencies are respected and used most effectively. Overlapping and perhaps contradictory regulations between national jurisdictions is also an issue that should be monitored so that no regulatory vacuum is allowed to develop (*i.e.* issues slipping through in which no authority has explicit responsibility) and to minimise the costs for corporations to comply with multiple legislative systems.

How does the corporate governance framework ensure the equitable treatment of shareholders? Do national characteristics of the corporate ownership and control structures call for strengthening any particular aspects of the corporate governance framework?

In the developing and emerging market economies that participate in the Regional Roundtables on Corporate Governance, as well as in many OECD countries, major shareholders control most companies, in some cases through differential voting rights or complex ownership and control structures that allow them to maintain control with relatively little equity. In many of these countries, most of these controlling shareholders are individuals or families. Controlling groups may also play a role, and less commonly, a foreign multinational or major bank. In other cases, ownership is controlled by the state, raising additional governance challenges which are touched upon under the last three questions of this chapter.

The ownership structure has important implications for the corporate governance framework. Controlling shareholders have strong incentives to closely monitor the company and its management, and can have a positive impact on the governance of the company. However, their interests may also conflict with the interest of other shareholders – minority shareholders. This conflict is most destructive when the controlling shareholders extract private benefits at the expense of minority shareholders. Thus, while the OECD Principles are intended to apply to the full range of ownership structures found in listed companies, and are also considered useful for non-listed companies, certain aspects of the Principles, such as protection of minority rights and equitable treatment of all shareholders, may receive increased attention in economies where majority control is dominant, especially through techniques which involve little equity.

Minority shareholders are not the only victims of poor corporate governance. Controlling shareholders themselves pay the cost of poor corporate governance in the form of lower valuations, restricted access to equity finance, and difficulties with respect to succession planning and accessing outside talent. And the economy pays through reduced productivity, as scarce investment funds are allocated less efficiently. To reduce these costs, some controlling shareholders take voluntary measures to improve their own corporate governance and improve their reputations with other shareholders. The creation of institutions like special stock market tiers and voluntary corporate governance codes can facilitate these voluntary measures by allowing companies to credibly signal markets that they have high standards of corporate governance. However, there are limits to what voluntary actions can achieve. In the long run, controlling shareholders may actually benefit from legally binding and effectively enforced measures to improve investor protection.

This should include protection of certain property rights. For example, an equity share in a publicly traded company can be bought, sold or transferred, and entitles the investor to participate in the company's profits. It also provides a right to obtain information about and influence the company, primarily by voting at shareholder meetings. All these rights carry an intrinsic economic value. In order for investors to buy equity they therefore need to be confident that their entitlement to these and other rights that they have purchased are properly recognised and protected.

> **What are the procedures and institutional structures for legal redress in cases of violation of shareholder rights? Do they function as a credible deterrent to such violations?**

One of the ways in which shareholders can enforce their rights is to initiate legal and administrative proceedings against board members and management (particularly executive management serving on the board). Experience has shown that an important determinant of the degree to which shareholder rights are protected is whether effective methods exist to obtain redress for grievances at a reasonable cost and without excessive delay. The confidence of minority investors is enhanced when the legal system provides mechanisms for minority shareholders to bring lawsuits when they have reasonable grounds to believe that their rights have been violated. The provision of such enforcement mechanisms is a key responsibility of legislators and regulators.

There is some risk that a legal system, which enables any investor to challenge corporate activity in the courts, can become prone to excessive litigation. Thus, many legal systems have introduced provisions to protect board members against litigation abuse in the form of tests for the sufficiency of shareholder complaints, so-called safe harbours for board member actions (such as the business judgement rule) as well as safe harbours for the disclosure of information. In the end, a balance must be struck between allowing investors to seek remedies for infringement of ownership rights and avoiding excessive litigation, which may also cause management and boards to become excessively risk averse. Many countries have found that alternative adjudication procedures, such as administrative hearings or arbitration procedures organised by the securities regulators or other regulatory bodies, are an efficient method for dispute settlement, at least at the first instance level.

The great majority of countries that participate in the Regional Roundtables on Corporate Governance have laws and regulations that seem to offer strong protection to shareholders. Yet these shareholders, including not only smaller investors but also large institutional investors such as pension funds and international investment firms, still have their rights violated, in large part because the procedures and institutional structures for legal redress often result in ineffective enforcement of these laws and regulations. Without the appropriate institutional framework, new laws, whether they are transplanted or domestically developed, may simply be ignored or in a few cases, create new difficulties.

An effective judiciary is essential for providing a credible deterrent to abuse of shareholder rights. In countries with a weak judiciary, lengthy legal processes with unpredictable outcomes undermine the incentives for shareholders to pursue their rights. As mentioned above, some countries place greater emphasis on use of alternative mechanisms for resolving disputes in order to reduce reliance upon the courts. However, an unaccountable regulator can be the source of other abuses. The securities regulator should not only ensure transparency in financial markets, but its own transparency as well. The regulator should explain and publish its rulings, and develop new regulation in an open manner. Even as national securities regulators seek to enhance the efficiency and effectiveness of enforcement of shareholder rights through their own enforcement and due process systems, checks and balances to ensure equitable treatment under the law remains important. Thus, strengthening the courts' ability to effectively address corporate disputes will remain critical.

What measures are in place to monitor and prevent abusive related party transactions and inhibit other ways for corporate insiders and controlling owners to extract private benefits?

Certain types of corporate activities involve inherent conflicts of interest on the part of the participating parties, for example managers, board members and controlling shareholders. It is therefore important for the market to know if such activities are carried out with due regard to the interests of all shareholders. Abusive self-dealing involving persons who exploit their close relationships to the company to the detriment of the company and investors, as well as insider trading entailing manipulation of the capital markets should be prohibited and enforced. To this end, it is also essential that companies fully disclose material related party transactions to the market, either individually, or on a grouped basis, including whether they have been executed at arms-length and on normal market terms. In discussing the content and coverage of such measures, consideration should of course be given to a workable definition of related parties. It will also be necessary to address the individual's responsibility for announcing a conflict of interest and the role of the board of directors in assessing the material implications of such a conflict.

An inquiry about the quality of the regulatory framework with respect to related party transactions would benefit from a special discussion about transactions that involve major shareholders (or their families), either directly or indirectly. It should also address the obligation of shareholders to report transactions and the nature of the transactions with related parties, grouped as appropriate.

> **What procedures and institutions are in place to ensure that shareholders have the ability to significantly influence the company? For example, are there sufficient notification procedures for general shareholders meetings and adequate procedures for proxy voting to effectively allow voting for those unable to directly participate?**

Participation in general shareholder meetings is a fundamental shareholder right that is critical to their ability to influence the company and the quality of corporate governance. It is during these meetings that decisions about key issues, such as dividends and the election of the board of directors, are made. In order for shareholders to be able to participate effectively in decisions made at the shareholders' meeting, either directly or by proxy, they need to be informed about the meeting in a timely and orderly fashion. Also, the rules and procedures for casting votes must be designed with an aim to facilitate and encourage shareholder participation in the decision-making process at a reasonable cost.

In this context, it is of particular importance to consider the timeliness and the quality of any information that is distributed with the purpose to inform shareholders about the issues that will be discussed and decided at the shareholders' meeting. Does content and procedure provide the background and time that is required for them to inform themselves and consult on the issues that will be discussed and decided?

Access to information and reliable proxy procedures are particularly important in the case of foreign investors who often hold their shares through chains of intermediaries. Shares are typically held in accounts with securities intermediaries, that in turn hold accounts with other intermediaries and central securities depositories in other jurisdictions, while the listed company resides in a third country. Such cross-border chains often give raise to special challenges with respect to determining the entitlement of foreign investors to use their voting rights in order to influence key decisions, such as the election of directors, and the process of communicating with such investors. The obvious risks are of course that information from the company doesn't reach the ultimate shareholder and that the opinion of the ultimate shareholder does not reach the shareholder's meeting. It is therefore important to address to what extent the legal and regulatory framework clarifies the duties and procedures for informing about the shareholders' meeting, and the procedures for voting of shares that are held by foreign owners.

More generally, the requirement for delegating voting rights to custodians should be regulated in some detail. When shaping such rules, special attention should be given to those situations where financial institutions, such as banks and brokerage firms, hold shares in custody for investors.

By what standards and procedures do companies meet the market demand for timely, reliable and relevant disclosure, including information about the company's ownership and control structure?

A strong disclosure regime that promotes real transparency is a pivotal feature of a market-based corporate governance system that allows shareholders to exercise their ownership rights on a fully informed and equal basis. It underpins confidence in the stock market and is a powerful tool for influencing the behaviour of companies and for protecting investor rights.

Present and potential shareholders require access to regular, reliable and comparable information in sufficient detail for them to assess the stewardship of management, and make informed decisions about the valuation, ownership and voting of the company's shares. Insufficient or ambiguous information will hamper the ability of the markets to function. It will increase the cost of capital and result in a poor allocation of resources.

Arguably, failures of governance can often be linked to the failure to disclose the "whole picture", particularly where off-balance sheet items are used to provide guarantees or similar commitments between related companies. It is therefore important that a discussion about the quality of disclosure standards also take into account how transactions relating to an entire group of companies are treated and how information about contingent liabilities, off-balance sheet transactions and special purpose entities are disclosed.

A discussion about the content of disclosure standards and the dissemination procedures will naturally address numerous trade-offs that relate to the completeness, quality and cost of establishing and disseminating the information. In order to determine what information should be disclosed at a minimum, many countries apply the concept of materiality. Material information can be defined as information whose omission or misstatement could influence the economic decisions taken by users of information.

A particular transparency issue in many markets relates to the complex ownership and control structures. Transparent reporting regarding ownership is essential in order to curb, among other things, abusive transactions among related parties. The OECD template on Options for Obtaining Beneficial Ownership and Control Information serves as a reference for improving the availability of such information.

In the course of developing a strong disclosure regime, it should always be kept in mind that the channels, timing and procedures for disseminating corporate information can be just as important as the content of the information itself. There is no use in issuing material information if it doesn't reach the market and the concerned authorities in a predictable and timely fashion. While the disclosure of information is often provided for by legislation, filing and access to information can be cumbersome and costly. Filing of statutory reports has been greatly enhanced in some countries by electronic filing and data retrieval systems. Some countries are now moving to the next stage by integrating different sources of company information, including shareholder filings. The Internet and other information technologies also provide the opportunity for improving information dissemination.

How does the corporate governance framework ensure the strategic guidance of the company, the effective monitoring of management by the board, and the board's accountability to the company and its shareholders? Does the framework also recognise the rights of stakeholders established by law or through mutual agreements, and encourage active co-operation between corporations and stakeholders in creating wealth, jobs and the sustainability of financially sound enterprises?

While board structures and procedures vary across countries, the board everywhere should play a central role in the governance of the company. Together with guiding corporate strategy, the board is chiefly responsible for monitoring managerial performance (and replacing it if necessary), and achieving an adequate return for shareholders. It should also monitor and manage potential conflicts of interest of management, board members and shareholders and ensure the balancing of competing demands on the corporation.

Controlling shareholders are frequently in a position to choose all members of the board. These board members may be quite effective at furthering the interest of the controlling shareholders, perhaps even seeing themselves as the delegate for the controlling shareholder. In turn, minority shareholders have demanded to have their own delegates on the board.

However, the *Principles* assert that regardless of how they are chosen, in order for boards to effectively fulfil their responsibilities, they must be able to exercise informed, objective and independent judgement, acting as representative of all shareholders. Important board responsibilities include overseeing systems designed to ensure that the corporation obeys applicable laws, including tax, competition, labour, environmental, equal opportunity, health and safety laws. These are normally formalised as a duty of care and loyalty, and it is important that these concepts are firmly anchored in law and jurisprudence, and in the understanding and practices of the board members themselves. In some countries, companies have found it useful to explicitly articulate the responsibilities that the board assumes and those for which management is accountable.

The board is not only accountable to the company and its shareholders but also has a duty to act in their best interests. In addition, boards are expected to take due regard of, and deal fairly with, other stakeholder interests including those of employees, creditors, customers, suppliers and local communities. Corporations should recognise that the contributions of stakeholders constitute a valuable resource for building competitive and profitable companies, contributing to the long-term success of the corporation. The rights of stakeholders as established by law or mutual agreement should be respected. Observance of environmental and social standards is relevant in this context (also see Chapter 7 on Responsible Business Conduct).

Examples of specific reforms include clarification of board member duties in the law; requiring greater numbers of "independent" board members; encouraging the use of specialized committees, especially audit committees; developing the infrastructure for the ongoing training of board members; and in some cases making greater use of cumulative voting, which may strengthen the representation of board members considered independent of the controlling shareholder.

> **What has been done and what more should be done in terms of voluntary initiatives and training to encourage and develop a good corporate governance culture in the private sector?**

In dealing with corporate governance issues, countries use a varying combination of legal and regulatory instruments on the one hand, and voluntary codes and initiatives on the other. The *Principles* do not prescribe a single approach, and country experience varies widely depending in part on history, legal traditions, efficiency of the courts, the political structure of the country and the stage of enterprise development. Many countries, hoping to minimize compliance costs and to provide greater flexibility within a market framework, have developed and sought to promote greater use of voluntary codes and initiatives to improve their corporate governance. Suggesting that a "one size fits all" approach is not efficient, some countries have sought to implement their codes through "comply or explain" provisions that do not require compliance, but require an explanation when the provision is not followed. In some countries, such codes are implemented by stock markets through listing requirements. However, while such measures can play an important role in improving corporate governance arrangements, they might leave shareholders and other stakeholders with uncertainty concerning their status and implementation. When codes and principles are used as a national standard or as an explicit substitute for legal or regulatory provisions, market credibility requires that their status in terms of coverage, implementation, compliance and sanctions is clearly specified.

Corporate governance institutes or institutes of boards of directors have also sprung up in many countries, increasingly in the last five years, with an aim to promote awareness and to train directors to better understand corporate governance objectives and requirements. Increasing the supply of competent directors and improving the quality of their supervision has been a particular concern. Some institutes have also engaged in media training programmes as another means for increasing public understanding of corporate governance.

> **Has a review been undertaken of the national corporate governance system against the OECD Principles of Corporate Governance? Has the result of that review been made public?**

The World Bank has completed 48 corporate governance reviews of some 40 developing and transition economies, known as Reports on Observance of Standards and Codes (ROSCs), using the *OECD Principles* as the reference for these exercises. Subject to the agreement of the country's government to have the review publicly disclosed, the World Bank publishes these ROSCs on their Web site at *www.worldbank.org/ifa/rosc_cg.html*. In addition, the OECD, as part of its work to develop an updated methodology for such reviews, has undertaken a pilot review of an OECD country's experience with implementation of the *Principles*. While participation in and public disclosure of these reviews are voluntary, their disclosure, and better yet, public discussion of these reviews, can provide a useful basis for building awareness of and support for changes needed to strengthen the corporate governance framework and overall environment for investment.

Policy dialogue among the range of policy-makers, institutions and stakeholders concerned with improving corporate governance has proven to be an effective way of building consensus for corporate governance improvements on a national and regional basis. The Regional Roundtables on Corporate Governance (in Asia, Eurasia, Latin America, Southeast Europe and Russia), which have been meeting since the year 2000, are continuing to meet regularly to promote implementation of White Paper recommendations setting out action plans for change. These and other regional policy dialogue programmes (in Africa, the Middle East and North Africa, and the Caribbean), with the strong support of the Global Forum on Corporate Governance and local partners, co-founded under a partnership agreement between the World Bank and OECD, have helped to build consensus for regional and country-based action, and for follow-up on implementation. Participation in such regional policy dialogue can provide a means for accessing international expertise and building capacity for change.

6.4. Corporate governance of state-owned enterprises

The *OECD Principles of Corporate Governance* apply to state-owned enterprises, particularly to listed SOEs, but the *OECD Guidelines on Corporate Governance of SOEs* have been developed because of a number of specific challenges associated with the state's role in governing SOEs.[5] SOEs indeed often suffer from passive ownership by the state, or on the contrary, from undue political interference. SOEs in many cases are also notorious for having a soft budget constraint, being largely protected from the takeover and bankruptcy threats that are essential tools for monitoring management in private sector corporations. More fundamentally, SOEs have a complex chain of agents (management, board, ownership entities, ministries, the government), without clearly and easily identifiable principals. Structuring this complex Web of accountabilities in order to ensure efficient decisions and good corporate governance is a challenge.

Moreover, globalisation in most industries and technological changes and liberalization in many infrastructure sectors and network industries, traditionally dominated by SOEs, have also made necessary certain readjustments or restructuring of the state sectors. In order to promote overall investment and economic development, the state should ensure that the private sector may compete on a level playing field with SOEs, including safeguarding against conflicts of interest between the state as owner and as market regulator within the same sectors. In a few cases, severe financial difficulties of highly visible SOEs, with the resulting heavier budgetary burden, subsidisation and indebtedness, have triggered strong reactions and a demand for the reorganisation of the exercise of ownership rights by the state.

To face these specific challenges and to respond to these difficulties and even backlashes, a number of governments have undertaken significant reforms in the way they exercise their ownership rights. This is true for the OECD countries, but is also true for a number of non-OECD countries where, in many cases, state ownership is even more prevalent. How SOEs are run is crucial to the economic efficiency and competitiveness of the countries where they are based. Poor corporate governance practices in SOEs have a series of serious consequences. Badly governed SOEs may have unclear objectives and take decisions which impair their efficiency and development potential. This will have an impact on the quality of services and products delivered to citizens, in turn impacting on the economic infrastructure and general development capacity of the countries concerned. This also leads to decreased profits or even losses that tend to be borne by the public budget, thus increasing the general fiscal burden and indebtedness. Frequent undue political interference in the management of SOEs and lack of transparency on both their objectives and performance also contribute to the general poor public governance. Moreover, SOEs are widely recognised for being an important source of corruption, particularly in weak institutional environments.

While the *Guidelines* provide more comprehensive background on addressing the challenges mentioned above, the questions below touch upon a few of the key considerations to be addressed.

How is the ownership function of state-owned enterprises structured to ensure a level playing field, competitive market conditions and independent regulation? What are the processes in place to enable the state to act as an active and informed owner, while not interfering in day-to-day management of SOEs?

How the ownership function of the state is organised – that is, the functioning of the entities responsible for establishing and implementing the state's ownership policies – can influence the overall investment environment. In particular, it is important that the ownership function is clearly identified and separated from other state functions, including regulatory oversight. This helps to ensure a level playing field for all investors, especially with regard to compliance with laws and regulations.

The organisation of the ownership function within the state administration varies from one country to another. The ownership function might be centralised within one ownership entity, shared between two ministries or entities, or decentralised over the different sector ministries concerned. To reinforce the ownership function and ensure its clear identification, the Guidelines recommend at least to set up a strong co-ordinating entity or, more appropriately, to centralise this ownership function. Such centralisation helps in clarifying the ownership policy and ensures a more consistent implementation of this policy. Moreover, it could also facilitate "pooling" together relevant expertise on key matters.

The objective of the ownership entity is to implement the ownership policy as developed by the government. This ownership policy typically defines the overall objectives of state ownership and describes the state role in the corporate governance of SOEs. It also explains how the state plans to implement its ownership policy.

It is the role of the ownership entity to develop an appropriate framework to ensure that the state exercises its ownership rights actively and in an informed manner. The state's primary responsibilities as an owner are as follows: *i)* to be represented in the general shareholders meeting and to vote the state shares; *ii)* to establish a well-structured and transparent board nomination process; *iii)* to set up reporting systems allowing regular monitoring and assessment of SOE performance; *iv)* when possible to maintain continuous dialogue with external auditors and state control organs; *v)* to ensure that remuneration schemes for SOE board members are adequate.

While being an active and informed owner, it is crucial that the state does not interfere in the day-to-day management of SOEs and let their boards carry out their responsibilities. In this case, SOEs enjoy full operational autonomy to realise their defined objectives.

> **What are the processes in place to ensure that SOE board members are nominated in a transparent manner and based on their competencies and experience, so that they may effectively carry out their role of strategic oversight, rather than to serve as a conduit for undue political pressure?**

In order to carry out their role, SOE boards should actively *i)* formulate, monitor and review corporate strategy within the framework of overall corporate objectives; *ii)* establish appropriate performance indicators and identify key risks; *iii)* monitor the disclosure and communication processes, ensuring that the financial statements fairly present the affairs of the SOEs and reflect the risks incurred; *iv)* assess and follow management performance; *v)* develop effective succession plans for key executives. To underline the board's responsibilities, a Directors' Report should be provided along with annual statements, and should give information on the organisation, financial performance, material risk factors, significant events, relations with stakeholders, and the effects of directions from the co-ordinating or ownership entity. The board should also develop, implement and communicate compliance programmes for internal codes of ethics based on country norms and in conformity with broader codes of behaviour, including the OECD Guidelines for Multinational Enterprises.

In view of this wide range of responsibilities, it is crucial that SOE boards have adequate authority, the necessary competencies and sufficient objectivity to effectively carry out their functions of strategic guidance and monitoring of management. Experience in most countries reveals that often SOE boards do not bear the responsibility for SOE performance and are not fully accountable to the owners. Political influence in the nomination process is strong in a number of countries, with the process often degenerating into political interference. This is often identified as a main weakness of SOE governance.

A crucial task for the ownership entities is thus to set up a structured and transparent nomination process for SOE boards. The objective is to ensure that board members are selected based on their competencies and experience and that they are independent enough to carry out their fiduciary duty. If employees from the ownership entity or other civil servants are elected on SOE boards, they still need to meet the required competence level for all board members and in no case should they act as a conduit for undue political influence. In this regard, it is also important to insist on the fiduciary duty of SOE board members. They should carry out their duties in an even-handed manner with respect to all shareholders, acting in the best interests of the company as a whole. They should not act as individual representatives of the constituencies that appointed them.

> **How are SOEs effectively held accountable to the government, the public, and in the case of listed SOEs, to other shareholders, including through adequate reporting by the ownership entity and SOEs themselves?**

Another challenge regarding the corporate governance of SOEs is to improve their transparency. Adequate reporting on SOE objectives and performance both by the SOEs themselves and by the ownership entities allows the media, the Parliament and the public to have a clear idea about how the state fulfils its ownership function. To ensure adequate transparency requires that SOEs are subjected to the same high-level accounting and auditing standards as listed companies. This also requires that SOEs develop efficient internal audit procedures and are subject to an annual independent external audit based on international standards.

Adequate disclosure of material information as described in the OECD Principles is also often a weak point in SOE governance practices. The Guidelines more particularly draw attention to specific areas of concern: i) the company objectives and their fulfilment; ii) the ownership and voting structure; iii) risk factors and any measures taken to manage such risks; iv) any financial assistance received from the state and commitments made on behalf of the state; v) any material transactions with related entities. These later transactions are often an important source of abuses, particularly in weak institutional environments, and it is crucial to consider closely the procedures in place to control and disclose such transactions.

Finally, consistent aggregate reporting by the ownership entity is instrumental in ensuring accountability to the public and the media on SOE performance. A growing number of countries are publishing annually an aggregate report on SOEs, focusing on their financial performance and their valuation, and giving an overview of their evolution. Such reports might also provide a general statement on the state ownership policy and on how it is implemented. Information on the organisation of the ownership function and on SOE boards is often included, as well as changes in these boards.

The Guidelines also call for reinforcing the accountability of the ownership entities vis-à-vis representative bodies such as the Parliament. However, it is important to fine-tune the accountability mechanisms to ensure that they do not unduly restrict the ownership entities or SOEs' autonomy and to provide reasonable guarantees regarding confidentiality issues. This is often a delicate balance to be struck.

Notes

1. Corporate governance, as set out in the Preamble to the OECD *Principles of Corporate Governance*, refers to a set of relationships between a company's management, its board, its shareholders and other stakeholders. It also provides the structure through which the objectives of the company are

set, and the means by which attaining those objectives and monitoring performance are determined.

2. For background information on the *Policy Framework for Investment*, see DAF/INV/TF(2006)1. In addition to corporate governance, the policy areas in the *Framework* include investment policy; investment promotion and facilitation; trade policy; tax policy; competition policy; policies for promoting responsible business conduct; human resource development; infrastructure and financial sector development; and public governance.

3. See the Declaration of heads of state and government, "Confronting the challenges of financing for development: a global response", issued on 22 March, 2002 at the UN Financing for Development conference in Monterrey, Mexico.

4. The above section is largely excerpted from an article by Mats Isaksson, OECD Corporate Affairs Division Head, "Corporate Governance and Public Policy" (2004) published in *The Future of Corporate Governance*, Corporate Governance Forum, Stockholm.

5. These Guidelines are primarily oriented to SOEs using a distinct legal form (*i.e.* separate from the public administration) and having a commercial activity (*i.e.* with the bulk of their income coming from sales and fees).

References and Further Policy Resources

Berglof, Erik (2005), Corporate Governance and Investment: the Developing Country Context (unpublished draft).

Berglof, Erik and Stijn Claessens (2003), Discussion Paper No. 5: Enforcement and Corporate Governance, Global Corporate Governance Forum, Washington, DC.

Corporate Governance Forum (2004), The Future of Corporate Governance, Editors: Mats Isaksson and Rolf Skog, Stockholm, Sweden.

Chong, Alberto and Florencio Lopez-de-Silanes (2003), The Truth About Privatisation in Latin America Inter-American Development Bank, October.

Defond, Mark L., and Mingyi Hung (2003), Investor Protection and Corporate Governance: Evidence from Worldwide CEO Turnover, mimeo, University of Southern California – Leventhal School of Accounting.

EBRD (2001-2003), Transition Report, European Bank for Reconstruction and Development, London.

Isaksson, Mats (2004), Corporate Governance and Public Policy, pp. 131-140 in the Corporate Governance Forum, The Future of Corporate Governance.

Oman, Charles, editor (2003), Corporate Governance in Development: The Experiences of Brazil, Chile, India and South Africa. OECD Development Centre and Center for International Private Enterprise, Paris and Washington, DC.

OECD (2002a), White Paper on Corporate Governance in Russia. Organisation for Economic Co-operation and Development, Paris.

OECD (2002b), Options for Obtaining Beneficial Ownership and Control Information: A Template. Organisation for Economic Co-operation and Development, Paris.

OECD (2003a), White Paper on Corporate Governance in Asia. Organisation for Economic Co-operation and Development, Paris.

OECD (2003b), White Paper on Corporate Governance in Latin America. Organisation for Economic Co-operation and Development, Paris.

OECD (2003c), White Paper on Corporate Governance in South Eastern Europe. Organisation for Economic Co-operation and Development, Paris.

OECD (2004a), OECD Principles of Corporate Governance. Organisation for Economic Co-operation and Development, Paris. See *http://www.oecd.org/daf/corporate-affairs*.

OECD (2004b), Experiences from the Regional Corporate Governance Roundtables. Organisation for Economic Co-operation and Development, Paris.

OECD (2004c), Survey of Corporate Governance Developments in OECD Countries. Organisation for Economic Co-operation and Development, Paris.

OECD (2004d), Corporate Governance in Eurasia, A Comparative Overview. Organisation for Economic Co-operation and Development, Paris.

OECD (2005), Guidelines on Corporate Governance of State-Owned Enterprises. Organisation for Economic Co-operation and Development, Paris.

OECD (2006, forthcoming), Principles of Corporate Governance Assessment Methodology. Organisation for Economic Co-operation and Development, Paris.

ANNEX 6.A1

The OECD Principles of Corporate Governance

I. Ensuring the basis for an effective corporate governance framework

The corporate governance framework should promote transparent and efficient markets, be consistent with the rule of law and clearly articulate the division of responsibilities among different supervisory, regulatory and enforcement authorities.

A. The corporate governance framework should be developed with a view to its impact on overall economic performance, market integrity and the incentives it creates for market participants and the promotion of transparent and efficient markets.

B. The legal and regulatory requirements that affect corporate governance practices in a jurisdiction should be consistent with the rule of law, transparent and enforceable.

C. The division of responsibilities among different authorities in a jurisdiction should be clearly articulated and ensure that the public interest is served.

D. Supervisory, regulatory and enforcement authorities should have the authority, integrity and resources to fulfil their duties in a professional and objective manner. Moreover, their rulings should be timely, transparent and fully explained.

II. The rights of shareholders and key ownership functions

The corporate governance framework should protect and facilitate the exercise of shareholders' rights.

A. Basic shareholder rights should include the right to: 1) secure methods of ownership registration; 2) convey or transfer shares; 3) obtain relevant and material information on the corporation on a timely and regular basis; 4) participate and vote in general shareholder meetings; 5) elect and remove members of the board; and 6) share in the profits of the corporation.

B. Shareholders should have the right to participate in, and to be sufficiently informed on, decisions concerning fundamental corporate changes such as: 1) amendments to the statutes, or articles of incorporation or similar governing documents of the company; 2) the authorisation of additional shares; and 3) extraordinary transactions, including the transfer of all or substantially all assets, that in effect result in the sale of the company.

C. Shareholders should have the opportunity to participate effectively and vote in general shareholder meetings and should be informed of the rules, including voting procedures, that govern general shareholder meetings:

1. Shareholders should be furnished with sufficient and timely information concerning the date, location and agenda of general meetings, as well as full and timely information regarding the issues to be decided at the meeting.

2. Shareholders should have the opportunity to ask questions to the board, including questions relating to the annual external audit, to place items on the agenda of general meetings, and to propose resolutions, subject to reasonable limitations.

3. Effective shareholder participation in key corporate governance decisions, such as the nomination and election of board members, should be facilitated. Shareholders should be able to make their views known on the remuneration policy for board members and key executives. The equity component of compensation schemes for board members and employees should be subject to shareholder approval.

4. Shareholders should be able to vote in person or in absentia, and equal effect should be given to votes whether cast in person or in absentia.

D. Capital structures and arrangements that enable certain shareholders to obtain a degree of control disproportionate to their equity ownership should be disclosed.

E. Markets for corporate control should be allowed to function in an efficient and transparent manner.

1. The rules and procedures governing the acquisition of corporate control in the capital markets, and extraordinary transactions such as mergers, and sales of substantial portions of corporate assets, should be clearly articulated and disclosed so that investors understand their rights and recourse. Transactions should occur at transparent prices and under fair conditions that protect the rights of all shareholders according to their class.

2. Anti-take-over devices should not be used to shield management and the board from accountability.

F. The exercise of ownership rights by all shareholders, including institutional investors, should be facilitated.

1. Institutional investors acting in a fiduciary capacity should disclose their overall corporate governance and voting policies with respect to their investments, including the procedures that they have in place for deciding on the use of their voting rights.

2. Institutional investors acting in a fiduciary capacity should disclose how they manage material conflicts of interest that may affect the exercise of key ownership rights regarding their investments.

G. Shareholders, including institutional shareholders, should be allowed to consult with each other on issues concerning their basic shareholder rights as defined in the Principles, subject to exceptions to prevent abuse.

III. The equitable treatment of shareholders

The corporate governance framework should ensure the equitable treatment of all shareholders, including minority and foreign shareholders. All shareholders should have the opportunity to obtain effective redress for violation of their rights.

A. All shareholders of the same series of a class should be treated equally.

1. Within any series of a class, all shares should carry the same rights. All investors should be able to obtain information about the rights attached to all series and classes of shares before they purchase. Any changes in voting rights should be subject to approval by those classes of shares which are negatively affected.

2. Minority shareholders should be protected from abusive actions by, or in the interest of, controlling shareholders acting either directly or indirectly, and should have effective means of redress.

3. Votes should be cast by custodians or nominees in a manner agreed upon with the beneficial owner of the shares.

4. Impediments to cross border voting should be eliminated.

5. Processes and procedures for general shareholder meetings should allow for equitable treatment of all shareholders. Company procedures should not make it unduly difficult or expensive to cast votes.

B. Insider trading and abusive self-dealing should be prohibited.

C. Members of the board and key executives should be required to disclose to the board whether they, directly, indirectly or on behalf of third parties, have a material interest in any transaction or matter directly affecting the corporation.

IV. The role of stakeholders in corporate governance

The corporate governance framework should recognise the rights of stakeholders established by law or through mutual agreements and encourage active co-operation between corporations and stakeholders in creating wealth, jobs, and the sustainability of financially sound enterprises.

A. The rights of stakeholders that are established by law or through mutual agreements are to be respected.

B. Where stakeholder interests are protected by law, stakeholders should have the opportunity to obtain effective redress for violation of their rights.

C. Performance-enhancing mechanisms for employee participation should be permitted to develop.

D. Where stakeholders participate in the corporate governance process, they should have access to relevant, sufficient and reliable information on a timely and regular basis.

E. Stakeholders, including individual employees and their representative bodies, should be able to freely communicate their concerns about illegal or unethical practices to the board and their rights should not be compromised for doing this.

F. The corporate governance framework should be complemented by an effective, efficient insolvency framework and by effective enforcement of creditor rights.

V. Disclosure and transparency

The corporate governance framework should ensure that timely and accurate disclosure is made on all material matters regarding the corporation, including the financial situation, performance, ownership, and governance of the company.

A. Disclosure should include, but not be limited to, material information on:

1. The financial and operating results of the company.

2. Company objectives.

3. Major share ownership and voting rights.

4. Remuneration policy for members of the board and key executives, and information about board members, including their qualifications, the selection process, other company directorships and whether they are regarded as independent by the board.

5. Related party transactions.

6. Foreseeable risk factors.

7. Issues regarding employees and other stakeholders.

8. Governance structures and policies, in particular, the content of any corporate governance code or policy and the process by which it is implemented.

B. Information should be prepared and disclosed in accordance with high quality standards of accounting and financial and non-financial disclosure.

C. An annual audit should be conducted by an independent, competent and qualified, auditor in order to provide an external and objective assurance to the board and shareholders that the financial statements fairly represent the financial position and performance of the company in all material respects.

D. External auditors should be accountable to the shareholders and owe a duty to the company to exercise due professional care in the conduct of the audit.

E. Channels for disseminating information should provide for equal, timely and cost-efficient access to relevant information by users.

F. The corporate governance framework should be complemented by an effective approach that addresses and promotes the provision of analysis or advice by analysts, brokers, rating agencies and others, that is relevant to decisions by investors, free from material conflicts of interest that might compromise the integrity of their analysis or advice.

VI. The responsibilities of the board

The corporate governance framework should ensure the strategic guidance of the company, the effective monitoring of management by the board, and the board's accountability to the company and the shareholders.

A. Board members should act on a fully informed basis, in good faith, with due diligence and care, and in the best interest of the company and the shareholders.

B. Where board decisions may affect different shareholder groups differently, the board should treat all shareholders fairly.

C. The board should apply high ethical standards. It should take into account the interests of stakeholders.

D. The board should fulfil certain key functions, including:

1. Reviewing and guiding corporate strategy, major plans of action, risk policy, annual budgets and business plans; setting performance objectives; monitoring implementation and corporate performance; and overseeing major capital expenditures, acquisitions and divestitures.

2. Monitoring the effectiveness of the company's governance practices and making changes as needed.

3. Selecting, compensating, monitoring and, when necessary, replacing key executives and overseeing succession planning.

4. Aligning key executive and board remuneration with the longer term interests of the company and its shareholders.

5. Ensuring a formal and transparent board nomination and election process.

6. Monitoring and managing potential conflicts of interest of management, board members and shareholders, including misuse of corporate assets and abuse in related party transactions.

7. Ensuring the integrity of the corporation's accounting and financial reporting systems, including the independent audit, and that appropriate systems of control are in place, in particular, systems for risk management, financial and operational control, and compliance with the law and relevant standards.

8. Overseeing the process of disclosure and communications.

E. The board should be able to exercise objective independent judgement on corporate affairs.

1. Boards should consider assigning a sufficient number of non-executive board members capable of exercising independent judgement to tasks where there is a potential for conflict of interest. Examples of such key responsibilities are ensuring the integrity of financial and non-financial reporting, the review of related party transactions, nomination of board members and key executives, and board remuneration.

2. When committees of the board are established, their mandate, composition and working procedures should be well defined and disclosed by the board.

3. Board members should be able to commit themselves effectively to their responsibilities.

F. In order to fulfil their responsibilities, board members should have access to accurate, relevant and timely information.

ISBN 92-64-02586-3
Policy Framework for Investment
A Review of Good Practices
© OECD 2006

Chapter 7

Policies for Promoting Responsible Business Conduct*

* This background document was prepared by Kathryn Gordon, Investment Division, OECD Directorate for Financial and Enterprise Affairs.

7.1. Introduction

Governments can use a broad range of public policies to promote recognised concepts and principles for responsible business conduct, such as those recommended in the OECD Guidelines for Multinational Enterprises. These policies help attract investments and enhance their contribution to sustainable development. This background document looks at how governments can work to help companies to ensure that their operations "are in harmony with government policies, to strengthen the basis of mutual confidence between enterprises and the societies in which they operate … and to enhance [their] contribution to sustainable development".[1]

Policies that promote responsible business conduct include: providing an enabling environment that clearly defines the respective roles of government and business; promoting dialogue on norms for business conduct; providing for adequate disclosure so that investors can be held accountable for their actions; supporting companies' efforts to comply with law; encouraging responsible business conduct through partnership and promotion; and participating in intergovernmental cooperation in order to promote agreed concepts and principles for responsible business conduct.

7.2. Clear separation of government and business roles

How does the government make clear for investors the distinction between its own role and responsibilities and those ascribed to the business sector? Does it actively assume its responsibilities (*e.g.* by effectively enforcing laws on respecting human rights, environmental protection, labour relations and financial accountability)?

The core mission of business is to identify and manage investment projects that yield competitive returns to suppliers of capital. In fulfilling this core function, responsible business conduct also consists above all of complying with legal and regulatory requirements; in addition, it includes responding to societal expectations that might be communicated through channels other than law. The view of responsible business conduct developed in this paper reflects earlier Investment Committee work. A summary of this work, drawn from the Committee's Report to Ministers [C/MIN(2001)4], appears in Annex 7.A.

The role of governments is to look after the collective interests of their citizens. As part of this role, they work with companies, trade unions and other civil society organisations to create enabling environments for responsible business conduct. If this enabling environment is well designed, including through a clearly communicated distinction between the respective roles and responsibilities of government and business, uncertainty over expectations concerning responsible business conduct are lowered, thus encouraging investment, and private and public sector actors will be encouraged to play mutually-supporting roles in enhancing economic, social and environmental well-being.[2] Government and business roles need to remain distinct and they cannot substitute for one another – each sector needs to assume its responsibilities.

7.2.1. Business roles

The business sector's contribution to sustainable development has many facets, the most important of which is the conduct of business itself. As noted above, its core mission is to identify and manage investment projects that yield competitive returns to suppliers of capital. In the process, investors spur economic growth and provide jobs and produce goods and services that consumers want to buy.

Of course, the responsibilities of business go beyond this core function. Businesses also have to comply with legal and regulatory requirements and, as a practical matter, must often respond to societal expectations that might be communicated through channels other than law.

OECD research shows that many companies have invested heavily in improving their abilities to comply with law and to respond to other societal expectations. They make these investments because they recognise their inter-dependence with societies in which they operate – if these societies are not doing well, business will not prosper either.

7.2.2. Government roles

Of course, governments also play an important role in nurturing this interdependent relationship. The role of governments is to define and implement policies that serve the collective interests of their citizens, including their interest in having a dynamic and efficient business sector. Governments play an essential role in creating the policy environment in which business can flourish. The Policy Framework for Investment provides considerations for good practice in many of the relevant policy areas (*e.g.* competition, corporate governance, taxation, human resource development, infrastructure and financial services). If the enabling environment is well designed, all parties – governments, business and other elements of civil society – will be encouraged to assume their respective roles in supporting sustainable development.

This background document provides a broad overview of government roles in this area. The range of policies that form part of this enabling environment is vast – they include protecting the rights framework, engaging in responsive, efficient and effective law making; promoting other forms of two-way communication between business and the rest of society; forming partnerships for compliance with business; The rest of this background document examines these government roles.

7.2.3. Trade union, NGO and other civil society roles

Trade unions and other elements civil society also have a role to play in fostering and monitoring responsible business conduct. Like the business sector, they control resources that they can use to improve the quality of the dialogue relevant to the formation of both business and government policy. In particular, they can contribute their knowledge of situations in specific locations and workplaces and bring a wider array of perspectives (other than those of government and business).

7.3. Promoting effective two-way communication: law-making and other forms of dialogue

> What steps does the government take to promote communication on expected responsible business conduct to investors? How does the government endeavour to protect the rights framework that underpins effective communication?

Law-making is the key channel for communicating societal expectations to companies, thus creating a stable, predictable environment conducive to investment. Expectations concerning responsible business conduct are also communicated through a multitude of other channels and these also affect the quality of the investment environment. Such communication can take place within the workplace, with local communities, with trade unions in the course of industrial relations and collective bargaining, through discussions with investors, dialogue with other civil society organisations, via the press and so forth. These two-way communication channels provide inputs that can be valuable for setting company policies and evaluating performance. These other channels complement the information communicated to companies through formal legal and regulatory processes.

7.3.1. Law-making

Law-making (developing legal statutes, regulations and administrative procedures; law enforcement; and design and maintenance of the judicial system) is central to the public sector's role in creating an enabling environment for responsible business – law is a key channel for communicating societal expectations to companies. The other chapters of the Policy Framework for Investment propose considerations for law-makers in diverse policy areas that are relevant for business.

While acknowledging the central place of law making in the government role in communicating societal expectations, it is also worth noting the limits of law. It is not possible for law codes to describe the conduct that should be adopted in every conceivable business situation. Even if it were possible to foresee every possible situation and to write down the corresponding appropriate conduct, the resulting legal codes would be too long for anyone to read. Thus, those covered by law almost always need to interpret the implications of law in specific business situations.[3] This interpretation of law or drawing out the implications of law for specific business circumstances is a key role for responsible business and one that business is uniquely qualified to play (since businesses are likely to have the most information about their own business processes).

In addition, laws are made within national jurisdictions, whereas many of the relevant business behaviours are international in scope and may occur in investment environments where legal systems do not work well.[4] In such circumstances, international instruments provide a particularly useful complement to national laws.

The use of other communication channels (*e.g.* social dialogue and development of international instruments for responsible business conduct) as complements to national laws are addressed in the rest of this section.

7.3.2. *Other channels for communication*

Societies also channel their expectations through *other channels for communication* (*e.g.* with employees in the workplace, with local communities, through discussions with investors, via the press and so forth). As noted above, these communications channels provide inputs that can be valuable for setting company policies and evaluating performance and they often complement formal legal and regulatory processes.

Governments play several roles in ensuring that these channels work well:

● *Protecting rights.* While the protection of human rights (political, social, civil, labour and property) is a fundamental objective in itself, it is also a pre-condition for such communication to take place.[5] This removes threats of rights violations so that many voices, including those of investors, can be heard. Thus, protection of the rights framework is a key responsibility of governments.

● *Promoting effective communication between companies and the rest of society.* Governments sometimes encourage such communication by participating in it directly or by requiring that it take place among private parties. Box 7.1 describes how the government of Brazil participated in a dialogue that led to the development of a National Tri-partite Agreement on Benzene (a hazardous chemical). Box 7.2 describes Ghana's requirement that such dialogue take place with a view to protecting local communities affected by lumbering operations.

International instruments for corporate responsibility are also important channels for communicating with business. These are often derived from the broader framework of international declarations and conventions (*e.g.* the Universal Declaration of Human

---

Box 7.1. **The National Tripartite Agreement on Benzene, Brazil**

Brazilian trade unions, the petrochemical, iron and steel industry, and the national government concluded the National Tripartite Agreement on Benzene. The Agreement provides a model of employer-union cooperation in support of sustainable development. Work on the Agreement began as follow up on a campaign led by the Unified Workers Confederation.

The Agreement recognises benzene as a hazard and requires companies and subcontractors to carry, store or handle it and its derivatives in a prescribed manner. It also requires them to register its use and to implement a "Prevention Programme" in every workplace. Standards and procedures define objectives, applications, and responsibilities for each workplace party and a technical standard for safe exposure determined by workers, employers and government.

Strict evaluation procedures are established and workers are involved in monitoring. A "Representative Group of Workers" in each plant is trained and made responsible for monitoring and enforcing the designated programme for Prevention of Occupational Exposure to Benzene. Workers also have equal representation on the Permanent National Commission for Benzene that oversees developments, monitors compliance, promotes research, supplements laws and regulation and issues Certificates for the controlled use of Benzene to companies. Periodic seminars organised under the Agreement provide for joint evaluation.

Source: International Confederation of Free Trade Unions and TUAC. FOX, Tom, Halina Ward and Bruce Howard (2002), *Public Sector Roles in Strengthening Corporate Social Responsibility: A Baseline Study.* The World Bank Corporate Responsibility Practice. Washington DC, Boxes 4 and 24.

Box 7.2. **Social Responsibility Agreements, Ghana**

The reform of forest policy in Ghana resulted in a new regulation stipulating that companies tendering for timber cutting permits would be assessed in terms of their respect for the social and environmental values of local residents. Under the new law, which came into operation in 1998, logging companies are required to secure a "Social Responsibility Agreement" with the customary owners of the land.

This Agreement follows a standard pattern. It includes a code of conduct setting forth commitments for the company's environmental, employment and cultural practices. It also involves a pledge to make specific contributions to local development. Each Agreement must be fully negotiated with the local community and must follow a procedure for negotiating with local representatives and the district forest office before submission to a central evaluation committee.

Source: FOX, Tom, Halina Ward and Bruce Howard (2002),.

Source: Public Sector Roles in Strengthening Corporate Social Responsibility: A Baseline Study. The World Bank Corporate Responsibility Practice. Washington DC, Box 14.

Rights, the International Labour Organisation's declarations and conventions).[6] Most corporate responsibility instruments draw on this broader framework (*e.g.* the OECD Guidelines and the UN Global Compact).[7] Box 7.3 describes the OECD Guidelines for Multinational Enterprises, one of the world's foremost corporate responsibility instruments. The Guidelines contain government-backed recommendations in such areas as human rights, supply chain management, employment and industrial relations, the environment, combating bribery, consumer interests, science and technology, disclosure of information, competition and taxation. They do not aim to introduce differences of treatment between multinational and domestic enterprises; they reflect good practices for all. While it is acknowledged that small- and medium-sized enterprises may not have the same capacities as larger enterprises, governments adhering to the Guidelines nevertheless encourage them to observe the Guidelines recommendations to the fullest extent possible. Other important international initiatives that have benefited from government involvement are the *ILO Tripartite Declaration of Principles concerning Multinational Enterprises and Social Policies* and *the Voluntary Principles on Security and Human Rights*.

7.4. Providing an adequate framework for corporate disclosure

Does the government ensure that an adequate framework is in place to support the financial and non-financial disclosure that companies make about their business activities? Is this framework flexible enough to allow scope for innovation, for tailoring practices to the needs of investors and their stakeholders?

Clear and complete information on enterprises is important to a variety of users ranging from shareholders and the financial community to other constituencies such as employees, local communities, special interest groups and society at large.

Box 7.3. **The OECD Guidelines for Multinational Enterprises**

Relative to other major instruments that promote responsible business, the OECD Guidelines' engage government responsibilities in a unique way – they are the only comprehensive code of conduct involving recommendations addressed by governments to business. In addition, the Guidelines are promoted via a government-backed follow-up mechanism.

The recommendations of the Guidelines are both comprehensive and detailed – they contain relatively specific recommendations on a broad range of issues. The recommendations cover such areas as respecting human rights, encouraging good conduct in supply chains, whistleblower protection, disclosing financial and non-financial information, respecting all core labour standards, environmental protection, combating bribery, protecting consumer interests, enhancing technology transfer to host societies, fair competition and making tax payments (see Annex for more detailed description of coverage).

Thirty nine countries adhere to the Guidelines (the thirty OECD member countries plus 9 non-members).[1] The National Contact Points (NCPs; government offices located in each adhering country that promote observance of the Guidelines among companies operating in or from their territories) are the most concrete sign of adhering government commitment to the Guidelines. The NCPs are expected to further the effectiveness of the Guidelines in accordance with the core criteria of visibility, accessibility, transparency and accountability. The NCPs report annually on their activities.

Among other responsibilities, the National Contact Point is asked to provide conciliation and mediation in which companies and other interested parties may discuss concrete issues of business ethics. The facility is called the "specific instances procedure". Specific instances involve voluntary dialogue on whether or not a company has observed the Guidelines in a particular business situation. They are the only international conciliation and mediation facility that can be used to address a broad range of business ethics issues. The specific instances procedure has been used 72 times since its creation in June 2000.[2] Discussions have covered a broad array of business situations including labour management practices in an export processing zone in Guatemala, forced labour in Myanmar, the resettlement of local populations in the Zambian copper belt and managing the risks of employing child labour in supply chains in the Indian sporting goods industry. Thus, the Guidelines provide a unique channel for communications among governments, business, trade unions and civil society and for promoting appropriate standards of business conduct.

1. The 9 non-member adherents are: Argentina, Brazil, Chile, Estonia, Israel, Latvia, Lithuania, Romania and Slovenia.
2. See "Summary Report of the Chair of the Meeting on the Activities of the National Contact Points" in the *2005 Annual Report on the OECD Guidelines for Multinational Enterprises*. Forthcoming. This report can be accessed at: *www.oecd.org/dataoecd/20/13/35387363.pdf*.

Rules and guidance for reporting by companies are already well developed in most countries (see also Question 6.5), although the framework for non-financial reporting, particularly in relation to voluntary initiatives, is still evolving. Governments can enhance the quality of the investment environment by ensuring that an adequate framework is in place, whether through legislation or self-regulation, to support clear communication of all relevant rules and guidance for both financial and non-financial disclosure. When disclosures are mandatory, governments need to ensure that the application and enforcement of these requirements is non-discriminatory. At the same time, governments should seek to avoid unnecessary regulatory burdens and to allow innovation and adaptation to particular company circumstances to take place.

7.5. Enlisting business as a partner in the legal and regulatory system

> **How can the government support companies' efforts to comply with the law?**

Effective and transparent enforcement of the law motivates compliance in a particularly straightforward way – by creating costs for non-compliance (*e.g.* the costs of investigations, legal costs, fines, imprisonment and damage to reputation) and by having a "deterrent" effect. Complying with law is a challenge and requires the knowledge of specific business circumstances and deployment of managerial expertise and of formal management systems.

Governments can facilitate and motivate companies' efforts by seeking out companies' views on laws and enforcement practices. They can also provide conciliation and ombudsman facilities so that investors and others have the right to complain about government decisions that they believe are unjust. In addition, governments can acknowledge and support private initiatives to enhance compliance by providing guidance on appropriate compliance management practices.

7.5.1. *Investing in management capabilities*

Complying with law can be a formidable management challenge, especially for companies that have thousands of employees and products and that straddle numerous legal jurisdictions and business cultures. Compliance in such companies requires the knowledge of specific business circumstances and deployment of significant managerial expertise and of formal management systems.

OECD research suggests that OECD and non-OECD businesses have invested heavily in developing management know-how and systems that make such compliance possible in complex, international business settings.[8] These systems generally involve developing formal expressions of company policy (*e.g.* codes of conduct), related management systems (involving, for example, information flow, financial incentives, hierarchical controls, hiring and firing practices, internal audit, external monitoring and whistle-blowing facilities) and associated disclosure of management practices and company performance.

Investments in these management capabilities have been a major trend in international business.[9] An OECD study[10] shows variable, but often high rates of adoption of formal compliance practices and management systems by publicly-traded companies around the world, including those based in emerging markets. For example, rates of publication of anti-corruption codes by listed companies in emerging markets are around 70 per cent for the African (essentially South African) and Latin American samples of listed companies (Figure 7.1). Similarly, almost 70 per cent of the African listed companies have implemented anti-corruption management systems, a rate which is close to those seen in OECD business sectors (Figure 7.2). In contrast, adoption of such management practices in Central and Eastern Europe is comparatively low. Thus, the global picture is that adoption

Figure 7.1. **Published codes on fighting corruption and promoting business integrity**

Companies reporting as a percentage of national sample of companies

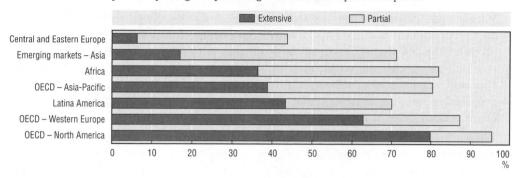

Figure 7.2. **Extent of anti-corruption management systems**

Companies reporting as a percentage of national sample of companies

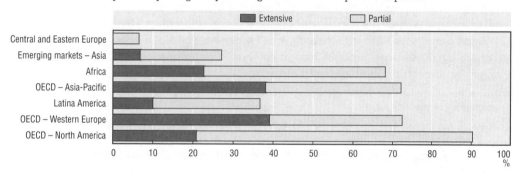

Source: OECD (2005), "Corporate Responsibility Practices of Emerging Market Companies – A Fact Finding Study", Annual Report on the OECD Guidelines for Multinational Enterprises, Paris, 2005.

of such practices is widespread in both the OECD and non-OED areas, but there are significant regional variations in practice. The rest of this section looks at the roles governments can play in encouraging innovation, learning and adoption of good management and compliance practices.

7.5.2. *Acknowledging and supporting private initiatives*

Only companies have the management expertise and the knowledge of their individual business circumstances and sectors that are needed to design and implement systems for complying with law and responding to other societal expectations. Thus, they control information and management resources that make them indispensable partners in successful regulatory systems. Business (often working through business associations and in multi-stakeholder settings) has undertaken many initiatives in an effort to play its role in this partnership more effectively. For example, Box 7.4 presents the International Association of Oil and Gas Producers' Reputational Risk Management Tool. This helps companies to select employees and business partners that are less likely to engage in corrupt or other criminal activities. Other examples include the Wolfsberg Standards (dealing with the financial sector's role in combating money laundering) and Responsible Care (for improving health and safety in the chemicals industry). These and other sectoral initiatives help individual companies to meet the compliance challenges facing their industries and, in that sense, they complement formal enforcement by public authorities.

Box 7.4. **The OGP Guidelines on reputational due diligence**

The International Association of Oil and Gas Producers' (OGP) Reputational Risk Management Guidelines recognise that companies are more vulnerable to violating anti-corruption laws when they do not have good knowledge of their employees and business partners. The OGP Guidelines aim to help companies to carry out appropriate and lawful research on associates, employees and business environments, especially when contemplating business relationships with previously unknown parties or when considering mergers, acquisitions or business in new markets where dependence on others is likely to be greater.

The purpose of conducting such research prior to entering into a business relationship is to develop a reasonable objective basis upon which the company can proceed in good faith that the employee or associate will not make improper payments to government officials or commit other illegal or unethical acts.

The OGP Guidelines outline good practices in such areas as initial risk assessment and screening; collection and verification of basic information; assessment and reports to management; proper documentation and records; integrity management of the business relationship to ensure the maintenance of longer term commitment to the required ethical policies and standards by the associate or employee. The Guidelines also note that, in certain circumstances, proof of having conducted appropriate due diligence research might be successfully used in a court of law.

Source: International Association of Oil and Gas Producers' Guidelines on Reputational Due Diligence. *www.ogp.org.uk/pubs/356.pdf.*

7.5.3. *Promoting voluntary compliance – personal conviction and informal peer pressure*[11]

Binding law and associated deterrence are not the only determinants of individual and organisational compliance with law. Indeed, compliance is often high where the amount spent on deterrence is low. In fact, the determinants of decisions to engage in socially-acceptable or anti-social behaviour appear to be remarkably complex. People comply with law and other behavioural norms not only because they fear sanctions, but because they believe in them, because they value their affiliation with the group issuing the law or norm, and because they are under informal social pressure to do so.

Widespread acceptance by business and other actors is increasingly viewed as an essential element for effective regulation – one that lowers enforcement costs and increases compliance. Private initiatives can help build up such acceptance by developing and reinforcing personal belief in and commitment to accepted norms and by strengthening informal, social pressures for compliance (*e.g.* peer pressures within business or professional associations). Examples of how this is done include:

- Some governments (*e.g.* Austria, Finland, Netherlands and Sweden) seek to do this through national initiatives that endorse and publicise good corporate practices and that create a social dynamic in favour of responsible business conduct. Government support of private anti-corruption initiatives are another example.

- Governments can facilitate and motivate companies' compliance efforts by seeking out companies' views on laws and enforcement practices. Consultation of this type can enhance the quality of the design and enforcement of law and can facilitate and motivate companies' compliance efforts.

● Governments can provide conciliation and ombudsman facilities so that investors and others have the right to complain about government decisions that they believe are unjust. This recognition of investors' and others rights to seek redress against unjust acts by the government also can reinforce acceptance of and willingness to comply with law and regulation.

7.6. Strengthening the business case for responsible business conduct

How does the government through partnership (*e.g.* by participating in the development of standards that lower costs of adopting responsible business policies) and through promotion (*e.g.* by improving the information on responsible business practices to customers and the public) help to strengthen the business case for responsible business conduct?

The "business case" for responsible behaviour is often clear-cut. For example, environmentally friendly production processes can decrease costs. Likewise, careful control of labour practices in supply chains can boost productivity at production sites and protect brand capital in consumer markets (*i.e.* it can improve profitability and help the company to manage business risks). The existence of a business case depends very much on particular circumstances (for example, the desire to protect brand capital would not be relevant for companies positioned in non-branded market segments). To the extent that the business case exists, private initiatives are self-enforcing (that is, government intervention is not required to make them happen).

Governments can act to reinforce the business case by providing information about responsible practices (*e.g.* good performance in the environmental field; see Box 7.5) and by lowering the costs of developing and adopting responsible practices, such as through support for industry initiatives (*e.g.* the International Association of Oil and Gas Producers Guidelines on Reputational Due Diligence). They can also promote internationally accepted concepts and principles, such as those embodied in the *OECD Guidelines for Multinational Enterprises*. The numerous initiatives and experiences of governments aimed at developing closer partnerships with investors on issues relating to the promotion of responsible business conduct, including through their purchasing, contracting and other business relations with private companies, provide a rich source of policy guidance.

Box 7.5. **Reinforcing the business case for environmental protection: The Green Business Award, Chinese Taipei**

The Environmental Protection Administration (EPA) of Chinese Taipei has run an annual Green Business Award since 1992 to "commend industrial organisations that have made a contribution to the environmental protection in Taiwan". The EPA exhibits practices from award-winning companies to create a demonstration effect for other companies. The EPA holds a high profile award ceremony and arranges for winning companies to meet with the President. The EPA believes that Chinese Taipei's high ranking in the ISO 14 000 certification (fifth in the word with over 560 organisations certified) can be linked to the promotion effect of the Green Business Award.

Source: FOX, Tom, Halina Ward and Bruce Howard (2002) Public Sector Roles in Strengthening Corporate Social Responsibility: A Baseline Study. The World Bank Corporate Responsibility Practice, Washington DC.

7.7. Intergovernmental co-operation

> Does the government participate in intergovernmental co-operation in order to promote international concepts and principles for responsible business conduct, such as the OECD Guidelines for Multinational Enterprises, the ILO Tripartite Declaration of Principles concerning Multinational Enterprises and Social Policies and the United Nations Global Compact?

Governments are co-operating with each other and with other actors to strengthen the international legal and policy framework in which business is conducted. The post-war period has seen the development of this framework, starting with the adoption in 1948 of the Universal Declaration of Human Rights. Multilateral instruments dealing with responsible business conduct, such as the OECD Guidelines for Multinational Enterprises and the ILO Tripartite Declaration of Principles concerning Multinational Enterprises and Social Policies, draw on this broader framework of international declarations and conventions. They communicate and promote concepts and principles for appropriate business conduct. Thirty-nine countries have committed to promoting responsible business conduct of their multinational enterprises – wherever they operate in the world – under the *OECD Guidelines for Multinational Enterprises*. While the Guidelines recommendations are addressed to business, governments – through their network of National Contact Points – have committed to promoting the Guidelines, handling enquiries and helping to resolve issues that arise in specific instances. Nine non-OECD members have adhered to the OECD Declaration on International Investment and Multinational Enterprises, which the Guidelines are a part of. The OECD encourages the adherence of other non-OECD members.

Global corporate responsibility instruments, such as the OECD Guidelines for Multinational Enterprises, communicate and promote a dynamic international framework of concepts and principles for appropriate business conduct. Intergovernmental cooperation in this field can make several contributions:

- *Broadening awareness and increasing the perceived legitimacy of concepts.* By promoting intergovernmental co-operation in this field, governments can help to broaden awareness of basic principles for appropriate conduct. As pointed out above, respect of basic principles for appropriate conduct is enhanced if these principles are widely known and accepted as legitimate. Governments can provide especially authoritative backing and support for such concepts and principles. Increased global acceptance of common principles for business conduct also helps to reduce the likelihood that responsible business conduct could become a competitive disadvantage for investors.

- *Exploring regional perspectives on global principles.* Regional intergovernmental processes allow countries to explore the meaning of international concepts and principles in the regional context (*e.g.* in light of institutional, political and cultural characteristics). For example, while the four regional human rights initiatives draw on the main international human rights instruments, they also exhibit distinctive features that reflect special regional interests or concerns. The Organisation of American States (OAS) Declaration deals with duties as well as rights of individuals. The African Union Charter covers the rights of "peoples" (that is, not just individual rights). The Arab Charter on Human Rights explicitly invokes a religious basis for human rights principles.[12]

● *Developing the international framework.* The framework of public and private instruments for corporate responsibility is in constant evolution. International and regional anti-corruption instruments have seen particularly remarkable development. Starting with the OAS' Inter-American Convention against Corruption (1996), initiatives have been developed by the OECD, the United Nations, the Council of Europe, the Southern African Development Community and the African Union Convention.

Notes

1. First paragraph of the *Preface* of the *OECD Guidelines for Multinational Enterprises*.

2. In some cases, usually referred to as "weak governance zones", governments are unable or unwilling to assume their responsibilities. In these situations, the guidance provided in international instruments such as the OECD Guidelines for Multinational Enterprises are particularly valuable for companies.

3. See the "Summary of Roundtable Discussions" for a discussion of the need for business, trade unions, NGOs and governments to make further investments in clarifying the meaning of anti-corruption laws. Facilitation payments, political contributions, use of agents and other business partners and subsidiaries were cited as priority areas for further work. The "Summary" is published in the *2003 Annual Report on the OECD Guidelines for Multinational Enterprises*. OECD 2003. Pages 120-121.

4. The OECD Investment Committee is developing a Risk Management Tool for Investors in Weak Governance Zones (these are defined as countries where governments and unwilling or unable to assume their responsibilities). This tool, which is addressed to business, is complementary to the *Policy Framework for Investment,* which is addressed to governments.

5. Protecting the rights of whistleblowers is deemed to be particularly important in the corporate responsibility field. Recommendation II.9 of the *OECD Guidelines* asks companies to "refrain from discriminatory or disciplinary action against employees who make *bona fide* reports to management or, as appropriate, to the competent public authorities on practices that contravene the law, the Guidelines or the enterprise's policies".

6. The *OECD Guidelines for Multinational Enterprises* and related Commentary cite 20 external instruments as important influences on the Guidelines' recommendations. For a more detailed review of the normative sources of the Guidelines, see "Multilateral Influences on the OECD Guidelines". *2005 Annual Report on the OECD Guidelines*. Forthcoming. or *www.oecd.org/dataoecd/29/40/35666447.pdf*.

7. For more information on the UN Global Compact, see *www.globalcompact.org*.

8. See Chapters 1-4 and 6 of *Corporate Responsibility: Private Initiatives and Public Goals*. Paris (2001). See also the background documentations prepared for the 2002 Roundtable (on responsible supply chain management), the 2003 Roundtable (on the business role in combating corruption), the 2004 Roundtable (on responsible environmental management) and the 2005 Roundtable (on corporate responsibility and developing countries). These background documents can be found at: *www.oecd.org/daf/investment/guidelines*.

9. Business associations, trade unions, NGOs and international organisations have sought to help individual companies develop these systems by issuing management system standards (*e.g.* the ISO 14000 management systems series and the International Chamber of Commerce and Transparency International's work on anti-corruption management systems). These standards help to lower companies' development and implementation costs.

10. The OECD study "Corporate Responsibility Practices of Emerging Market Companies – A Fact-Finding Study" is based on a sample of 127 publicly-listed companies in 21 emerging markets. Where possible the findings are compared to existing data on 1 740 listed companies in a range of high-income OECD countries. The 127 companies analysed comprised 22 per cent of the emerging market companies on FTSE's All-World index. The companies were selected so that sample would consist of the largest companies on their respective stock exchanges and so that the emerging market sample would have wide geographical coverage. *www.oecd.org/dataoecd/29/38/35666512.pdf*.

11. The basis for this section can be found in Chapter 1 of *Corporate Responsibility: Private Initiatives and Public Goals* (OECD 2001). Chapter 1 discusses social capital, "voluntary compliance" and the importance of consensus.

12. See "Multilateral Influences on the OECD Guidelines for Multinational Enterprises" in the 2005 *Annual Report on the OECD Guidelines for Multinational Enterprises*. OECD (2005a). This paper can also be accessed at: *www.oecd.org/dataoecd/29/40/35666447.pdf*.

References and Further Policy Resources

ILO (2000), Tripartite Declaration of Principles concerning Multinational Enterprises and Social Policies: Revised 2000, Geneva.

OECD (2000), Guidelines for Multinational Enterprises: Revision, Paris.

OECD (2001), Corporate Responsibility: Private Initiatives, Public Goals, Paris.

OECD (2005), Environment and the OECD Guidelines for Multinational Enterprises, Paris.

OECD (forthcoming), Risk Management Tool for Investors in Weak Governance Zones, Paris.

OECD, Annual Report on the Guidelines for Multinational Enterprises (various years), Paris.

OECD, Declaration on International Investment and Multinational Enterprises, Paris.

ANNEX 7.A1

Extracts from the Report to OECD Ministers by the Investment Committee on "Private Initiatives for Corporate Responsibility" [C/MIN(2001)4]

Paragraph 3:

The key findings are as follows:

- *Global phenomenon.* Voluntary initiatives are a global phenomenon, but there are significant intra-regional variations in practice.

- *Strong motivations exist that reinforce these initiatives' credibility.* Although the initiatives are often referred to as "voluntary", some firms have strong motivations to comply. These stem from legal and regulatory arrangements, employees' expectations, the need to protect brand or reputation capital and the interest of civil society. For some firms, however, such motivations can be weak (for example, for those with low public visibility).

- *Divergences of commitment and management practices.* There appear to be wide divergences in the content of codes of conduct even in relatively narrowly defined issue areas (*e.g.* labour standards in branded apparel, environmental and human rights commitments in extractive industries, the fight against bribery, science and technology transfer). This is not necessarily a problem, since there can be no "one-size-fits-all" approach to corporate responsibility due to the varying business contexts facing individual companies. On the other hand, these divergences may point to a need for continued public debate on what exactly constitutes appropriate behaviour for the different ethical challenges that confront international business. Similarly, management practices vary significantly. Some firms have adopted advanced practices while others have yet to translate their codes into management controls. The Guidelines have an important role to play in helping to build international consensus and to spread knowledge about advanced management practices in support of corporate responsibility.

- *Steps toward global norms for business conduct.* Private initiatives for corporate responsibility have provided an international channel through which various actors – businesses, business associations, public authorities, trade unions, intergovernmental organisations and NGOs – can debate various standards of business conduct and management practice. The amount of dialogue and mutual influence among these actors has been significant and it is important that this continues. This dialogue can be facilitated when companies choose to make their corporate responsibility practices public. The Guidelines institutions provide an important forum for discussion of norms for business conduct.

- *Accumulation of managerial expertise in ethical and legal compliance.* Voluntary initiatives in corporate responsibility have promoted the accumulation of the management expertise needed to translate law, regulation and less formal societal expectations into the day-to-day operations of companies. The institutional supports for this expertise – management standards, professional societies, specialised consulting and auditing services – help lower the costs of legal and ethical compliance as well as making it more effective. Non-financial auditing and reporting standards are a more recent phenomenon and, while advances are being made, they are still relatively weak.

- *The costs of voluntary initiatives for corporate responsibility.* Little information on the costs of these initiatives in specific business settings is available. It is expected that, as experience with the initiatives grows, businesses will add to their knowledge of both costs and benefits. Uncertainty also gives rise to the possibility that well-intended initiatives might have adverse, unforeseen effects. The risk of unintended consequences underscores the need to proceed carefully and with adequate knowledge of local circumstances.

- *The benefits for individual companies and for society.* The potential benefits of these initiatives are numerous. For companies, they include improved legal compliance, management of litigation risks, brand and reputation enhancement and smoother relations with shareholders and with society. Some initiatives have also deflected calls for formal regulation. Finally, companies use the initiatives to improve employee morale and to promote a "culture of integrity" within the firm. For societies, the benefits include better compliance with law and regulation and an enhanced contribution by the business sector to economic, social and environmental welfare.

- *The effectiveness of voluntary initiatives.* To promote compliance with law and appropriate responses to other societal expectations, companies often need to communicate effectively with thousands of employees and to use diverse compliance tools, effectively deployed in a coherent management system. Private initiatives are the expression of managerial expertise that allows companies to blend profitability objectives with other legal and ethical considerations into coherent business activity and response. Non-financial auditing and reporting systems are now emerging to make companies' efforts in this area more effective and more credible. However, the business sector is not the only actor to play a crucial role in promoting the success of these initiatives. If private initiatives are successful, this attests not only to the competence of the business community, but also to the abilities of societies to formulate and communicate reasonable expectations for appropriate business conduct. Thus, the effectiveness of these initiatives is closely linked to the effectiveness of the broader systems of private and public governance from which they emerge – private initiatives cannot work well if other parts of the system work poorly.

ANNEX 7.A2

Declaration on International Investment and Multinational Enterprises

27 June 2000

ADHERING GOVERNMENTS[1]

CONSIDERING:

- That international investment is of major importance to the world economy, and has considerably contributed to the development of their countries;

- That multinational enterprises play an important role in this investment process;

- That international co-operation can improve the foreign investment climate, encourage the positive contribution which multinational enterprises can make to economic, social and environmental progress, and minimise and resolve difficulties which may arise from their operations;

- That the benefits of international co-operation are enhanced by addressing issues relating to international investment and multinational enterprises through a balanced framework of inter-related instruments;

DECLARE:

Guidelines for Multinational Enterprises	I.	That they jointly recommend to multinational enterprises operating in or from their territories the observance of the Guidelines, set forth in Annex 1 hereto,[2] having regard to the considerations and understandings that are set out in the Preface and are an integral part of them
National Treatment	II.1.	That adhering governments should, consistent with their needs to maintain public order, to protect their essential security interests and to fulfil commitments relating to international peace and security, accord to enterprises operating in their territories and owned or controlled directly or indirectly by nationals of another adhering government (hereinafter referred to as "Foreign-Controlled Enterprises") treatment under their laws, regulations and administrative practices, consistent with international law and no less favourable than that accorded in like situations to domestic enterprises (hereinafter referred to as "National Treatment");

2.   That adhering governments will consider applying "National Treatment" in respect of countries other than adhering governments;

3.   That adhering governments will endeavour to ensure that their territorial subdivisions apply "National Treatment";

4.   That this Declaration does not deal with the right of adhering governments to regulate the entry of foreign investment or the conditions of establishment of foreign enterprises;

Conflicting Requirements

III.   That they will co-operate with a view to avoiding or minimising the imposition of conflicting requirements on multinational enterprises and that they will take into account the general considerations and practical approaches as set forth in Annex 2 hereto.[3]

International Investment Incentives and Disincentives

IV.1   That they recognise the need to strengthen their co-operation in the field of international direct investment;

2   That they thus recognise the need to give due weight to the interests of adhering governments affected by specific laws, regulations and administrative practices in this field (hereinafter called "measures") providing official incentives and disincentives to international direct investment;

3.   That adhering governments will endeavour to make such measures as transparent as possible, so that their importance and purpose can be ascertained and that information on them can be readily available;

Consultation Procedures

V.   That they are prepared to consult one another on the above matters in conformity with the relevant Decisions of the Council;

Review

VI   That they will review the above matters periodically with a view to improving the effectiveness of international economic co-operation among adhering governments on issues relating to international investment and multinational enterprises

Notes

1. As at 27 June 2000 adhering governments are those of all OECD members, as well as Argentina, Brazil, Chile and the Slovak Republic. The European Community has been invited to associate itself with the section on National Treatment on matters falling within its competence.

2. The text of the Guidelines for Multinational Enterprises is reproduced in Appendix II of this publication.

3. The text of General Considerations and Practical Approaches concerning Conflicting Requirements Imposed on Multinational Enterprises is available from the OECD Web site *www.oecd.org/daf/investment/*.

ANNEX 7.A3

The OECD Guidelines for Multinational Enterprises: Text and Implementation Procedures

Text

Preface

1. The *OECD Guidelines for Multinational Enterprises* (the *Guidelines*) are recommendations addressed by governments to multinational enterprises. They provide voluntary principles and standards for responsible business conduct consistent with applicable laws. The *Guidelines* aim to ensure that the operations of these enterprises are in harmony with government policies, to strengthen the basis of mutual confidence between enterprises and the societies in which they operate, to help improve the foreign investment climate and to enhance the contribution to sustainable development made by multinational enterprises. The *Guidelines* are part of the *OECD Declaration on International Investment and Multinational Enterprises* the other elements of which relate to national treatment, conflicting requirements on enterprises, and international investment incentives and disincentives.

2. International business has experienced far-reaching structural change and the *Guidelines* themselves have evolved to reflect these changes. With the rise of service and knowledge-intensive industries, service and technology enterprises have entered the international marketplace. Large enterprises still account for a major share of international investment, and there is a trend toward large-scale international mergers. At the same time, foreign investment by small and medium-sized enterprises has also increased and these enterprises now play a significant role on the international scene. Multinational enterprises, like their domestic counterparts, have evolved to encompass a broader range of business arrangements and organisational forms. Strategic alliances and closer relations with suppliers and contractors tend to blur the boundaries of the enterprise.

3. The rapid evolution in the structure of multinational enterprises is also reflected in their operations in the developing world, where foreign direct investment has grown rapidly. In developing countries, multinational enterprises have diversified beyond primary production and extractive industries into manufacturing, assembly, domestic market development and services.

4. The activities of multinational enterprises, through international trade and investment, have strengthened and deepened the ties that join OECD economies to each

other and to the rest of the world. These activities bring substantial benefits to home and host countries. These benefits accrue when multinational enterprises supply the products and services that consumers want to buy at competitive prices and when they provide fair returns to suppliers of capital. Their trade and investment activities contribute to the efficient use of capital, technology and human and natural resources. They facilitate the transfer of technology among the regions of the world and the development of technologies that reflect local conditions. Through both formal training and on-the-job learning enterprises also promote the development of human capital in host countries.

5. The nature, scope and speed of economic changes have presented new strategic challenges for enterprises and their stakeholders. Multinational enterprises have the opportunity to implement best practice policies for sustainable development that seek to ensure coherence between social, economic and environmental objectives. The ability of multinational enterprises to promote sustainable development is greatly enhanced when trade and investment are conducted in a context of open, competitive and appropriately regulated markets.

6. Many multinational enterprises have demonstrated that respect for high standards of business conduct can enhance growth. Today's competitive forces are intense and multinational enterprises face a variety of legal, social and regulatory settings. In this context, some enterprises may be tempted to neglect appropriate standards and principles of conduct in an attempt to gain undue competitive advantage. Such practices by the few may call into question the reputation of the many and may give rise to public concerns.

7. Many enterprises have responded to these public concerns by developing internal programmes, guidance and management systems that underpin their commitment to good corporate citizenship, good practices and good business and employee conduct. Some of them have called upon consulting, auditing and certification services, contributing to the accumulation of expertise in these areas. These efforts have also promoted social dialogue on what constitutes good business conduct. The *Guidelines* clarify the shared expectations for business conduct of the governments adhering to them and provide a point of reference for enterprises. Thus, the *Guidelines* both complement and reinforce private efforts to define and implement responsible business conduct.

8. Governments are co-operating with each other and with other actors to strengthen the international legal and policy framework in which business is conducted. The post-war period has seen the development of this framework, starting with the adoption in 1948 of the Universal Declaration of Human Rights. Recent instruments include the ILO Declaration on Fundamental Principles and Rights at Work, the Rio Declaration on Environment and Development and Agenda 21 and the Copenhagen Declaration for Social Development.

9. The OECD has also been contributing to the international policy framework. Recent developments include the adoption of the Convention on Combating Bribery of Foreign Public Officials in International Business Transactions and of the OECD Principles of Corporate Governance, the OECD Guidelines for Consumer Protection in the Context of Electronic Commerce, and ongoing work on the OECD Guidelines on Transfer Pricing for Multinational Enterprises and Tax Administrations.

10. The common aim of the governments adhering to the *Guidelines* is to encourage the positive contributions that multinational enterprises can make to economic, environmental and social progress and to minimise the difficulties to which their various operations may

give rise. In working towards this goal, governments find themselves in partnership with the many businesses, trade unions and other non-governmental organisations that are working in their own ways toward the same end. Governments can help by providing effective domestic policy frameworks that include stable macroeconomic policy, non-discriminatory treatment of firms, appropriate regulation and prudential supervision, an impartial system of courts and law enforcement and efficient and honest public administration. Governments can also help by maintaining and promoting appropriate standards and policies in support of sustainable development and by engaging in ongoing reforms to ensure that public sector activity is efficient and effective. Governments adhering to the *Guidelines* are committed to continual improvement of both domestic and international policies with a view to improving the welfare and living standards of all people.

I. Concepts and principles

1. The *Guidelines* are recommendations jointly addressed by governments to multinational enterprises. They provide principles and standards of good practice consistent with applicable laws. Observance of the *Guidelines* by enterprises is voluntary and not legally enforceable.

2. Since the operations of multinational enterprises extend throughout the world, international co-operation in this field should extend to all countries. Governments adhering to the *Guidelines* encourage the enterprises operating on their territories to observe the *Guidelines* wherever they operate, while taking into account the particular circumstances of each host country.

3. A precise definition of multinational enterprises is not required for the purposes of the *Guidelines*. These usually comprise companies or other entities established in more than one country and so linked that they may co-ordinate their operations in various ways. While one or more of these entities may be able to exercise a significant influence over the activities of others, their degree of autonomy within the enterprise may vary widely from one multinational enterprise to another. Ownership may be private, state or mixed. The *Guidelines* are addressed to all the entities within the multinational enterprise (parent companies and/or local entities). According to the actual distribution of responsibilities among them, the different entities are expected to co-operate and to assist one another to facilitate observance of the *Guidelines*.

4. The *Guidelines* are not aimed at introducing differences of treatment between multinational and domestic enterprises; they reflect good practice for all. Accordingly, multinational and domestic enterprises are subject to the same expectations in respect of their conduct wherever the *Guidelines* are relevant to both.

5. Governments wish to encourage the widest possible observance of the *Guidelines*. While it is acknowledged that small- and medium-sized enterprises may not have the same capacities as larger enterprises, governments adhering to the *Guidelines* nevertheless encourage them to observe the *Guidelines* recommendations to the fullest extent possible.

6. Governments adhering to the *Guidelines* should not use them for protectionist purposes nor use them in a way that calls into question the comparative advantage of any country where multinational enterprises invest.

7. Governments have the right to prescribe the conditions under which multinational enterprises operate within their jurisdictions, subject to international law. The entities of a

multinational enterprise located in various countries are subject to the laws applicable in these countries. When multinational enterprises are subject to conflicting requirements by adhering countries, the governments concerned will co-operate in good faith with a view to resolving problems that may arise.

8. Governments adhering to the *Guidelines* set them forth with the understanding that they will fulfil their responsibilities to treat enterprises equitably and in accordance with international law and with their contractual obligations.

9. The use of appropriate international dispute settlement mechanisms, including arbitration, is encouraged as a means of facilitating the resolution of legal problems arising between enterprises and host country governments.

10. Governments adhering to the *Guidelines* will promote them and encourage their use. They will establish National Contact Points that promote the *Guidelines* and act as a forum for discussion of all matters relating to the *Guidelines*. The adhering Governments will also participate in appropriate review and consultation procedures to address issues concerning interpretation of the *Guidelines* in a changing world.

II. General policies

Enterprises should take fully into account established policies in the countries in which they operate, and consider the views of other stakeholders. In this regard, enterprises should:

1. Contribute to economic, social and environmental progress with a view to achieving sustainable development.

2. Respect the human rights of those affected by their activities consistent with the host government's international obligations and commitments.

3. Encourage local capacity building through close co-operation with the local community, including business interests, as well as developing the enterprise's activities in domestic and foreign markets, consistent with the need for sound commercial practice.

4. Encourage human capital formation, in particular by creating employment opportunities and facilitating training opportunities for employees.

5. Refrain from seeking or accepting exemptions not contemplated in the statutory or regulatory framework related to environmental, health, safety, labour, taxation, financial incentives, or other issues.

6. Support and uphold good corporate governance principles and develop and apply good corporate governance practices.

7. Develop and apply effective self-regulatory practices and management systems that foster a relationship of confidence and mutual trust between enterprises and the societies in which they operate.

8. Promote employee awareness of, and compliance with, company policies through appropriate dissemination of these policies, including through training programmes.

9. Refrain from discriminatory or disciplinary action against employees who make *bona fide* reports to management or, as appropriate, to the competent public authorities, on practices that contravene the law, the *Guidelines* or the enterprise's policies.

10. Encourage, where practicable, business partners, including suppliers and sub-contractors, to apply principles of corporate conduct compatible with the *Guidelines*.

11. Abstain from any improper involvement in local political activities.

III. Disclosure

1. Enterprises should ensure that timely, regular, reliable and relevant information is disclosed regarding their activities, structure, financial situation and performance. This information should be disclosed for the enterprise as a whole and, where appropriate, along business lines or geographic areas. Disclosure policies of enterprises should be tailored to the nature, size and location of the enterprise, with due regard taken of costs, business confidentiality and other competitive concerns.

2. Enterprises should apply high quality standards for disclosure, accounting, and audit. Enterprises are also encouraged to apply high quality standards for non-financial information including environmental and social reporting where they exist. The standards or policies under which both financial and non-financial information are compiled and published should be reported.

3. Enterprises should disclose basic information showing their name, location, and structure, the name, address and telephone number of the parent enterprise and its main affiliates, its percentage ownership, direct and indirect in these affiliates, including shareholdings between them.

4. Enterprises should also disclose material information on:

   1. the financial and operating results of the company;

   2. company objectives;

   3. major share ownership and voting rights;

   4. members of the board and key executives, and their remuneration;

   5. material foreseeable risk factors;

   6. material issues regarding employees and other stakeholders;

   7. governance structures and policies.

5. Enterprises are encouraged to communicate additional information that could include:

   a) Value statements or statements of business conduct intended for public disclosure including information on the social, ethical and environmental policies of the enterprise and other codes of conduct to which the company subscribes. In addition, the date of adoption, the countries and entities to which such statements apply and its performance in relation to these statements may be communicated.

   b) Information on systems for managing risks and complying with laws, and on statements or codes of business conduct.

   c) Information on relationships with employees and other stakeholders.

IV. Employment and industrial relations

Enterprises should, within the framework of applicable law, regulations and prevailing labour relations and employment practices:

1. a) Respect the right of their employees to be represented by trade unions and other *bona fide* representatives of employees, and engage in constructive negotiations, either individually or through employers' associations, with such representatives with a view to reaching agreements on employment conditions.

    b) Contribute to the effective abolition of child labour.

    c) Contribute to the elimination of all forms of forced or compulsory labour.

    d) Not discriminate against their employees with respect to employment or occupation on such grounds as race, colour, sex, religion, political opinion, national extraction or social origin, unless selectivity concerning employee characteristics furthers established governmental policies which specifically promote greater equality of employment opportunity or relates to the inherent requirements of a job.

2. a) Provide facilities to employee representatives as may be necessary to assist in the development of effective collective agreements.

    b) Provide information to employee representatives which is needed for meaningful negotiations on conditions of employment.

    c) Promote consultation and co-operation between employers and employees and their representatives on matters of mutual concern.

3. Provide information to employees and their representatives which enables them to obtain a true and fair view of the performance of the entity or, where appropriate, the enterprise as a whole.

4. a) Observe standards of employment and industrial relations not less favourable than those observed by comparable employers in the host country.

    b) Take adequate steps to ensure occupational health and safety in their operations.

5. In their operations, to the greatest extent practicable, employ local personnel and provide training with a view to improving skill levels, in co-operation with employee representatives and, where appropriate, relevant governmental authorities.

6. In considering changes in their operations which would have major effects upon the livelihood of their employees, in particular in the case of the closure of an entity involving collective lay-offs or dismissals, provide reasonable notice of such changes to representatives of their employees, and, where appropriate, to the relevant governmental authorities, and co-operate with the employee representatives and appropriate governmental authorities so as to mitigate to the maximum extent practicable adverse effects. In light of the specific circumstances of each case, it would be appropriate if management were able to give such notice prior to the final decision being taken. Other means may also be employed to provide meaningful co-operation to mitigate the effects of such decisions.

7. In the context of *bona fide* negotiations with representatives of employees on conditions of employment, or while employees are exercising a right to organise, not threaten to transfer the whole or part of an operating unit from the country concerned nor transfer employees from the enterprises' component entities in other countries in

order to influence unfairly those negotiations or to hinder the exercise of a right to organise.

8. Enable authorised representatives of their employees to negotiate on collective bargaining or labour-management relations issues and allow the parties to consult on matters of mutual concern with representatives of management who are authorised to take decisions on these matters.

V. Environment

Enterprises should, within the framework of laws, regulations and administrative practices in the countries in which they operate, and in consideration of relevant international agreements, principles, objectives, and standards, take due account of the need to protect the environment, public health and safety, and generally to conduct their activities in a manner contributing to the wider goal of sustainable development. In particular, enterprises should:

1. Establish and maintain a system of environmental management appropriate to the enterprise, including:

   a) collection and evaluation of adequate and timely information regarding the environmental, health, and safety impacts of their activities;

   b) establishment of measurable objectives and, where appropriate, targets for improved environmental performance, including periodically reviewing the continuing relevance of these objectives; and

   c) regular monitoring and verification of progress toward environmental, health, and safety objectives or targets.

2. Taking into account concerns about cost, business confidentiality, and the protection of intellectual property rights:

   a) provide the public and employees with adequate and timely information on the potential environment, health and safety impacts of the activities of the enterprise, which could include reporting on progress in improving environmental performance; and

   b) engage in adequate and timely communication and consultation with the communities directly affected by the environmental, health and safety policies of the enterprise and by their implementation.

3. Assess, and address in decision-making, the foreseeable environmental, health, and safety-related impacts associated with the processes, goods and services of the enterprise over their full life cycle. Where these proposed activities may have significant environmental, health, or safety impacts, and where they are subject to a decision of a competent authority, prepare an appropriate environmental impact assessment.

4. Consistent with the scientific and technical understanding of the risks, where there are threats of serious damage to the environment, taking also into account human health and safety, not use the lack of full scientific certainty as a reason for postponing cost-effective measures to prevent or minimise such damage.

5. Maintain contingency plans for preventing, mitigating, and controlling serious environmental and health damage from their operations, including accidents and emergencies; and mechanisms for immediate reporting to the competent authorities.

6. Continually seek to improve corporate environmental performance, by encouraging, where appropriate, such activities as:

   a) adoption of technologies and operating procedures in all parts of the enterprise that reflect standards concerning environmental performance in the best performing part of the enterprise;

   b) development and provision of products or services that have no undue environmental impacts; are safe in their intended use; are efficient in their consumption of energy and natural resources; can be reused, recycled, or disposed of safely;

   c) promoting higher levels of awareness among customers of the environmental implications of using the products and services of the enterprise; and

   d) research on ways of improving the environmental performance of the enterprise over the longer term.

7. Provide adequate education and training to employees in environmental health and safety matters, including the handling of hazardous materials and the prevention of environmental accidents, as well as more general environmental management areas, such as environmental impact assessment procedures, public relations, and environmental technologies.

8. Contribute to the development of environmentally meaningful and economically efficient public policy, for example, by means of partnerships or initiatives that will enhance environmental awareness and protection.

VI. Combating bribery

Enterprises should not, directly or indirectly, offer, promise, give, or demand a bribe or other undue advantage to obtain or retain business or other improper advantage. Nor should enterprises be solicited or expected to render a bribe or other undue advantage. In particular, enterprises should:

1. Not offer, nor give in to demands, to pay public officials or the employees of business partners any portion of a contract payment. They should not use subcontracts, purchase orders or consulting agreements as means of channelling payments to public officials, to employees of business partners or to their relatives or business associates.

2. Ensure that remuneration of agents is appropriate and for legitimate services only. Where relevant, a list of agents employed in connection with transactions with public bodies and state-owned enterprises should be kept and made available to competent authorities.

3. Enhance the transparency of their activities in the fight against bribery and extortion. Measures could include making public commitments against bribery and extortion and disclosing the management systems the company has adopted in order to honour these commitments. The enterprise should also foster openness and dialogue with the public so as to promote its awareness of and co-operation with the fight against bribery and extortion.

4. Promote employee awareness of and compliance with company policies against bribery and extortion through appropriate dissemination of these policies and through training programmes and disciplinary procedures.

5. Adopt management control systems that discourage bribery and corrupt practices, and adopt financial and tax accounting and auditing practices that prevent the establishment of "off the books" or secret accounts or the creation of documents which do not properly and fairly record the transactions to which they relate.

6. Not make illegal contributions to candidates for public office or to political parties or to other political organisations. Contributions should fully comply with public disclosure requirements and should be reported to senior management.

VII. Consumer interests

When dealing with consumers, enterprises should act in accordance with fair business, marketing and advertising practices and should take all reasonable steps to ensure the safety and quality of the goods or services they provide. In particular, they should:

1. Ensure that the goods or services they provide meet all agreed or legally required standards for consumer health and safety, including health warnings and product safety and information labels.

2. As appropriate to the goods or services, provide accurate and clear information regarding their content, safe use, maintenance, storage, and disposal sufficient to enable consumers to make informed decisions.

3. Provide transparent and effective procedures that address consumer complaints and contribute to fair and timely resolution of consumer disputes without undue cost or burden.

4. Not make representations or omissions, nor engage in any other practices, that are deceptive, misleading, fraudulent, or unfair.

5. Respect consumer privacy and provide protection for personal data.

6. Co-operate fully and in a transparent manner with public authorities in the prevention or removal of serious threats to public health and safety deriving from the consumption or use of their products.

VIII. Science and technology

Enterprises should:

1. Endeavour to ensure that their activities are compatible with the science and technology (S&T) policies and plans of the countries in which they operate and as appropriate contribute to the development of local and national innovative capacity.

2. Adopt, where practicable in the course of their business activities, practices that permit the transfer and rapid diffusion of technologies and know-how, with due regard to the protection of intellectual property rights.

3. When appropriate, perform science and technology development work in host countries to address local market needs, as well as employ host country personnel in an S&T capacity and encourage their training, taking into account commercial needs.

4. When granting licenses for the use of intellectual property rights or when otherwise transferring technology, do so on reasonable terms and conditions and in a manner that contributes to the long term development prospects of the host country.

5.   Where relevant to commercial objectives, develop ties with local universities, public research institutions, and participate in co-operative research projects with local industry or industry associations.

IX. Competition

Enterprises should, within the framework of applicable laws and regulations, conduct their activities in a competitive manner. In particular, enterprises should:

1.   Refrain from entering into or carrying out anti-competitive agreements among competitors:

   a) to fix prices;

   b) to make rigged bids (collusive tenders);

   c) to establish output restrictions or quotas; or

   d) to share or divide markets by allocating customers, suppliers, territories or lines of commerce.

2.   Conduct all of their activities in a manner consistent with all applicable competition laws, taking into account the applicability of the competition laws of jurisdictions whose economies would be likely to be harmed by anti-competitive activity on their part.

3.   Co-operate with the competition authorities of such jurisdictions by, among other things and subject to applicable law and appropriate safeguards, providing as prompt and complete responses as practicable to requests for information.

4.   Promote employee awareness of the importance of compliance with all applicable competition laws and policies.

X. Taxation

It is important that enterprises contribute to the public finances of host countries by making timely payment of their tax liabilities. In particular, enterprises should comply with the tax laws and regulations in all countries in which they operate and should exert every effort to act in accordance with both the letter and spirit of those laws and regulations. This would include such measures as providing to the relevant authorities the information necessary for the correct determination of taxes to be assessed in connection with their operations and conforming transfer pricing practices to the arm's length principle.

Implementation Procedures

Decision of the OECD Council on the OECD Guidelines for Multinational Enterprises

June 2000

THE COUNCIL,

Having regard to the Convention on the Organisation for Economic Co-operation and Development of 14th December 1960;

Having regard to the OECD Declaration on International Investment and Multinational Enterprises (the "Declaration"), in which the Governments of adhering countries ("adhering countries") jointly recommend to multinational enterprises operating in or from their territories the observance of Guidelines for Multinational Enterprises (the "Guidelines");

Recognising that, since operations of multinational enterprises extend throughout the world, international co-operation on issues relating to the Declaration should extend to all countries;

Having regard to the Terms of Reference of the Investment Committee, in particular with respect to its responsibilities for the Declaration [C(84)171(Final), renewed in C/M(95)21];

Considering the Report on the First Review of the 1976 Declaration [C(79)102(Final)], the Report on the Second Review of the Declaration [C/MIN(84)5(Final)], the Report on the 1991 Review of the Declaration [DAFFE/IME(91)23], and the Report on the 2000 Review of the Guidelines [C(2000)96];

Having regard to the Second Revised Decision of the Council of June 1984 [C(84)90], amended June 1991 [C/MIN(91)7/ANN1];

Considering it desirable to enhance procedures by which consultations may take place on matters covered by these Guidelines and to promote the effectiveness of the Guidelines;

On the proposal of the Investment Committee:

DECIDES:

To repeal the Second Revised Decision of the Council of June 1984 [C(84)90], amended June 1991 [C/MIN(91)7/ANN1], and replace it with the following:

I. National Contact Points

1. Adhering countries shall set up National Contact Points for undertaking promotional activities, handling inquiries and for discussions with the parties concerned on all matters covered by the Guidelines so that they can contribute to the solution of problems which may arise in this connection, taking due account of the attached procedural guidance. The business community, employee organisations, and other interested parties shall be informed of the availability of such facilities.

2. National Contact Points in different countries shall co-operate if such need arises, on any matter related to the Guidelines relevant to their activities. As a general procedure, discussions at the national level should be initiated before contacts with other National Contact Points are undertaken.

3. National Contact Points shall meet annually to share experiences and report to the Investment Committee.

II. The Investment Committee

1. The Investment Committee ("the Committee") shall periodically or at the request of an adhering country hold exchanges of views on matters covered by the Guidelines and the experience gained in their application.

2. The Committee shall periodically invite the Business and Industry Advisory Committee to the OECD (BIAC), and the Trade Union Advisory Committee to the OECD (TUAC) (the "advisory bodies"), as well as other non-governmental organisations to express their views on matters covered by the Guidelines. In addition, exchanges of views with the advisory bodies on these matters may be held at their request.

3. The Committee may decide to hold exchanges of views on matters covered by the Guidelines with representatives of non-adhering countries.

4. The Committee shall be responsible for clarification of the Guidelines. Clarification will be provided as required. If it so wishes, an individual enterprise will be given the opportunity to express its views either orally or in writing on issues concerning the Guidelines involving its interests. The Committee shall not reach conclusions on the conduct of individual enterprises.

5. The Committee shall hold exchanges of views on the activities of National Contact Points with a view to enhancing the effectiveness of the Guidelines.

6. In fulfilling its responsibilities for the effective functioning of the Guidelines, the Committee shall take due account of the attached procedural guidance.

7. The Committee shall periodically report to the Council on matters covered by the Guidelines. In its reports, the Committee shall take account of reports by National Contact Points, the views expressed by the advisory bodies, and the views of other non-governmental organisations and non-adhering countries as appropriate.

III. Review of the Decision

This Decision shall be periodically reviewed. The Committee shall make proposals for this purpose.

Procedural Guidance

I. National Contact Points

The role of National Contact Points (NCP) is to further the effectiveness of the Guidelines. NCPs will operate in accordance with core criteria of visibility, accessibility, transparency and accountability to further the objective of functional equivalence.

A. *Institutional arrangements*

Consistent with the objective of functional equivalence, adhering countries have flexibility in organising their NCPs, seeking the active support of social partners, including the business community, employee organisations, and other interested parties, which includes non-governmental organisations.

Accordingly, the National Contact Point:

1. May be a senior government official or a government office headed by a senior official. Alternatively, the National Contact Point may be organised as a co-operative body, including representatives of other government agencies. Representatives of the business community, employee organisations and other interested parties may also be included.

2. Will develop and maintain relations with representatives of the business community, employee organisations and other interested parties that are able to contribute to the effective functioning of the Guidelines.

B. *Information and promotion*

National Contact Points will:

1. Make the Guidelines known and available by appropriate means, including through on-line information, and in national languages. Prospective investors (inward and outward) should be informed about the Guidelines, as appropriate.

2. Raise awareness of the Guidelines, including through co-operation, as appropriate, with the business community, employee organisations, other non-governmental organisations, and the interested public.

3. Respond to enquiries about the Guidelines from:

   a) other National Contact Points;

   b) the business community, employee organisations, other non-governmental organisations and the public; and

   c) governments of non-adhering countries.

C. *Implementation in specific instances*

The NCP will contribute to the resolution of issues that arise relating to implementation of the Guidelines in specific instances. The NCP will offer a forum for discussion and assist the business community, employee organisations and other parties concerned to deal with the issues raised in an efficient and timely manner and in accordance with applicable law. In providing this assistance, the NCP will:

1. Make an initial assessment of whether the issues raised merit further examination and respond to the party or parties raising them.

2. Where the issues raised merit further examination, offer good offices to help the parties involved to resolve the issues. For this purpose, the NCP will consult with these parties and where relevant:

    a) seek advice from relevant authorities, and/or representatives of the business community, employee organisations, other non-governmental organisations, and relevant experts;

    b) consult the National Contact Point in the other country or countries concerned;

    c) seek the guidance of the CIME if it has doubt about the interpretation of the Guidelines in particular circumstances;

    d) offer, and with the agreement of the parties involved, facilitate access to consensual and non-adversarial means, such as conciliation or mediation, to assist in dealing with the issues.

3. If the parties involved do not reach agreement on the issues raised, issue a statement, and make recommendations as appropriate, on the implementation of the Guidelines.

    a) In order to facilitate resolution of the issues raised, take appropriate steps to protect sensitive business and other information. While the procedures under paragraph 2 are under way, confidentiality of the proceedings will be maintained. At the conclusion of the procedures, if the parties involved have not agreed on a resolution of the issues raised, they are free to communicate about and discuss these issues. However, information and views provided during the proceedings by another party involved will remain confidential, unless that other party agrees to their disclosure.

    b) After consultation with the parties involved, make publicly available the results of these procedures unless preserving confidentiality would be in the best interests of effective implementation of the Guidelines.

4. If issues arise in non-adhering countries, take steps to develop an understanding of the issues involved, and follow these procedures where relevant and practicable.

D. *Reporting*

1. Each National Contact Point will report annually to the Committee.

2. Reports should contain information on the nature and results of the activities of the National Contact Point, including implementation activities in specific instances.

II. Investment Committee

1. The Committee will discharge its responsibilities in an efficient and timely manner.

2. The Committee will consider requests from NCPs for assistance in carrying out their activities, including in the event of doubt about the interpretation of the Guidelines in particular circumstances.

3. The Committee will:

   a) Consider the reports of NCPs.

   b) Consider a substantiated submission by an adhering country or an advisory body on whether an NCP is fulfilling its responsibilities with regard to its handling of specific instances.

   c) Consider issuing a clarification where an adhering country or an advisory body makes a substantiated submission on whether an NCP has correctly interpreted the Guidelines in specific instances.

   d) Make recommendations, as necessary, to improve the functioning of NCPs and the effective implementation of the Guidelines.

4. The Committee may seek and consider advice from experts on any matters covered by the Guidelines. For this purpose, the Committee will decide on suitable procedures.

ISBN 92-64-02586-3
Policy Framework for Investment
A Review of Good Practices
© OECD 2006

Chapter 8

Human Resource Development Policy*

---

* This background document was prepared by Jonathan Coppel, Investment Division, OECD Directorate for Financial and Enterprise Affairs, based upon inputs provided by the World Bank. .

8.1. Introduction

This chapter deals with how human resource development policies can contribute to an environment that is attractive to domestic and foreign investors and can enhance the benefits of investment to society. The chapter serves as background documentation to the PFI checklist and annotations dealing with human resource development (HRD).

A premise of the chapter is the linkage between government and private investments in education, training and population health with other kinds of investment: increased investment in human resource development attracts higher capital spending by enterprises, provided the general business environment is appropriate. The objectives of the chapter, therefore, are to examine and distil the lessons learnt from how government human resource development policies, including labour market policy, bear on business investment decisions and the key features that determine their success from a wider development perspective.

8.2. Human resource development promotes investment: the overall relationship

> **Has the government established a coherent and comprehensive human resource development (HRD) policy framework consistent with its broader development and investment strategy and its implementation capacity? Is the HRD policy framework periodically reviewed to ensure that it is responsive to new economic developments and engages the main stakeholders?**

In this chapter HRD[1] is interpreted broadly as having four main elements. These are educational attainment, workforce skills, population health and the set of employment policies that connect people to business enterprises with the required skills to reap the maximum benefit from economic opportunities and to quickly adapt to new challenges. Each of these areas is thus a key driver in creating a favourable environment for both domestic and foreign enterprises to grow through new investment. Their relative roles and the overall importance of HRD depend, of course, on individual country circumstances, particularly the economic structure.

However, the quality of HRD policies cannot be seen in isolation. Attempts to boost workforce skills through vocational training without considering their interaction with basic educational attainment or flanking labour market policies are likely to be ineffective. Rather, it is important to tackle low HRD through a comprehensive strategy that takes full account of the linkages between, for example, improved population health on educational attainment and, depending on employment policies, on labour productivity. This chapter, therefore, aims to identify the key elements of education, health and employment policies within an overall institutional framework for promoting the development of HRD and attracting investment.

Particular emphasis needs to be attached to the flexibility of the institutional framework to accommodate the consequences of rapidly changing technologies and economic structures. Continued improvements in and the falling cost of information and communication technologies, for instance, is raising the demand for skilled workers, making low human resource development a bigger obstacle to inward investment. The same forces, however, also represent an opportunity for developing countries to more quickly integrate into the global economy, as businesses restructure their supply chain and operations to gain from regional comparative cost advantages. As well, international enterprises are strategically well positioned to build-up human and intellectual assets as the knowledge economy develops. HRD policies must, therefore, be adaptable and constantly fine-tuned in order to quickly respond to the changing skill needs created by new challenges and to ensure the contribution of investment for development. For this to happen, close co-operation between policy makers and the main stakeholders is crucial and periodic assessments of the impact of HRD policies on the business and investment environments are needed.

8.3. Fostering a skilled and healthy workforce: a public and private partnership

Human resources are the principal asset of every country and required by all business enterprises. But without investments in developing the capacity to acquire skills, build knowledge and innovate, the potential for human resources to attract investment is limited. More broadly, human resource development contributes to civil liberties, political stability, improved population health and reduced crime and corruption, advancing economic development and further attracting inward FDI.[2] This complementarity creates a virtuous cycle and a potentially sizeable source of sustainable economic growth. Many countries, however, under-invest in human capital. This section of the chapter deals with five fields of HRD policies to foster a skilled and healthy workforce.

8.3.1. Start with the basics

> **What steps has the government taken to increase participation in basic schooling and to improve the quality of instruction so as to leverage human resource assets to attract and to seize investment opportunities?**

Access to basic education for girls and boys is a human right and educational attainment at the primary and lower secondary levels are a minimum necessary condition for development. Wide access to basic education also underpins a healthy investment environment. A joint OECD/UNESCO study has found, for instance, that investment in human capital over the past 2 decades has accounted for about ½ a percentage point in the annual growth rate of 17 emerging market economies and among OECD member countries one more year of schooling can increase GDP per capita by 4 to 7 per cent (OECD, 2003a). These are the average impacts and individual developing country experiences span within a wide and not always propitious range, depending on the quality and delivery of education and on the incentives firms face to hire more skilled workers.[3] Concerning the relationship between education and FDI, a recent study of 36 developing countries found that human capital, using 3 different proxy measures, is one of the most important determinants of the investment location decision and its importance has become greater through time

(Noorbakhsh, *et al.*, 2001).[4] In another study covering Latin America and the Caribbean, a one per cent decline in the illiteracy rate was found to increase FDI by about 2.6 per cent (Daude, Mazza and Morrison, 2003).

Formal educational attainment also provides the foundations for further learning and safeguards the capacity to seize future investment opportunities. Indeed, mastering core competencies of literacy and numeracy are pre-requisites for effective training programmes later on. Countries with very low basic education thus risk, down the road, missing out on opportunities to move up the value chain by upgrading worker skills. Positive developments in schooling enrolment rates over recent decades have lowered this risk, though in many countries progress has been slow.

Too often families living in poverty and unable to access credit markets have no option, but to prematurely withdraw their children from schooling, even though it is in their long term interest to continue. In these circumstances, without policy intervention, investment in early childhood, primary and lower secondary education will be sub optimal, perpetually feeding under-skilled workers into the labour market, disconnected with the requirements of business. Sub-Saharan Africa and South Asia offer a stark example. According to the World Bank, in year 2000 more than 40 per cent of those aged 25 and over in these regions had not completed any formal education.

Basic education is an area especially prone to be shaped by country specific constraints. Moreover, successful basic education systems vary widely, making general policy guidelines hard to formulate. But not just anything goes. First, governments need to aim to extend access to all, not just the elite. Second, they should consider further development of basic education by, for instance, extending the length of compulsory education to at least the lower-secondary level. Better quality of basic education is also important. This can be facilitated through streamlining of learning objectives designed to impart core competencies and promote creativity, and by strengthening the relationships of accountability.

One of the risks attached to a strategy that tries to rapidly boost the level of access and quality of primary and lower-secondary level education is it encounters supply constraints, delaying the improvements to the investment climate that flow from better human resources. This risk can be reduced by better service delivery procedures, such as voucher schemes and by giving schools and communities more autonomy for budget management, provided they meet pre-defined performance criteria.[5]

8.3.2. *Ensure appropriate economic incentives to acquire a higher formal education*

Is the economic incentive sufficient to encourage individuals to invest in higher education and life-long learning, supporting the improvement in the investment environment that flows from better human resources? What measures are being taken to ensure the full benefit of a countries' investment in its own human resources accrues, including the attraction of nationals who have completed their studies abroad? What mechanisms exist to promote closer co-operation between education institutions and business and to anticipate future labour force skill requirements?

Higher secondary and tertiary educated workers are essential to help secure the full benefits of investment. The potential gains stemming from the wider adoption of new and more productive technologies by businesses in high value-added activities depend on a skilled workforce. Further, new technologies typically require organisational changes, which a skilled workforce is better able to handle (Bresnahan, Brynjolfsson and Hitt, 2002). A more skilled workforce also gives firms a stronger incentive to engage in growth enhancing activities, raising both the private and social returns to education.

The externalities and market failures that characterise basic education tend to be less present in the case of upper secondary and tertiary education. Graduates are usually able to mostly internalise the benefits in the form of job opportunities offering a higher wage (See Box 8.1). However, there is a danger that the benefits to society and the local business community are forfeited to the extent that freshly-minted graduates permanently emigrate, or those who studied abroad do not return. The evidence indicates that this risk

---

Box 8.1. **How big are the returns to investment in education?**

Beyond compulsory education the decision by individuals to continue to participate in learning programmes is mostly shaped by economic incentives. The internal rate of return is a summary measure that is widely used to gauge the overall size of the economic incentive to invest in human capital and as a measure of the economic sustainability of such investments.[*] It is the discount rate that equalises the costs of education during the period of study to the expected benefits from education following thereafter. The higher are the costs of education relative to the benefits, the lower the internal rate of return. Internal rates of return can be calculated for the individual and for society. They usually differ because the individual often only shoulders a fraction of the total cost of providing education and because the returns to society may include a range of indirect benefits, such as lower crime, better health and more social cohesion to name a few. In practice, however, it is difficult to attach a monetary value to every indirect benefit needed in rate of return calculations.

A variety of factors influence estimates of the internal rate of return. The costs side depends on the size of the tuition fees less any resources made available to the student in the form of grants and loans and the foregone net of tax earnings over the length of the course of study (adjusted for the probability of being in employment). The benefits are calculated as the estimated gains in post-tax earnings (adjusted for the higher probability of being in employment) less any repayments of public support during the period of study (e.g. student loans). Estimates are sensitive to the many assumptions made, particularly the age of the individual when the course is completed, the length of the course of study and the wage premium earned by a higher educated individual.

Bearing in mind the caveats, OECD estimates of the private internal rate of return to upper-secondary education for young graduates in member countries are positive everywhere and generally high, compared to rates of return on other productive assets, providing a strong incentive for individuals to continue to invest in human capital. Likewise, estimates of the social rate of return to upper-secondary education are typically above 5 per cent, suggesting that investment in education is likely be a productive use of public resources. Moreover, these estimates ignore the likely gains from a range of positive externalities. There are also a multitude of estimates of the internal rate of return to upper secondary education for non-OECD economies, which as well show large, but a wide dispersion across countries in the size of the returns to education.

[*] Non-pecuniary benefits are also relevant, but these are hard to quantify at an aggregate level.

Source: OECD (2001 and 2004a) and Psacharopoulos and Patrinos (2004).

---

is greater in small-sized economies. In the larger economies, high-skilled worker migration is also indisputable, but its nature is more aptly described as "brain circulation", since return migration is common, likely further benefiting the business environment via the new skills and work experience gained while abroad (Dumont and Lemaître, 2005). In countries where these benefits are not forthcoming, policy measures that favour return migration have a role to play in addition to initiatives aimed at improving the business climate.[6]

Higher educational institutions themselves obviously play a key role in equipping youngsters with the workforce skills needed by businesses. But these needs change quickly and often learning institutions are slow to respond. In this regard, stronger links between universities, businesses and other stakeholders can help reshape course offerings to stay closely in line with evolving demands for specific skills. In Ireland, for example, the Industrial Development Agency (Ireland's investment promotion authority) works in partnership with educators and the business community to identify likely future skill requirements by industry. Co-operation can also bring a number of other benefits favouring the investment environment. For instance, it fosters an environment conducive to innovation and the diffusion of new knowledge more quickly (Borensztein, De Gregorio and Lee, 1995).

To provide an incentive to individuals to invest in human capital and to help secure all the spillover benefits of investment are squeezed-out, governments can focus on education policies in three dimensions:

● *Increase total resources for higher and tertiary education.* Since in many countries private internal rates of return at the tertiary level tend to be high and lie substantially above social returns, increased total resources for education and broader access to tertiary education could be facilitated by having graduates finance more of their studies. In those countries where rates of return are low, short, focussed programmes and the removal of obstacles that compress the wage structure raise private returns, strengthening the incentive to pursue higher education, including among older adults. More generally, a better business environment lifts the financial returns to investing in education. Funding support for students from poor or disadvantaged backgrounds and addressing failures in financial markets so that students are able to finance tertiary education through loans that use future labour income as credit collateral, would also improve access to higher education.

● *Raise the quality and efficiency of tertiary education.* These goals are more likely to be achieved if universities are meritocratic, granted more autonomy and competition among universities is allowed. The latter involves winding back policies, where they exist, that discriminate in favour of public sector providers. At the same time, minimum quality standards and quality assurance mechanisms through certification or accreditation schemes, with transparent procedures, covering both public and private providers is essential. Tightening links with the business community is also important to enhance the relevance of higher education.

● *Improve framework conditions.* Rent seeking associated with lack of competition in product markets, employment policies that inhibit labour turnover and job creation and the inability to exploit investment opportunities because of underdeveloped financial markets are some of the reasons why earlier efforts to increase resources in education sometimes failed to result in economic development and to improve the business and investment environment. The experience underscores the importance attached to framework policies that favour well functioning product and labour markets (see below).[7] Some policy guidelines that improve framework conditions in product markets are covered in the PFI chapters dealing with competition, trade and public governance policies.

8.3.3. Training helps business to stay competitive

To what extent does the government promote training programmes and has it adopted practices that evaluate their effectiveness and their impact on the investment environment? What mechanisms are used to encourage businesses to offer training to employees and to play a larger role in co-financing training?

While formal education equips individuals with the skills needed to learn, new recruits tend to lack the firm-specific knowledge that businesses require to unlock the full productive potential of its employees and invested capital. Transmitting these firm-specific skills is the domain of on-the-job training and specialised off-site training. However, as with basic education, market failures lead to too little training by businesses and, what limited training has been undertaken, is concentrated within a narrow group of individuals (OECD, 2003c and 2004b). One reason for this predicament is that training invariably conveys both firm specific and portable skills. The cost of the latter cannot be fully internalised in the employee's remuneration, exposing employers to the risk that workers leave the firm shortly after completing their training and before being able to recoup the cost incurred.

The shortage of trained workers is thus an obstacle to expanding investment and makes it particularly hard to attract high-skill industries to developing countries (Marin, 2004). The problem is universal, but is especially acute in many developing countries (Figure 8.1),and notably among smaller firms and those that plan to innovate and expand

Figure 8.1. **In many countries, businesses are constrained by skilled-worker shortages**

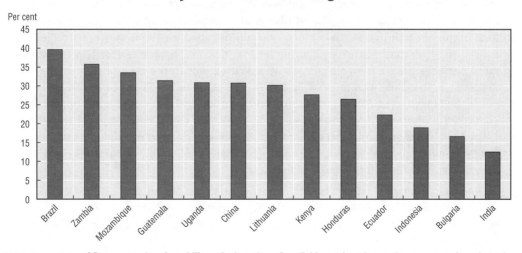

Note: Percentage of firms reporting that skills and education of available workers is a major or severe obstacle to the operation and growth of their business.

Source: World Bank Investment Climate Surveys.

(World Bank, 2005). As a consequence, and since multinational enterprises invest relatively more in worker training than domestically owned businesses (Tan and Batra, 1996), there is a danger that developing countries enter a cycle of under-trained workers that is subsequently hard to escape from. The macroeconomic costs in terms of lost potential output can also be sizeable, given the productivity gains linked to training (Batra and Tan, 1995) and because of the spillovers that training by multinational enterprises transmit to local firms (Miyamoto, 2003).

This suggests that there is a role for government to support training programmes, which in tandem with formal education improves the business environment and attracts foreign investors in high-skill industries (see Box 8.2). Policy instruments to support training are many, including co-financing arrangements where payroll levies are used to fund training grants to employers, or through levy exemptions for employers that spend a given proportion of their payroll on training, tax incentive schemes and subsidies.[8]

Evaluations of these instruments in a developing country context are scant and in any case are likely to be country specific. In these circumstances what is important from the investment environment perspective is to ensure stable training programmes that are in

---

Box 8.2. **Singapore as a location for multinational enterprise regional headquarters**

Singapore's highly skilled workforce has acted like a magnet, drawing many multinational enterprises to locate their regional headquarters in the city state. Of the approximately six thousand foreign enterprises operating in Singapore today, nearly two thirds have regional responsibilities and headquarter functions. But it was not always the case. After independence in 1959 it adopted, like many other developing countries, an import substitution strategy. With Singapore's small domestic market, this failed and was replaced in 1965 by an outward-focussed development strategy. There were many components to the strategy, but one of the central elements was an emphasis on developing and maintaining a skilled workforce, capable of adapting to new needs.

Initially, great importance was placed on secondary education, vocational training and the creation of technical universities. Businesses were encouraged to invest in human capital with funding financed by a skills-development fund and to protect and bolster Singapore's intellectual assets, inward-investing enterprises were required to provide and fund employee training. Further, since 1987 all Singaporean children are instructed in English and they must also study another language. With Singapore's economy becoming more services based the role played by a skilled workforce has gained further in importance. To ensure workforce skills are responsive to and evolve in line with business needs the Singaporean education system works closely with the Economic Development Board (the Investment Promotion Agency). In 1997, they established together the World Class Universities Programme. It aims to attract 10 world class educational institutions to locate branch campuses in Singapore and to deliver quality courses and research and development in line with the needs of industry.

The case of Singapore offers a concrete example of the importance of a skilled workforce developed through an emphasis on both formal education and training to attract FDI, and of the need to adapt human resource development policies in response to changing economic opportunities.

Source: Miyamoto (2003) and Brown (2000).

---

line with business requirements and coupled with evaluations to favour those schemes which have a proven track record of high rates of return. As well, OECD experience shows that governments can contribute to promote training by creating the structural pre-conditions for raising the benefits of training, improving delivery and quality control and through efforts to improve co-ordination between the relevant stakeholders to ensure coherence and to secure the wider contribution of investment to sustainable economic development (OECD, 2005). In addition, foreign businesses can make a positive addition to promoting training. In this regard, the 39 OECD and non-OECD countries that have adhered to the OECD *Guidelines for Multinational Enterprises* recommend efforts to offer and to encourage training to local employees (See also Box 8.5).

8.3.4. Population health matters for investment decisions and performance

> **Does the government have a coherent strategy to tackle the spread of pandemic diseases and procedures to evaluate public health expenditures aimed at improving public health outcomes and, through inter linkages, the investment environment?**

Pandemic and epidemic diseases, such as malaria and HIV/AIDS, are a human tragedy, ravaging societies through the premature loss of lives and entrapping many others in poverty. They negatively influence investment decisions too, risking a vicious cycle between poor health, less investment, job creation and entrepreneurship and hence slower economic growth and fewer resources for tackling the sources of treatable diseases and disabilities (see Box 8.3 on the economic cost of HIV/AIDs).

However, the links between health, education and economic growth can equally work in a virtuous way. A less disease prone country strengthens the ability and increases the incentive to invest in, and the returns from investment in education and from worker experience. More generally, it boosts morale, strengthens confidence in the future and increases the willingness to save and invest. These effects favour both higher productivity and participation in the economy and thus higher household incomes. There is also a direct impact on productivity, since a healthy population is more physically and mentally robust and less prone to absenteeism due to illness or the need to care for other family members.

Apart from the human and macroeconomic gains, population health promotes investment. This is because of the effect of good health on worker productivity and because domestic and foreign businesses tend to avoid sending employees into areas where their health could be damaged and where access to health care is limited. In addition, uncertainty, a feature of uncontrollable, infectious diseases makes investors wary, leading to much larger economic costs in terms of foregone investment than is warranted by the size of the risk. This dimension of the investment environment was clearly illustrated following the outbreak of Severe Acute Respiratory Syndrome (SARS) in 2003, when FDI into China fell sharply (Tam, 2003). While investment inflows were restored once SARs had been brought under control, it demonstrated the sizeable adverse impacts that sustained epidemics, such as malaria and HIV/Aids can have on investment.

Box 8.3. **The economic cost of HIV/AIDS**

Over past centuries epidemics have had catastrophic effects on human well-being. The plague that swept through Europe in the mid-14th century took with it one third of the population and between 1918 and 1919 the Spanish influenza claimed more than 40 million lives. The HIV/AIDS epidemic is the most prominent contemporary pandemic disease. Worldwide, an estimated 42 million people live with HIV/AIDS and 22 million have already lost their life to the disease. A disproportionate number of these people and over three quarters of new infections in 2003 were located in Sub-Saharan Africa. In the most affected African countries, life expectancy at birth has dropped by more than 10 years to around 50 years and is projected to fall to as low as 30 years over the next two decades (UN, 2003).

When the declines in health status are this large, the economic impact is big as well. Estimates of the macroeconomic impact of AIDS vary widely. A review of 11 studies that quantified the effect on GDP per capita in Africa concluded that the net effect of HIV/AIDS is negative and substantial, with bigger impacts found in the most recent studies (Dixon, McDonald and Roberts, 2002). These recent studies suggest that the income and output loss associated with the epidemic has slowed the pace of economic growth in the region by 2 to 4 per cent per annum. Moreover, such estimates do not fully capture the dynamic losses associated with lower physical investment, the destruction of human capital and the weaker transmission of knowledge and abilities from one generation to another. All of these effects are harder to quantify, because they take decades before they become fully felt and because of the slow progression of AIDS.

The HIV/AIDS epidemic also imposes large costs on households and businesses. Since most fatalities from AIDS are adults in the prime of life, businesses lose skilled workers and valuable know-how accumulated through worker experience, and incur higher costs of employee health benefit schemes, where they exist. Productivity is also reduced due to increased absenteeism and possibly as a result of a wider impact on staff morale. In a survey of African businesses, nearly all respondents said they were concerned about HIV/AIDS and quantified its impact on the region's economic productivity at around 1 per cent of GDP.

Source: Bell and Lewis (2005), Bloom, Rosenfield and River Path Associates (1999), Dixon, McDonald and Roberts (2003), UN (2003) and World Bank (2005).

The longer lasting effects of poor population health on foreign direct investment were investigated in a study of 51 low- and middle-income countries. It found that a one year improvement in life expectancy – roughly proxying the health of a country's population – led to about a 9 per cent increase in gross FDI inflows (Alsan, Bloom and Canning, 2004). The overall impact would likely be even greater if domestic investment is also taken into account. The potential benefits in terms of economic development are also substantial. A range of studies have found that a five year gain in life expectancy – equivalent to the average increase over the past two decades – leads to about 0.4 per cent faster growth in GDP per capita per year (Strauss and Thomas, 1998).

The payoffs to controlling epidemic diseases are thus multifaceted and include increased investment. But designing the policies with limited resources that favour a virtuous cycle between health, investment and sustainable development is hard to get right. It takes time before the impact of policies is felt, making it less certain which factors play the fundamental role and difficult to justify sustained funding. Nonetheless, and in addition to ensuring broad access to essential medicines there are several lessons to be drawn from successful experiences. The first is the importance of a coherent framework of policies; there is no magic bullet. The provision of clean water and sanitation, control of disease vectors – the organism that transmits a disease – vaccination programmes and health education, are all needed to prevent epidemic outbreaks and to contain them in the event they occur. A second lesson is the need for regular evaluations of public health programmes to evaluate their effectiveness (*e.g.* treatment or preventative), since what works well in one country may not always be effective in a different country context. Thirdly, policies that exploit known inter linkages are important. A better educated population, for example, indirectly improves health, because it leads to greater awareness and access to information and also an improved capability by health authorities to respond to and manage public health matters.

8.3.5. Bolster – don't undermine – a competitive labour climate

To create the business conditions to spur investment and to reap their full output expanding potential also requires a competitive labour force so that resources freely move towards their most productive uses. In most situations markets generally do a good job of allocating the most effective use of resources, but can also result in outcomes unacceptable to society. Governments, therefore, intervene in the labour market to achieve social and other objectives. But the design of policy interventions and how they are implemented and enforced may also, advertently or inadvertently, compromise the ability of businesses to adapt to changed circumstances, harming the investment environment.

This, of course, does not mean that governments should shy away from regulatory interventions. But rather care is needed to craft regulatory strategies that focus both on the aimed-for benefits, taking a wide range of interests into account and to ensure overall efficiency losses are minimised. Within this framework there are several dimensions to a competitive labour climate. These relate to the basic rights of workers, or core labour standards, labour market regulations that govern employment conditions and regulations that relate to the ability of workers from investor source countries to relocate to the host country. In each of these areas the considerations that need to be taken into account and how they bear on the investment environment differ and are therefore treated separately.

Enforce core labour standards

> **What mechanisms are being put in place to promote and enforce core labour standards?**

Core labour standards relate to fundamental principles and basic human rights in the workforce. As such, they are distinct from labour standards regarding work conditions (discussed below). The international community, largely through the ILO, has made significant progress in developing a consensus with respect to the concept and recognition of a set of core labour standards. Core labour standards are also part of the ILO Decent Work Agenda, adopted in 2000.

According to the ILO *Declaration on Fundamental Principles and Rights at Work* these core standards relate to eliminating all forms of forced or compulsory labour; abolishing child labour; non-discrimination in respect of employment and occupation; and ensuring the freedom of association and the right to collective bargaining. Specific definitions of these principles are spelled out in a series of ILO Conventions, which a growing number of countries have ratified, establishing core labour standards, regardless of a country's stage of development. As of February 2006, two thirds of ILO member states had ratified all 8 of the ILO conventions, compared with one third six years ago and less than one fifth in 1996 (ILOLEX, 2006 and OECD, 2000).

The rapid and widespread ratification of the ILO core labour standard conventions can be explained by the fact that they serve countries' economic self interest. They are a key element in the healthy functioning of market economies, create a level playing field for all investors, foreign and domestic, and improve economic performance. According to a study by Palley (1999) covering 17 mostly developing countries, reforms that introduce greater freedom of association, raise GDP growth by 1.9 percentage points in the following five year period. And in a series of influential works, Rodrik (1997 and 1999) showed that democratic institutions have a positive effect on wages, reduce economic volatility and foster greater resilience to economic shocks. These results reflect the stronger incentives core labour standards give workers to improve skills and to the younger generation to accumulate human capital. Efficiency gains are also achieved through less discrimination in the workplace and possibly via a more favourable social climate and political stability.

Even though countries benefit from the adoption of core labour standards, compliance is uneven across signatory states, particularly in relation to child labour and in different forms of discrimination.[9] In some cases, violations are deliberate. For instance, a number

---

Box 8.4. **Do core labour standards discourage foreign direct investment?**

It is often claimed that low labour standard countries are a location criteria for foreign investors, because they ensure a competitive advantage due to lower labour costs. This has sparked fears that there might be a "race to the bottom" on fundamental worker rights. But the empirical support for this conventional wisdom is lacking. All of the available studies find no statistically robust connection between weaker measures of workers rights and greater inflows of foreign direct investment. Most of the variation in labour costs across countries disappears once adjusted for differences in productivity (Rodrik, 1999).

In fact, more often, available research has identified that core labour standards actually help to attract FDI. One of the first studies to examine the relationship between compliance with core labour standards and FDI was undertaken by the OECD in 1996. It focussed on the rights of freedom of association and to collective bargaining in 76 OECD and non-OECD countries and found a small positive link between compliance with these rights and FDI inflows (OECD, 1996).

Since the OECD report, a range of other studies have tackled this issue, using various proxies for compliance with ILO labour standard Conventions (*e.g.* Rodrik, 1996, Kucera, 2001, Busse, 2002 and Daude, Mazza and Morrison, 2003). All of these studies find no evidence to support the conventional wisdom that multinational enterprises favour countries with lower respect for basic human and worker rights. And in line with OECD work, several of the researchers found that higher child labour standards and greater respect for freedom of association are positively associated with investment.

Source: Busse (2002), Busse and Braun (2002), Daude, Mazza and Morrison (2003), Kucera (2001), and OECD (1996 and 2000).

---

of governments waive certain components of the core labour standards within special export processing zones (EPZ) because the authorities fear multinational enterprises' investment may be deterred by their presence (see OECD, 2000 and ICFTU, 2005 for specific examples), or the perception it may help to attract FDI (see ILO, 1998).[10] However, there is no unequivocal empirical support for this concern. Indeed, many researchers find that multinational enterprises are more likely to invest in countries with stricter safeguards and enforcement of basic human and worker rights than in those countries where such rights are absent or poorly enforced (see Box 8.4).

The main policy lesson to draw from the above is the need to reinforce efforts to increase enforcement and compliance with the core labour standards. There is no simple well-targeted instrument to do this. A broad strategy is required. The key features need to embrace programmes that raise awareness of the problems associated with low compliance, including the damage it does to the investment environment and the provision of financial and technical assistance by donor countries to develop the administrative capacity needed to enforce core labour standards. Where they exist, the removal of fees for basic education and supply responsive funding arrangements indirectly reduce the incidence of child labour, as do broader initiatives to combat poverty.[11] Finally, the promotion of standards, such as the *OECD Guidelines for Multinational Enterprises* helps to foster responsible business practices.

Keeping the labour market competitive

> **To what extent do labour market regulations support job creation and the government's investment attraction strategy? What initiatives have been introduced that support policy coordination, balancing social objectives, the goal of a competitive workforce and the incentives for business to invest?**

As already observed, interventions in the labour market aim to improve market efficiency and achieve social objectives. From an investment environment perspective the issue is how well such interventions achieve their goals without compromising other determinants of economic performance. Badly designed labour market regulations can reduce the opportunities and incentives for businesses to make new investments and expand. This situation appears to be the case in some developing countries where labour regulations are reported to be a "major or severe" obstacle to business operations (Figure 8.2).[12]

The exact nature of the labour market regulations that are said to harm the business environment vary from country to country. But based on a World Bank Study (2005) and experience in OECD countries (OECD, 1994, 1999 and 2006) there are two areas of intervention where governments face a trade-off between promoting social goals and a conducive investment environment. The first relates to wage formation methods that result in labour costs too high to spur job creation and in underutilised labour resources, in particular female employment, preventing economies from making full benefit from its investments in HRD. The second source relates to interventions that escalate other non-wage labour costs (*e.g.* paid leave) which employers are unable to pass on to employees through lower monetary remuneration, making some businesses economically unviable.

Figure 8.2. **Firms rating regulations as a "major or severe" obstacle to doing business**

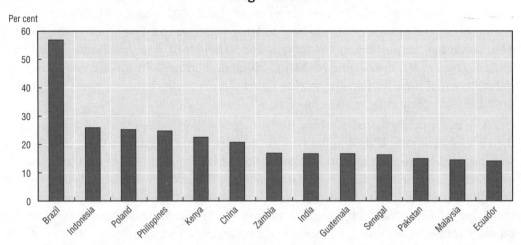

Note: Percentage of firms reporting that labour regulations were a major or severe obstacle to the operation and growth of their business.

Source: World Bank Investment Climate Surveys.

Another of the likely consequences is to give workers and employers an incentive to shift to the informal sector, or to stay there. According to World Bank research, regulations that affect business labour costs, such as worker hours and paid leave, are more stringent in developing countries than in many developed countries (Pierre and Scarpetta, 2004). Again, however, compliance and enforcement of statutory norms is weak.

There are a number of steps that the authorities can take to design labour interventions without unduly compromising a government's investment attraction strategy. For instance, the wage formation process and its responsiveness to labour market conditions could be reinforced through more effective co-ordination among the parties involved in negotiations. In practice, how this is achieved will depend on the specific circumstances in each country. Analytical work confirms that aggregate wage flexibility can be obtained in both centralised and decentralised wage bargaining systems (OECD, 2006). In contrast, the *OECD Jobs Strategy* concludes that wages tend to be rigid in countries with industry-based and uncoordinated bargaining (OECD, 2006). As a rule, other than setting minimum and economically responsible standards and facilitating an environment in which labour and management can bargain on an equal footing, governments should refrain from leading negotiations on work conditions. In this context, trade unions play an important role in co-ordinating and representing the interests and preferences of workers. Their impact on investment depends on having a constructive dialogue between freely elected associations of workers and employers.[13] At the same time, it is necessary to have institutional arrangements for conciliation, mediation or arbitration on a voluntary basis on issues and cases where no agreement can be reached.

The role of foreign workers

> **Do laws and regulations restrict the deployment of skilled workers from an enterprise investing in the host country? What steps have been taken to unwind unduly restrictive practices covering the deployment of workers from the investing enterprise and to reduce delays in granting work visas?**

Foreign investment often requires the deployment of experienced staff from more established parts of the organisation to ensure the smooth introduction of new facilities and the local implementation of corporate practices. Often, in time, these roles are passed on to locally-engaged employees. Some countries, however, put tight limits on the number of foreign employees granted work visas or impose local recruitment quotas linked to the number of expatriate staff. And frequently bureaucratic processes cause long delays in issuing work permits. These practices raise the cost of doing business and can discourage investment. As well as harming the investment environment, the country loses the opportunity of hosting skilled workers – a "brain gain" – and the local diffusion of knowledge and international business practices that it brings.

The main conclusion to draw from the above is that governments should reconsider restrictions that prevent the deployment of skilled foreign workers associated with new investments by multinational enterprises and governments need to evaluate the costs and benefits of performance requirements that oblige foreign companies to hire a minimum number of local workers (see also Chapter 1). In addition, procedures for applying and granting work and residence visas for foreign staff should be made transparent and delays shortened through less bureaucratic operations and the streamlining of qualification recognition procedures.[14]

8.4. Reaping the maximum benefit from investment: the role of human resource development in facilitating adjustment

Every economy is prone to upheaval, often linked to new technologies that lead to different work practices, opening fresh business opportunities and making others no longer viable. This puts businesses under constant pressure to innovate and adapt their operations. Those firms that are able to adapt quickly as the business environment changes are better placed to face new competition and to expand, by seizing the investment opportunities as they open. The ability to respond quickly is thus a key factor in the overall business environment, with the adaptability of labour markets playing a crucial role. This part of the chapter, therefore, deals with how human resource policies can underpin investment dynamism while cushioning the transition costs of adjustment and then examines labour market policies that maintain an adaptable workforce.[15]

8.4.1. Policies to cushion transition costs

Does the government support programmes designed to assist large-scale labour adjustment and indirectly the investment environment by better positioning firms to seize investment opportunities? Do the incentive mechanisms in these schemes encourage broad support for change? What role is business encouraged to play in easing the transition costs associated with labour adjustment?

In many economies as much as 10 to 20 per cent of the workforce turns over each year, as new firms are created and grow and as others contract or cease to operate (World Bank, 2005). This is one of the channels through which technologies and know how are diffused, boosting productivity. Indeed, it is this process of "creative destruction" that leads to higher output overall. But there are both winners and losers. The transition period can be a costly and traumatic experience for those employees affected, especially in the developing countries which have inadequate or non-existent social insurance mechanisms. This can cause resistance to change and, because of factors such as rent-seeking by interest groups, influence political processes to stall reforms that would otherwise benefit society asa whole.

Good policy can limit these dislocation costs and at the same time speed up the pace of adjustment. There are several elements to good policy practice. These include retraining and redeployment support, though these need to be well-targeted yet responsive to individual needs, put in place quickly and tailored to local circumstances, otherwise they

---

Box 8.5. **The OECD Guidelines for Multinational Enterprises on employment and industrial relations**

The *OECD Guidelines for Multinational Enterprises* constitute a set of voluntary recommendations by governments in all the major areas of business ethics. They are a multilaterally endorsed and comprehensive code of conduct that enjoys the backing of governments whose territories are home to almost 90 per cent of foreign direct investment flows and to 97 out of the top-100 multinational enterprises.

One of the Guideline chapters covers employment and industrial relations. In this respect, the principles and standards mostly relate to core labour standards, discussed above. However, they also cover certain aspects of working conditions, such as occupational health and safety. Concerning industrial relations, the Guidelines recommend that firms consult and inform employees. Specifically, it states: In considering changes in their operations which would have major effects upon the livelihood of their employees, in particular in the case of the closure of an entity involving collective lay-offs or dismissals, provide reasonable notice of such changes to representatives of their employees, and, where appropriate, to the relevant governmental authorities, and co-operate with the employee representatives and appropriate governmental authorities so as to mitigate to the maximum extent practicable adverse effects.

Promoting observance of the OECD Guidelines contributes to furthering human resource development in host countries.

Source: OECD (2004d).

risk failing to attract much demand. In countries where comprehensive social security is not available, employer pre-funded one-off severance payments can cushion the impact of restructuring and build support for change and thus quicken adjustment. In cases where adjustment is concentrated in a region and where a single enterprise dominates the local economy a wider range of support measures may be needed, including regional development programmes. Finally, full and early consultation and providing comprehensive information engages employees in the process of adjustment and helps to limit opposition to change. It forms a part of the recommendations made by the 39 countries that have adhered to the *OECD Guidelines on Multinational Enterprises* (see Box 8.5).

8.4.2. Maintaining an adaptable workforce

What steps are being taken to ensure that labour market regulations support an adaptable workforce and maintain the ability of enterprises to modify their operations and investment planning?

Investments in HRD help to maintain an adaptable and skilled workforce. However, this source of dynamism may fail to benefit the business environment if other interventions in the labour market create a context that blunts the process of workforce reorganisation and discourages business from investing in new productivity enhancing technologies. Against this background, it is notable that some developing countries have tighter labour laws than in developed economies (Figure 8.3). Their impact on the investment environment, however, also depends on their specific design.

The key issue for policy is how to reconcile the employers' need for flexibility in hiring and firing with that of workers for employment security. The *OECD Jobs Strategy* has

Figure 8.3. **Some developing countries have tighter labour laws than developed countries**

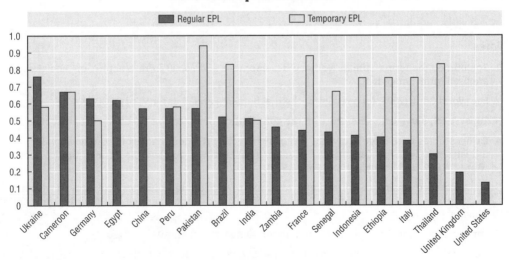

Note: The index of employment protection legislation (EPL) ranges between 0 and 1. Higher numbers mean more stringent employment protection laws.

Source: Pierre and Scarpetta (2004) and World Bank Doing Business Project.

highlighted innovative approaches to maintain labour market dynamism while also providing workers with adequate security exist. These include improving the efficiency of job protection regulations, for instance through implementation procedures that are quick and predictable and shifting the focus of interventions toward income support, coupled with re-employment services. However, in a developing country context, implementation of such a "flexicurity" approach is obviously a major challenge. Opportunities for improving the income support schemes and the pooling of risks across individuals may also exist. These include, for example, the introduction of pre-funded, financially feasible severance pay savings accounts. And the risks associated with job turnover that are born by individuals could be pooled through the introduction of unemployment insurance benefits. More generally, labour market regulations need to be crafted to reflect the interests of the whole working age population, not just those in employment in the formal sector and to consult with a wide range of stakeholders.

8.5. Conclusion

HRD policy is an integral part of the wider policy framework aimed at creating an environment conducive to attracting and encouraging investment and to ensure the maximum contribution of investment to sustainable economic development. The chapter has stressed the importance of establishing a coherent institutional framework for HRD policies and identified three principles that should guide the design of such a framework. These are a comprehensive focus on the role of educational attainment, workforce skills, population health and employment policies, an understanding of the linkages between these four areas of human resource development policy and their relationship with the investment environment, and thirdly adaptability to new challenges.

When moving from general principles to practical HRD policy guidelines to foster a favourable investment environment, one must recognise that country circumstances will differ, and possibly in ways that shape policy prescriptions. Against this background, the approach of the PFI is to identify the key issues and questions that policy makers need to consider in framing specific HRD policies which directly or indirectly influence investment decisions and to offer guidelines on good policy practices.

Notes

1. Sometimes the terms human resource development and social infrastructure, or "social capital" are used interchangeably.

2. See World Bank (2005) for a review of the mechanisms and chapter VI of OECD (2002).

3. Topel (1999) surveys the literature on the contribution of education to economic development.

4. Earlier studies were more equivocal, probably reflecting the dominance of FDI in lower value added industries 20 years ago, where the need for skilled workers is less. See, for example, Root and Ahmed (1979) and Schneider and Frey (1985).

5. For a detailed review of educational reforms in developing countries and drawing from this evidence the best practices in the delivery of basic education services, see World Bank (2004), Chapter 7.

6. For a review of the literature see Commander, Kangasniemi and Winters (2004).

7. OECD (2003b), Chapter VIII shows that framework conditions which support well-functioning labour markets attract inward FDI.

8. See OECD (2004c) for a review of co-financing of adult education and training, the policy issues involved and the evidence on their effectiveness in OECD countries.

9. As Busse (2002) showed, there is little correspondence between *de jure* ratification of the ILO Conventions and *de facto* compliance. The US and Myanmar, for example, have both signed only two of the ILO Conventions, yet no one would claim that these countries have the same respect for core labour standards.

10. On average, wages are higher and working conditions better in EPZs than in the rest of the economy, with most exceptions occurring in low-skilled labour intensive assembly operations, which account for a large number of workers in EPZs. Brown (2000) reviews labour standards in export processing zones.

11. Brazil offers an example of this strategy. In 1998 it introduced new funding arrangements for schools, tightened targeted income support programmes and made some entitlements conditional on child school enrolment, resulting in a very sharp increase in primary-age school enrolments (De Mello and Hoppe, 2005).

12. The business survey responses to questions on human resources closely match the relative stringency of *de jure* labour laws (Pierre and Scarpetta, 2004).

13. Aidt and Tzannatos (2002) survey and synthesise the economic literature on the impact of wage bargaining institutions, in particular collective bargaining, on economic performance.

14. This matter is also dealt with in the Investment Promotion and Facilitation chapter of the PFI.

15. Although treated separately here for the purposes of exposition, these two topics are intimately related and the policy implications are closely connected.

References and Further Policy Resources

Aidt, T. and Z. Tzannatos (2002), Unions and Collective Bargaining: Economic Effects in a Global Environment, the World Bank, Washington, DC.

Alsam, M., D. Bloom and D. Canning (2004), "The effect of population health on foreign direct investment", NBER Working Paper, No. 10596.

Batra, G. and H. Tan (1995), "Enterprise training in developing countries: overview of incidence, determinants and productivity outcomes", World Bank Private Sector Development Occasional Paper Series, No. 3170.

Bell, C. and M. Lewis (2005), "The economic implications of epidemics old and new", Centre for Global development Working Paper, No. 54.

Bloom, D. and D. Canning (2003), "The health and poverty of nations: from theory to practice", Journal of Human Development, Vol. 4, No. 1.

Bloom, D., A. Rosenfield and River Path Associates (1999), A Moment in Time: Aids and Business, American Foundation for AIDS Research, Washington DC.

Borensztein, E., J. De Gregorio and J. Lee (1995), "How does foreign direct investment affect economic growth?", NBER Working Paper, No. 5057.

Bresnahan, T., E. Brynjolfsson and L. Hitt (2002), "Information technology, workplace organisation and the demand for skilled labor: firm level evidence", Quarterly Journal of Economics, Vol. 117, No. 1.

Busse, M. and S. Braun (2002), "Trade and investment effects of forced labour: an empirical assessment", HWWA Discussion Paper, No. 200.

Busse, M. (2002), "Foreign direct investment and fundamental workers' rights", Journal of International Relations and Development, Vol. 5 No. 2.

Brown, D. (2000), "International trade and core labour standards: a survey of the recent literature", OECD Directorate for Education, Employment, Labour and Social Affairs Occasional Papers No. 43.

Commander, S., M. Kangasniemi and L. Winters (2004), "The brain drain: curse or boon? A survey of the literature", in R. Baldwin and L.A. Winters (eds.), Challenges to Globalisation: Analysing the Economics, University of Chicago Press.

Daude, C., J. Mazza and A. Morrison (2003), "Core labour standards and foreign direct investment in Latin America and the Caribbean: does lax enforcement of labour standards attract investors?" IADB mimeo.

Dixon, S., S. McDonald and J. Roberts (2002), "The impact of HIV and AIDS on Africa's economic development", BMJ, Vol. 324, No. 26.

Dumont, J.-C. and G. Lemaître (2005), "Counting immigrants and expatriates in OECD countries: a new perspective", OECD Social, Employment and Migration Working Papers, No. 25.

Golub, S. (2003), "Measures of restrictions on inward foreign direct investment for OECD countries", OECD Economics Department Working Papers, No. 357.

ICTFU (2005), Reports on Violations of Trade Union Rights, International Confederation of Free Trade Unions, posted at www.icftu.org.

ILO (1998), Labour and Social Issues Relating to Export Processing Zones, Geneva.

ILO (1998), ILO Declaration on Fundamental Principles and Rights at Work.

ILO Conventions (www.ilo.org).

Kucera, D. (2001), "The effects of core workers rights on labour costs and foreign direct investment: evaluating the 'conventional wisdom'", International Institute for Labour Studies Discussion Paper, DP/130/2001.

Marin, D. (2004), "A nation of poets and thinkers – less so with Eastern enlargement? Austria and Germany", CEPR Discussion Paper Series, No. 4358.

De Mello, L. and M. Hoppe (2005), "Education attainment in Brazil: the experience of FUNDEF", OECD Economics Department Working Papers, No. 424.

Miyamoto, K. (2003), "Human capital formation and foreign direct investment in developing countries", OECD Development Centre Working Paper, No. 211.

Mori Business (2004), Off-Shoring Survey 2004 Summary Report, London.

Nicoletti, G., S. Golub., D. Hajkova., D. Mirza and K. Yoo (2003), "Policies and international integration: influences on trade and foreign direct investment", OECD Economics Department Working Papers, No. 359.

Noorbakhsh, F., A. Paloni and A. Youssef (2001), "Human capital and FDI inflows to developing countries: new empirical evidence", World Development, Vol. 29, No. 9.

OECD (1994), The OECD Jobs Study, Evidence and Explanations, Paris.

OECD (1996), Trade, Employment and Labour Standards: A Study of Core Worker's Rights and International Trade, Paris.

OECD (1999), Implementing the OECD Jobs Strategy: Assessing Performance and Policy, Paris.

OECD (2000), International Trade and Core Labour Standards, Paris.

OECD (2001), OECD Economic Outlook, Chapter V. "Investment in human capital through post-compulsory education and training", Paris.

OECD and UNESCO (2002), Financing Education – Investments and Returns, Paris.

OECD (2002), Foreign Direct Investment for Development – Maximising Benefits, Minimising Costs, Chapter VI. "FDI and Human Capital Enhancement", Paris.

OECD (2003a), The Sources of Economic Growth in OECD Countries, Paris.

OECD (2003b), OECD Economic Outlook, Chapter VIII. "Policy influences on foreign direct investment", Paris.

OECD (2003c), Beyond Rhetoric: Adult Learning Policies and Practices, Paris.

OECD (2004a), Education at a Glance: OECD Indicators 2004, Paris.

OECD (2004b), OECD Employment Outlook, Chapter IV. "Improving skills for more and better jobs: does training make a difference?", Paris.

OECD (2004c), Co-Financing Lifelong Learning: Towards a Systematic Approach, Paris.

OECD (2004d), Annual Report on the OECD Guidelines for Multinational Enterprises, Paris.

OECD (2005), Promoting Adult Learning, Paris.

OECD (2006, forthcoming), OECD Jobs Strategy: Lessons from a Decade's Experience, Paris.

Palley, T. (1999), "The economic case for international labour standards: theory and some evidence", mimeo, AFL-CIO, Washington DC

Psacharopoulos, G. and H. Patrinos (2004), "Returns to investment in education: a further update", Education Economics, Vol. 12, No. 2.

Pierre, G. and S. Scarpetta (2004), "Do employers' perceptions square with actual labour regulations?", Background paper for the World Bank World Development Report 2005.

Rama, M. (2003), "Globalisation and workers in developing countries", World Bank Policy Research Discussion Paper, No. 2958.

Rodrik, D. (1996), "Labour standards in international trade: do they matter and what do we do about them?" in R.Z. Lawrence. R. Rodrik and J. Whalley (eds.) Emerging Agenda for Global Trade: High Stakes for Developing Countries, Overseas Development Council Essay No. 20, John Hopkins University Press, Washington DC.

Rodrik, D. (1997), "Democracy and economic performance", manuscript.

Rodrik, D. (1999), "Democracies pay higher wages", NBER Working Paper, No. 6364.

Root, F. and A. Ahmed (1979), "Empirical determinants of manufacturing direct foreign investment in developing countries", Economic Development and Cultural Change, Vol. 27.

Schneider, F. and B. Frey (1985), "Economic and political determinants of foreign direct investment", World Development, Vol. 13.

Strauss, J. and D. Thomas (1998), "Health, nutrition and economic development", Journal of Economic Literature, Vol. 36.

Tam, J. (2003), "SARS slashes FDI inflows by 62 per cent", The Standard Greater China's Business Newspaper, 30 September.

Tan, H. and G. Batra (1996), "Enterprise training in developing countries", Mimeo World Bank, Washington DC.

Topel, R. (1999), "Labor markets and economic growth", in Handbook of Labor Economics, edited by O.C. Ashenfelter and D. Card, Amsterdam.

United Nations (2003), World Population Prospects: The 2002 Revision, New York.

United Nations Development Programme (UNDP), The National Human Development Report (NHDR) Workspace (http://hdr.undp.org/nhdr/).

United Nations Educational, Scientific and Cultural Organization (UNESCO), instruments and other policy resources (www.unesco.org).

World Bank (2004), World Development Report 2004: Making Services Work for Poor People, Washington DC.

World Bank (2005), World Development Report 2005: A Better Investment Climate for Everyone, Washington DC.

World Health Organisation, research tools (www.who.int/research/).

ISBN 92-64-02586-3
Policy Framework for Investment
A Review of Good Practices
© OECD 2006

Chapter 9

Infrastructure and Financial Sector Development*

* This background document is based on Chapter 6 of the World Bank's 2005 World Development Report. It was prepared by Jonathan Coppel, Investment Division, OECD Directorate for Financial and Enterprise Affairs.

9.1. Introduction

Well functioning financial markets and good infrastructure promotes investment by connecting firms to their customers and suppliers and helping them to take advantage of modern production techniques and organisational structures. Conversely, inadequacies in infrastructure and financial services create barriers to opportunities and increase costs for all firms, from rural micro-entrepreneurs to multinational enterprises. By impeding new entry into markets (by either domestic or foreign firms), these inadequacies also limit competition, thus dulling incentives to innovate and to improve productivity.

One of the underlying problems often associated with investment in infrastructure can be traced to a specific market failure – market power associated with economies of scale. This has been the case with both private and public investment in infrastructure. In many cases, government attempts to overcome such market failures have made matters worse. Infrastructure investment has often been undermined by government use of state ownership or regulation to pursue objectives unrelated to efficient service delivery – typically favouring some groups over broader interests and introducing new sources of inefficiency. These problems usually hit smaller firms the hardest.

Governments have started confronting these issues. They are pursuing new approaches that recognise that infrastructure is a fundamental cornerstone of the investment climate. That is why many governments are taking steps to increase genuine competition among providers of infrastructure-related services (whether privately or publicly owned or controlled), securing property rights, and regulating providers in ways that recognise the potential for market failures to replace government failures, or *vice versa* . Governments are also working to improve management of public resources – to get more for their money when they finance or subsidize infrastructure services.[1]

This background document looks at experience in selected infrastructure areas: roads, ports, electricity, telecommunications, and water.[2] Although the chapter focuses on the impact of infrastructure services on the investment environment, improvements in the coverage and quality of these services also benefit households.

Well developed and functioning financial markets support the expansion of infrastructure investment, and play a pivotal role for the investment environment. Getting financial markets to work well, however, runs into market failures, associated with information asymmetries and problems of political economy. This chapter, therefore, also briefly considers selected aspects of financial market development policies. The focus is on the set of policies that help to foster macroeconomic stability, access to financial services and to the development of financial markets.

9.2. Common challenges in physical infrastructure

Building and maintaining roads, ports, electricity grids, telecommunications and water networks is expensive, so it is no surprise that infrastructure constitutes a significant economic bottleneck in many developing countries. However, the challenge of improving infrastructure is not just one of finding more money.

Market power, irreversible investments, and politics

> **What processes does the government use to evaluate its infrastructure investment needs? Does the national government work in co-operation with local and regional governments to establish infrastructure investment priorities? Does the government have clear guidelines and transparent procedures for the disbursement of public monies funding infrastructure projects? Are the regulatory agencies that oversee infrastructure investment and the operations of enterprises with infrastructure investments independent from undue political interference?**

The problem of infrastructure provision has its roots in the potential for market power that results from economies of scale. It rarely makes sense to have two competing roads between two points – or competing electricity grids. Indeed, all infrastructure activities were once thought to be "natural" monopolies, so that a particular market could be served at least cost by a single supplier. However, the potential abuse of market power in services that affect many consumers creates pressure for governments to intervene, either through intensive regulation of private suppliers or through provision by the public sector. Whether provision is public or private, governments tend to control tightly the prices that infrastructure providers charge and are often reluctant to allow prices to rise even when costs have.

This reluctance can create problems because of another feature of many infrastructure services – long-lived, immobile investments. Once built, a road or hydroelectric dam cannot sensibly be dismantled and moved elsewhere. Investors in infrastructure are often vulnerable, therefore, to shifts in government policies and changes to regulations, including those limiting prices. Before they invest, the government may promise them prices high enough to cover the costs of investment, but afterward the government, or subsequent governments may be tempted to please customers and voters by keeping prices low. So long as prices cover operating costs, the investors cannot credibly threaten to withdraw their services.

The underlying problem in the provision of much infrastructure is thus the combination of two concerns: customers fear that firms will use their market power to overcharge, and firms fear that governments will use their regulatory power to prevent them from covering their costs. Private firms originally created much of the world's infrastructure, but the playing out of these fears, combined with a prevailing scepticism about markets and private ownership, led to widespread nationalisation of infrastructure after World War II.[3]

Under public provision, however, the problems re-emerged in different guises and were joined by others. Infrastructure services remained highly politicised, and governments frequently kept prices below costs. The low prices were sometimes presented as necessary to help the poor, but the beneficiaries tended to be those who had access to services, so the poorest members of the community usually missed out. To take just one example, a study of the incidence of "lifeline" electricity tariffs in one Latin American country, under which the government subsidized the first block of household electricity consumption, found that about 80 per cent of the subsidies went to households that were not poor (Wodon, Ajwad and Siaens, 2003). Governments have also used their infrastructure agencies to channel assistance to particular regions and give jobs to favoured groups, increasing the agencies' costs and frustrating attempts to hold them accountable for the efficient delivery of services. With high costs and low prices, agencies have often been unable to finance investment from their own cash flows or borrow on their own credit (Box 9.1).

Box 9.1. **The political economy of electricity in India**

Indian electricity utilities generally provide unsatisfactory service to their customers, whether firms or households. In a recent budget document the central government noted that electricity shortages routinely lead to outages and voltage fluctuations that disrupt all aspects of economic life and require substantial investments in voltage stabilizers, generators and new motors. Most electricity is generated and supplied by state-owned electricity boards, which are experiencing severe financial difficulties and draining state budgets. Before privatising its electric utility in 2002, for example, the Delhi government provided it with implicit subsidies of $200 to $300 million a year, in loans unlikely to be repaid. Even so, the company still faced financial problems and provided poor service: power cuts were common in summer and winter. The problems in Delhi, in other parts of India and indeed in much of the developing world are political. Under pressure from well-organized groups of voters, governments have kept average prices below average costs, allowing politically influential customers to pay especially low prices. Farmers often receive electricity for irrigation pumps at prices well below costs. The subsidies became popular in the late 1970s. In Andhra Pradesh the government offered flat-rate tariffs to farmers as an election promise. Soon after, in Tamil Nadu, demonstrations by the Agriculturalists Association led to the provision of free electricity to some farmers. Other states then followed with their own agricultural subsidy programs. Many of the recipients are fairly well off land-owning farmers. Farmers are not the only beneficiaries: many customers steal their electricity, costing suppliers an estimated $4 billion a year. According to one report, utility employees who conspire in the theft of electricity can receive many times their annual salary in bribes. Although some farmers, employees, and politicians benefit, low prices discourage both the conservation of power and further investment in increasing supply and improving its reliability. That is why other users, including many firms, have to pay more.

Source: Agarwal, Alexander, and Tenenbaum (2003); Dubash and Rajan (2001); India – Ministry of Finance (2003); and Lal (2004).

As long as governments heavily subsidized public infrastructure agencies, the agencies could still operate and expand. Fiscal pressures and mounting dissatisfaction with public services, however, made governments reluctant to go on providing large subsidies. That, combined with a change in the prevailing views about markets and private ownership, led many governments to turn again to the private sector for at least some infrastructure services. While public provision remains important, private participation has now spread throughout much of the developing world, playing a role in achieving the UN's Millennium Development Goals.

Although private provision has often, though not always been associated with lowered costs and improved services, political economy problems remain. Many customers have opposed privatization, believing it will do more to enrich business and its political allies than improve public services. At the same time, many infrastructure investors have been disappointed by their returns in both developed and developing countries, often believing that governments have broken their promises on regulation for fear of losing votes. In other cases, a need to improve the skills and capacity of government officials to design and negotiate complex contracts and to operate large-scale infrastructure projects has been identified. Partly because of these problems, the amount of investment in private infrastructure projects in many countries has declined in the last few years.

Encouraging private investment in infrastructure

> **What measures has the government adopted to uphold the principle of transparency and procedural fairness for all investors bidding for infrastructure contracts, to protect investors' rights from unilateral changes to contract terms and conditions? What steps have been taken to attract investors to supply infrastructure at fair and reasonable prices, to ensure that investor-state contracts serve the public interest and to maintain public support for private involvement in infrastructure?**

Addressing these problems requires recognition that the performance of infrastructure providers is shaped by their investment climate. In some respects, the concerns of infrastructure firms – whether private or publicly owned but commercially run – are no different from those of other firms. All firms worry about the security of their property rights and the burdens imposed by regulation, taxation, and corruption.[4]

The problems arising specifically from market power and immobile investments in infrastructure highlight the central role of secure property rights. Private infrastructure firms in particular are concerned not only about outright expropriation, but also about whether governments will progressively undermine their profitability by imposing ever more severe regulation. The problems affect small providers as well as multinationals (Box 9.2). Governments must therefore take care to craft rules and institutions that constrain market power without unduly weakening property rights.

With this aim, governments often set out regulations and infrastructure investors' rights in contracts that cannot be changed unilaterally and allow disputes to be brought to and settled by domestic courts, international arbitration panels or independent regulatory agencies.[5] Decision-making about the implementation of rules is often delegated to independent regulatory agencies more insulated than politicians from day-to-day political pressures and can help to allay investor concerns about posterior government decisions that impinge on the economic viability of infrastructure investment and about the dual role of governments as contractual parties and regulators in investor-state contracts (Phillips, 1993 and Smith, 1997). When stabilisation clauses are used, governments need to

> ### Box 9.2. **Improving the investment climate for small private providers of infrastructure**
>
> Much private investment in infrastructure comes from multinationals from rich countries in Asia, Europe and North America. When concerns are expressed about the investment climate for infrastructure providers, it is these firms that most naturally come to mind. However, small (often informal) infrastructure providers are also important for electricity and telecommunications, especially in rural areas, and the investment climate for them matters, too.
>
> For example, in Bangladesh, with one of the world's lowest telephone densities and waiting times of many years for a fixed connection, village phone operators, most of them women, provide mobile phone access to their rural neighbours. Benefiting in many cases from loans from the Grameen Bank, village phone operators are present in thousands of villages. At low cost they enable villagers to communicate with people in markets in neighbouring towns – avoiding the need to walk there to find out the prices of commodities. However, valuable services such as these have sometimes been hampered by the state-owned companies that perceive a threat to their position, even though they do not serve the market in question.
>
> In Cambodia the biggest electricity supplier is the state-owned Electricité du Cambodge, which supplies Phnom Penh and a few towns. But several hundred small private providers supply electricity to more than 100 000 households and small firms in rural areas, sometimes by recharging batteries and sometimes through metered connections to small electricity grids. Although charging high prices, they supply customers who would otherwise have to supply themselves or go without. By law these private providers require licenses, which the government issues for a renewable term of three years. Because the capital invested in electricity grids can have a useful life of more than three years and the assets cannot be costlessly dismantled and moved elsewhere, uncertainty about license renewals creates a policy risk that can discourage investment and increase electricity prices. (It also encourages the substitution of easily moved investments for those less costly but less easily moved.) The providers do not know whether their license will be renewed – or what bribe they might be asked to pay to ensure its renewal. Most of the small providers are, in fact, unlicensed. They thus face a different policy risk: being prosecuted and closed down – or having to pay a bribe to avoid that. All providers are also vulnerable to a change in government policy that would give either Électricité du Cambodge or other providers exclusive rights to provide service. All are vulnerable to the possibility that, as they grow and become better established, the government will come under pressure to regulate the prices they charge in a way that undermines their profitability.
>
> *Source:* PPIAF and World Bank (2002); Burr (2000); and Cohen (2001).

balance their usefulness against the risk of circumscribing host government's right to regulate.

To work well, however, the government's approach must not only secure investors' property rights on paper. To be credible to firms, the arrangement must be sustainable, which means it must be perceived as reasonably fair and legitimate by consumers. Arrangements widely perceived as legitimate and fair thus reduce risks faced by providers, lower the returns that commercial investors must be promised, and so lower the prices that customers must pay, for any given degree of legal protection.

One cause of popular resistance to private participation in infrastructure in the 1990s was the opacity of some procedures used to privatize infrastructure businesses and adjust the tariffs the privatized business could charge. In the absence of transparency, suspicions were reasonably raised about whether bribes or the public interest had motivated policy. Responding to these concerns, most countries have turned to transparent competitive bidding to award contracts. Such countries as Brazil, Panama, and Peru now publish many infrastructure concession contracts on the Internet.[6] In 2002 Mexico passed a freedom-of-information law that will require information about such contracts to be made public.

The creation of independent regulatory agencies can be viewed as an attempt to reconcile the partly competing demands for investor protection and public legitimacy. If legitimacy could be ignored, investors' property rights would be most secure if contractual tariff adjustment rules were interpreted by independent international experts and serious disputes resolved by international arbitration. Using national regulatory agencies, courts, or arbitration increases one type of risk for investors, because the national institutions are more susceptible to political pressures to keep prices below costs – but decisions made by national institutions may be viewed as more legitimate, enhancing the sustainability of the arrangements.

Competition has the power to transform infrastructure industries by increasing legitimacy and strengthening investors' property rights. It pushes firms to become more efficient and cut prices. As a result, it helps assure customers that they are getting a reasonable deal. This in turn reduces pressure on governments to regulate in ways that weaken investors' property rights. Where competition works, it can thus help infrastructure provision avoid the problems that have traditionally afflicted it under both public and private provision. Competitive market prices may mean for some users and in some locations that prices charged are too expensive. In these circumstances and when governments aim to ensure access to essential infrastructure at affordable prices as a social goal, programmes based on instruments that maintain an economic incentive to invest in infrastructure and achieve their objective at least cost are preferable.

Private participation is often advocated because it provides an alternative source of financing to governments that have limited resources. Such reasoning is flawed – and can encourage privatization with few real benefits.[7] The big problem is paying for services, not financing them, and though private investors may finance services, they do not pay for them (see, for example, Klein and Hadjimichael, 2003).

The real advantage of well-designed private participation is different and deeper: it lies in changing the political economy of infrastructure provision. First, when the government is no longer a provider of services, it can more easily allow genuine competition. Private participation can be part of a strategy to help garner the benefits of competition – reducing costs and the property-rights problems of intensive regulation. Second, to attract private investment, a government needs to make a credible commitment to allow prices to cover costs and not interfere in commercial operations – a commitment it cannot make under public provision, because it can renege on commitments to public agencies with impunity. If a government can credibly make this commitment to investors by using the policies described above – and simultaneously persuade customers that their interests are being protected – it will have gone much of the way toward creating a good investment climate for infrastructure providers, thereby doing much to provide good infrastructure services to all firms and to their broader societies.[8]

Improving public management

Although private participation plays a powerful role, governments remain major financiers and providers of much infrastructure, especially roads. Even in sectors where a good deal of investment is private, complementary public investment in the parts of the sector owned by the government is often important. When governments do not provide or finance infrastructure, they often subsidize it – sometimes directly, sometimes indirectly through guarantees and other instruments. Because government budgets are always more limited than the plans of project proponents, governments need ways of deciding how much to spend on infrastructure, how to allocate that spending, both geographically and in the case of transportation networks across the different possible modes and how to administer it.

The questions are both technically difficult and politically charged. For example, if the government can afford to construct and maintain just one more transportation project in the next year, should it connect a poor rural area to the capital, or should it strengthen the network around a congested and more prosperous commercial centre, and should priority be given to the construction of roads, railways or other transportation modes, without ignoring the integration of transport networks? Answering requires technical capability to undertake cost-benefit analyses; financial reporting that reasonably reflects the true costs of different policies, and decision-making processes that give weight to the results of those analyses while allowing a socially acceptable balancing of competing interests.

When governments provide infrastructure, they need to think about the best way to organize themselves in order to do it. Traditionally, governments provided services through ministries, but a desire to free service providers from some of the constraints of bureaucratic procedures, to give them operational independence from ministers, and increase their accountability for results has led many governments to establish legally independent, though still wholly government-owned, infrastructure agencies.

Some governments have taken extra steps, such as making the state-owned agency subject to company law, appointing as directors people outside the government with commercial experience, and requiring the agency to prepare audited financial reports according to high-quality accounting standards. In South Africa, for example, the state-owned electricity agency, Eskom, is now a company with mainly outside directors with business experience, which reports according to international accounting standards. Even when all these steps are taken, however, it can be difficult for governments to resist political pressures to interfere in business decisions and keep prices below costs. This is part of the reason why many governments undertaking these reforms have eventually turned to private participation.

9.3. Infrastructure: connecting firms and expanding opportunities for investment

Firms with access to modern telecommunications services, reliable electricity supply, dependable water and sanitation services and efficient transport links stand out from firms without them. They invest more, and their investments are more productive. Yet in many countries, firms find themselves having to cope with infrastructure that fails to meet their needs. The problems, as expressed by firms, vary by region. They also tend to vary by infrastructure service and firm size – electricity is often the biggest problem, and larger firms express more concerns than smaller firms about all services.

The following sections examine six sectors that have a particularly important bearing on the investment climate: roads, ports, electricity, telecommunications and, water. The last section, as noted in the introduction, considers selected aspects of financial market development policy.

9.3.1. *Telecommunications – competition makes the difference*

In the telecommunications sector, does the government assess market access for potential investors and the extent of competition among operators? Does the government evaluate whether telecommunication pricing policies are competitive, favouring investment in industries that depend on reliable and affordable telecommunications?

Modern telecommunications are vital to the investment climate and have become more important to firms of all kinds. Telecommunication services allow enterprises to communicate rapidly and cheaply with distant suppliers and customers, to access the Internet, they underpin modern financial markets, and they help governments communicate with firms and citizens. In Bangladesh, China, Ethiopia, and India the World Bank's Investment Climate Surveys found that garment manufacturers are more productive, pay higher wages, and grow more quickly when telecommunications services are better (Dollar, Hallward-Driemeier and Mengistae, 2003). Among developed countries, investments in telecommunications in the last 20 years appear not only to have followed growth, but also to have fuelled it (Röller and Waverman, 2001). In Latin America, a 10 per cent increase in the number of main phone lines per worker has been estimated to increase output per worker by about 1.5 per cent (Calderón and Servén, 2003).

The extent to which telecommunications services meet firms' needs varies greatly from country to country, as well as within countries. A three-minute call to the United States costs $0.17 from Finland, but up to $9 in some African countries, where some governments cross-subsidize local calls and other services through higher prices on international calls. Getting a new phone line takes only a couple of days in Lithuania, but up to a year in parts of Sub-Saharan Africa.

On average, however, telecommunications services have improved dramatically. Over the last 20 years, prices have fallen at an average of 7 per cent a year, while the number of phone subscribers per capita in low-income countries has quintupled (Rossotto, Lewin, Gomez and Wellenius, 2003). The changes have been driven by changes in technology and by changes in policy. Most governments have at least partly privatized their country's main phone company and allowed at least some competition. The policy changes mean lower prices, shorter waiting times for connections and faster expansion of services (see, for example, Wallsten, 2001 and Boylaud and Nicoletti, 2001).

Although challenges remain, including the extension of access in rural areas (Box 9.3), the combination of technological change and liberalisation has transformed telecommunications. Providers need no longer be monopolies, and with the advent of wireless telecommunication services new investments are needed. Coupled with a predictable and independent industry regulator, these developments reduce the policy-

> ### Box 9.3. **Expanding rural access to electricity and telecommunications**
>
> For many years governments in developing countries relied on state-owned monopolies to bring electricity and telecommunications services to rural areas. Typically they required the monopolies to charge the same price in rural and urban areas, even though the costs were higher in the rural area. Because that made the rural services unprofitable, governments gave the monopolies budgetary subsidies and allowed them to benefit from cross-subsidies from low-cost, high-revenue customers. In many countries, however, the subsidies have been too small to finance rapid expansion. Even when expansion was affordable, the monopolies had a financial incentive to go slow. An alternative that some governments have used, especially in the last decade, is to rely on a combination of liberal regulation and well-targeted, output-based subsidies. Removing legal barriers to entry by new providers of electricity and telecommunications services helps ensure that profitable opportunities to extend service in areas un-served by the incumbent are seized quickly (as illustrated by Cambodia in Box 9.2). Liberal entry rules may not by themselves cause access to increase as fast as governments want. In such a case, governments may find carefully targeted direct subsidies more effective than cross-subsidies or subsidies aimed only at keeping providers afloat. Peru, for example, has used a least-subsidy approach to bring pay phone service to targeted rural areas. Some of the subsidy is paid up front, the rest in half-yearly instalments, conditional on the operator meeting its performance targets. Although the operators are struggling financially even with the subsidies, most results from the pilot project appear promising. For the scheme's beneficiaries the average distance to the nearest pay phone fell by more than 90 per cent. In addition, competitive bidding led to a subsidy 41 per cent lower than the government had budgeted for and 74 per cent lower than the subsidy previously requested by the incumbent. Similar schemes have been used for rural electrification in Argentina, Chile, and Guatemala.
>
> *Source:* Cannock (2001); Harris (2002); Tomkins (2001); Wellenius (1997); and Jadresic (2000).

related risks of investments in the telecommunication sector and raise the scope to inject greater competition among operators.

9.3.2. Electricity – *competition is not as easy but possible*

> **Has the government developed a strategy to ensure reliable access to electricity services by users, and economic incentives to invest and supply electricity? What programmes exist to ensure on a least-cost basis access to electricity services by a wide range of users. Are these programmes time-bound and based upon clear performance targets?**

Access to a reliable electricity supply at a reasonable price is vital for most firms – from small factories in rural areas to multinational firms. Most urban firms are served by utilities, but firms in small towns and rural areas in developing countries may have to supply themselves (Komives, Whittington and Wu, 2003). Firms with access to grid electricity seldom get good service. Temporary losses of supply are frequent in many countries, especially in Africa and South Asia, as are fluctuations in voltage that damage machinery. According to World Bank Investment Climate Surveys, firms in some regions have estimated that such outages cause them to lose on average around 5 per cent of their annual sales. Limited access in rural areas and poor quality in cities cause many firms to rely on self-supply, which is generally more expensive than a regular supply from a utility.

Many firms also pay higher than necessary prices for electricity, as governments direct utilities to hold down prices for (often middle class) households and effectively tax firms to make up some of the difference. The largest industrial users sometimes have enough influence to avoid such levies, leaving small- and medium-sized firms to bear most of the burden. In one Indian state, industrial users pay twice as much per kilowatt-hour as households, but commercial users – offices and shops – pay nearly twice as much again (World Energy Council, 2001).

Poor electricity supply makes existing investments less productive and discourages new investment. In Uganda firms that experienced fewer problems of supply from the Uganda Electricity Board invested less in self-supply and more in their own productive capacity (Reinikka and Svensson, 2002). In Bangladesh, China, Ethiopia, and Pakistan the World Bank's Investment Climate Surveys found that more reliable power supply increases garment manufacturers' total factor productivity and the growth rates of their output and employment (Roller, Hallward-Driemeier and Mengistae, 2003). In Latin America, a 10 per cent increase in electricity-generating capacity per worker has been estimated to increase GDP per worker by around 1.5 per cent (Calderón and Servén, 2003).

As in telecommunications, changes in technology, coupled with dissatisfaction with monopoly provision by state-owned enterprises, have led many governments to progressively liberalise – typically starting with supply to companies where fewer clients makes it easier to manage - and to introduce private participation. Economies of scale in generation declined in the 1980s, allowing more countries to have enough generating stations to make competition in the generation of electricity workable (Hunt and Shuttleworth, 1996). Countries that can distribute electricity to their neighbours have further opportunities.[9] Enabling the inter-connection of networks, where feasible, is also a possible solution to local shortages.

Almost all countries in the developed world and most in Latin America now allow at least some firms to choose their electricity supplier. Elsewhere the picture is mixed. Many countries have allowed a sort of competition in generation under which a state-owned utility contracts out the financing, construction, and operation of new power stations to privately owned independent power producers. The state-owned utility, however, usually retains a monopoly on selling electricity to customers, limiting the benefits of such competition. In addition, such projects can create disguised government debt.

Getting competition to work in electricity is harder than in telecommunications, as high profile problems in recent years in California have shown (see, for example, Besant-Jones and Tenenbaum, 2001). Many small countries have too few generators to allow real competition, while in larger countries, individual electricity companies may still have market power if they own many generation plants. Even when electricity generators do not have market power at most times of the day, they may have it when demand peaks, and like sellers in many markets, they may collude to increase prices. Competition is fostered by separating generation from transmission, and distribution from retail supply, so that the owners of the transmission and distribution lines cannot use their monopoly in these industry segments to stifle competition in generation.[10] But such unbundling makes it harder to coordinate investments among these segments of the industry, including investment to maintain and improve the grid infrastructure itself. It also requires an efficient and effective regulator of the grid.

Overall, the evidence suggests that competition (usually combined with commercial provision and new forms of regulation) has led to better service. Countries that early on introduced competition, private provision, and new forms of regulation – such as Argentina, Chile, and the United Kingdom – have benefited from lower prices and higher quality (see, for example, Pollitt, 2003 and Galal, Jones, Tandon and Vogelsang, 1994). In Chile, wholesale prices fell by 37 per cent and retail prices by 17 per cent between 1986 and 1996. Private companies were sufficiently confident in the market to invest in hydroelectric generation, transmission, and distribution (World Bank, 2004). More generally, competition in electricity has been found to increase labour productivity and generating capacity per capita (Zhang, Parker and Kirkpatrick, 2002). Competition also tends to lower prices for small- and medium-sized firms because they need no longer buy from a utility that overcharges them.

9.3.3. Transport – the dwindling importance of distance

> **What processes are followed to inform decisions on the development of new transport facilities, as well as the maintenance of existing investment in transport infrastructure? Are the requirements for all modes of transport regularly reviewed, taking into consideration investor needs and the links between different modes of transport infrastructure?**

Transport infrastructure creates opportunities for firms to buy and sell not only in neighbouring markets but also in the entire world. As governments eliminate import quotas and reduce import tariffs, transport becomes more important as a source of further gains in trade. Although global transport costs have been falling over the long term, further progress is important. For Chile and Ecuador transport costs to the United States are now 20 times larger than US tariffs (Clark, Dollar and Micco, 2002). If they could reduce their transport costs by 10 per cent, they could expect to increase their trade by 20 per cent (Limão and Venables, 2001). Other evidence suggests that they would also grow faster (Radelet and Sachs, 1998).

Transport costs depend on distance, so countries far from rich markets in Europe, North America, and East Asia face a disadvantage they can do nothing about. Yet poor infrastructure has been found to account for 40 per cent of the cost of transport in the average country and 60 per cent in landlocked countries. So while distance accounts for much of transport costs, shipping goods from efficient ports, such as those in Hamburg and Rotterdam – or inland cities benefiting from good infrastructure, such as Ankara and Vienna – is cheap for the distance. According to one study a country could lower its transport costs by an amount equivalent to moving several thousand kilometres closer to other countries if it could improve its transport (and telecommunications) infrastructure from the median to the 75th percentile (Limão and Venables, 2001).

Reducing transport costs requires paying attention to particular transport modes, such as ports and roads. Yet governments should not lose sight of the links among different modes: ports and airports, for example, become more valuable when served by good roads and railways. Transport costs are also affected by factors other than transport infrastructure, such as whether telecommunications systems allow companies to track their goods in transit and how quickly goods are cleared through customs.

Ports – many types of competition

More than 80 per cent by weight of the trade of developing countries goes through ports (World Bank, 2004). The efficiency of those ports affects exporters and importers directly and almost all firms indirectly. Improving one measure of port efficiency from the 25th to the 75th percentile – achievable in part by reducing the influence of organised crime – has been found to reduce shipping costs by more than 12 per cent (Clark, Dollar and Micco, 2002). As with improvements in other transport infrastructure, the reduction in costs is equivalent to moving thousands of kilometres closer to trading partners (Inter-American Development Bank, 2001).

Unlike the customers of electricity and telecommunications utilities, port customers are mainly firms, not households, which makes tariff setting less politicized. Ports, however, require immobile investments and often have market power, so they face many of the challenges common to infrastructure services. Under public ownership and restrictions on competition within and sometimes between ports, they have tended to be overstaffed, have restrictive labour practices, act as a magnet for corruption – and as a result offer slow and expensive service to firms (see, for example, Estache and Carbajo, 1996).

To improve the efficiency of ports, governments have tried to expose them to more competition, often while introducing private participation (Box 9.4). Colombia and

---

Box 9.4. Port reform in Colombia and India

Colombia and India show two ways of confronting the challenges posed by port reform. In Colombia port efficiency had become a major issue by the early 1990s. Early proposals involved the re organisation of Colpuertos, the state-owned company, but not private participation. President Gaviria, however, favoured a bolder approach and raised the issue in his inaugural address in 1990. Legislation to allow private participation in ports, including severance packages for workers, passed within 60 days. The overall program – liquidating Colpuertos, establishing new policymaking and regulatory bodies, concessioning the five major ports to private firms, and introducing competition in stevedoring in each port – was completed in three years. The combination of competition and private participation led to impressive improvements in performance.

India approached port reform differently from Columbia. Each of the 12 major ports in India is administered by a Port Trust representing various interest groups. Port reform began with the issuance of a new policy framework in 1994 and guidelines for private participation in 1996. Private participation was to start with the concessioning of the container terminal at Jawaharlal Nehru Port, established in 1989 as a satellite port to Mumbai. The implementation of reforms was left to the ports, and the Jawaharlal Nehru Port Trust (the majority of whose trustees represented the government or labour) chose to engage the main stakeholders in the reform process and to protect the interests of labour by keeping the existing port under public ownership. But they did allow a new private terminal to compete with it. The competition improved performance, with pre-berthing and turnaround time falling from around 11 days in 1996 to less than 3 days in 2002.

Source: Navarrete (2004) and Ray (2004).

Argentina split their national state-owned companies into several separate companies that compete with each other for some services. Governments can also create competition within a single port in services not inherently monopolistic: different terminals in a port can sometimes compete with each other, and different stevedoring companies can sometimes compete at the same terminal.[11]

The combination of private participation and increased competition has led to better services (Galal, Jones, Tandon and Vogelsang, 1994). In Colombia average vessel waiting time fell from 10 days before privatization and competition to a matter of hours afterward, throughput per hour increased, and the ports moved to all-year, all-day operation (Gaviria, 1998). In Argentina, the average stay fell from 72 hours to 33, throughput per worker rose from 900 tons to 4 850, and capacity increased fivefold (Trujillo and Serebriskey, 2003).

Roads

Almost all goods are transported by road at some stage, making a country's road network a critical part of its infrastructure and the investment climate (Box 9.5). Not surprisingly, the extent of the network has been found in many studies to be associated with better economic performance. In Latin America, a 10 per cent increase in the length of roads per worker has been estimated to increase GDP per worker by nearly 2 per cent (Calderón and Servén, 2003). Not all roads are equally valuable, of course; in the United States the interstate road building of the 1950s and 1960s seems to have significantly

---

Box 9.5. **The benefits of rural roads in Morocco and elsewhere**

When built in the right locations (and not "roads to nowhere"), good roads can create substantial new opportunities for entrepreneurs in rural areas and small towns, as illustrated by a Moroccan government program to pave gravel roads and dirt tracks. Upgrading the roads meant they were usable all year round, causing less damage to the vehicles using them. The new roads allowed farms and other firms to move their goods more often and more cheaply. In some cases the time it took to get to rural markets fell by half. The cost of shipping a truckload of merchandise also fell by half. In the areas benefiting from the road upgrading, the land is more productive, and the volume and value of agricultural produce is higher. As it became easier to ship produce quickly without damaging it, farmers shifted from low-value cereals to high-value fruit. As the price of bringing goods to the farms fell, farmers used more fertiliser. Improvements in the agricultural economy spurred the growth of other business. Off-farm employment grew twice as fast as in areas not benefiting from road improvement. The estimated economic rate of return to the projects ranged from 16 to 30 per cent. As is often the case, the improvement in infrastructure did not benefit only firms. It made it easier for children to go to school and, by making the delivery of butane more affordable, reduced the need for women and girls to collect firewood. After the road improvements, primary school enrolment rose from 28 per cent to 68 per cent. The Moroccan experience is not an isolated case. Recent work by the International Food Policy Research Institute suggests that Uganda's investment in rural feeder roads connecting farmers to otherwise remote markets has high returns in agricultural growth and rural poverty reduction. In China investment in rural roads is socially profitable. In India such investment is the most socially productive form of public investment in reducing poverty.

Source: World Bank (1996); Fan, Hazell, and Thorat (1999); Fan, Zhang, and Rao (2004); Fan, Zhang, and Zhang (2002).

---

boosted productivity, while recent spending on roads has had only modest benefits (Fernald, 1999). Even so, the evidence suggests that governments should pay close attention to the extent and quality of their road networks. The challenges relate to planning appropriate network expansion, executing the required investment and maintenance, and working out how best to pay for it.

All the typical challenges are more difficult because the transaction costs of imposing user fees (tolls) to fund roads are high, at least on city streets and rural roads. Even on intercity highways, where the transaction costs are lower, user fees remain uncommon. So prices rarely ration demand on congested roads, cover the costs of maintenance, or signal that new capacity is needed. One avenue for tackling these problems is thus to increase the use of tolls. The advent of electronic tolls and related information technology is making direct pricing feasible on more roads and, in the long term, it may make the road industry much more like other utilities. In the near future, however, only a small proportion of roads will have tolls. Therefore, many governments focus on using other sources of revenue linked to road use to pay for roads, such as use-related license fees and especially fuel taxes.

Many governments are assigning funds from fuel taxes and other sources to a road fund that operates with some autonomy from ministers. The funds are allocated to investment and maintenance projects according to a set of principles established by political authorities. Road users may be represented on the agency, and the agency may consult with road users and others on the allocation of funds. As in other areas, designing a system that gives the managers of the road fund the information, incentives, and capability to make decisions aligned with the public interest is crucial.

Developing countries often spend too little on maintenance compared with investment, perhaps because of donors' traditional preference for subsidizing capital rather than outputs, and perhaps because large investment projects offer opportunities for politicians to cut more ribbons or for decision makers to collect bigger bribes. Countries afflicted with higher levels of corruption seem to spend more on public investment in roads and other infrastructure, but less on maintenance, and seem accordingly to have poorer quality roads (Tanzi and Davoodi, 1997). There is no simple answer, but an emphasis on making decision-making more transparent can help reduce corruption and improve decisions. Governments can consult on, publish, and explain the principles for allocating funds and the decisions implementing those principles, and they can use open and transparent processes for awarding contracts to do the work.

Road agencies that decide on the allocation of funds need not build or maintain roads themselves. More road agencies now contract out such work to private firms, under output-based contracts. In Argentina, the highway authority maintains many roads by letting long-term maintenance contracts that require private firms to maintain roads to a defined standard. One review concludes that the program reduced the proportion of roads in poor condition from 25 per cent to less than 5 per cent, reducing road users' costs by more than 10 per cent (Liavtaud, 2001).

9.3.4. Financing investment in water[12]

> **Has the government evaluated the investment needs in water required to support its development goals? To what extent is the private sector involved in water management, supply and infrastructure financing?**

From the perspective of a country's investment climate, water matters for three reasons. First (and foremost), water is essential for a healthy population. Second, water serves as a direct input for certain businesses (*e.g.* soft drinks). Third, the water industry itself is an important destination for investments, public and private, domestic and foreign. The Millennium and Johannesburg Summits, and the publication of the "Camdessus Report", have helped to raise the profile of the water sector. However, other political and economic trends have worked in the opposite direction. Continued low incomes have impeded many developing countries from increasing investment in the water sector. Official Development Assistance flows have continued to decline, and are now at their lowest level in recent years. Commercial lending and private investment have also been scaled back significantly as the private sector has become more risk averse *vis-à-vis* the water sector, following a range of high-profile disputes on contract terms between the private sector and public sector agencies.

National governments are likely to remain the major source of finance, particularly capital investments: in the mid 1990s, they accounted for about two-thirds of such investments in the water sector. However this has a number of perverse effects, and shifting the financing burden from taxpayers to users would have several advantages: it would reduce demand and hence investment needs; it would help put the sector on a more financially sustainable basis; and it would promote better governance by enhancing accountability. The user pay principle does not forsake a government's ability to put in place policies designed to ensure access to water as a social goal. Devolution of responsibility, as well as the (financial) means to fulfil that responsibility, is also crucial. This is complex, but successful devolution is associated with transparent local government budgets and financial statements by water utilities, a multi year framework for annual budgets of local governments, a mid-term rolling investment plan, project selection based on clear rules, good creditworthiness that facilitates access to local capital and financial markets, and the ability to manage debt. Independent assessments of public investment programmes can help to enhance their credibility, and help attract additional finance.

For the foreseeable future, private sector operators are more likely to be a source of managerial and technical know-how rather than investors in the water sector in developing countries. However, more could be done to engage the private sector in other ways, particularly by improving municipalities' access to capital and financial markets. This was the approach followed in many OECD countries where borrowing from commercial banks (Europe) or issuing municipal bonds (North America) were important mechanisms for developing municipal infrastructure, including water and sanitation. Some interesting experience is developing with the use of municipal development funds in developing countries that blend capital from domestic and external sources for on-lending, thereby contributing to the deepening of local credit markets. Such approaches facilitate the transition to municipalities borrowing from banks directly or issuing bonds. The lessons learned from the US Development Credit Agency, for example, should be reviewed with a view to replicating successes more widely.

There is no "magic bullet" to solve the problem of financing water. Although reform and innovation is needed in financial architecture, a "paradigm shift" is unlikely. All existing financial sources will need to increase if the internationally agreed targets are to be realised. Different sources of finance will, however, need to be blended in "smart" ways to enhance synergies, avoid crowding out other sources, and to maximise leverage on the total flows.

Useful tools to facilitate smart blending of potential financial sources and instruments have recently been developed and applied with positive results. The FEASIBLE model developed jointly by the OECD/EAP Task Force and Denmark is a tool to help rationalise financing strategies of the water sector in several regions and countries in Central and Eastern Europe, Central Asia and China. At a project level, USAID has experience in financing water infrastructure using partial loan guarantees and technical assistance for pooled projects, which has helped these projects tap debt markets in local currency.

The elaboration of financing strategies should not be regarded as a one-off exercise; nor is it purely an analytical exercise. It should be treated as an iterative process, refined and modified in the light of data and experience, enabling decision-makers to make more informed trade-offs. All the main stakeholders should be involved in the process, and there should be regular feedback between policy makers and those involved in implementation and financing, especially if specific policy changes are needed.

9.3.5. Financial services: a special form of infrastructure

What process does the government use to evaluate the capacity of the financial sector, including the quality of its regulatory framework, to support effectively enterprise development? What steps has the government taken to remove obstacles, including restrictions on participation by foreign institutions, to private investment in the development of the financial sector?

Developed financial sectors provide payment services, mobilize savings, and allocate financing to firms wishing to invest. When they work well, they give firms of all types the ability to seize promising investment opportunities. They reduce firms' reliance on internally generated cash flows and money from family and friends – giving them access to external equity and debt, something that smaller firms in particular often lack. They allow poor entrepreneurs to grow their businesses, even though they have little money themselves. Well-functioning financial sectors also impose discipline on firms to perform, driving efficiency, both directly and by facilitating new entry into product markets. And they create opportunities for firms and households to manage risks. As a result, financial sector development leads to faster growth in productivity and output. Doubling private credit as a share of GDP is associated with an increase in average long-term growth of almost two percentage points.[13] Developed financial sectors also reduce poverty – directly and through their role in economic growth (Li, Squire and Zou, 1998).

Governments are learning from the past to overcome the problems holding back the development of financial sectors and taking new approaches that involve five key elements:

● ensuring macroeconomic stability;

● fostering competition;

● securing the rights of borrowers, creditors, and shareholders;

● transparency and facilitating the flow of information;

● controlling risk taking.

Ensuring macroeconomic stability

Macroeconomic stability – more specifically, low inflation, sustainable debt, and realistic exchange rates – is fundamental to the effective functioning of the financial sector. Macroeconomic instability increases the volatility of interest rates, exchange rates, and relative prices, imposing additional costs and risks on financial institutions and their clients. High inflation erodes the capital of financial institutions and makes it difficult to mobilize savings or to expand services. High fiscal deficits increase interest rates and spreads. The increase in holdings of government paper by banks, mutual funds, and investment funds crowds out credit to the private sector, because these providers of finance find it more profitable to hold government securities than to make loans to firms.

Fostering competition

Restrictions on competition between providers of finance can mean slower economic growth, reduced employment growth, and slower exit of mature firms in concentrated bank markets (see, for example, Black and Strahan, 2002 and Cetorelli, 2003). Policies that impede competition – such as entry restrictions, restrictions on foreign banks, and state ownership of banks – hurt the financial system and economic performance. In markets where the financial system is established and the institutions responsible for financial sector regulation function well, removing barriers to competition has been shown to improve banking stability, reduce interest margins, and expand access to finance (Demirgüc-Kunt, Laeven and Levine, 2003). In a more competitive financial sector environment, the organisation and functions of the regulation institutions themselves may also require some modifications.

One way to foster competition is to prudently issue new domestic banking licenses. In the United States the wave of mergers and acquisitions in the 1980s and 1990s created large banks, which may have reduced lending to new and small firms. Yet fairly liberal licensing policies allowed new banks to form in the United States to help offset any lack of supply and keep interest margins low (Berger, Demirgüc-Kunt, Levine and Haubrich, 2004). Competition is also benefiting from technological innovation, as in India's rural areas (Box 9.6).

Policymakers are sometimes concerned that the competition from foreign banks will weaken the banking system. However, evidence shows that foreign banks improve the efficiency and performance of domestic banks and reduce interest rate margins. This is what happened when the Philippines allowed more foreign bank competition – interest rate spreads fell and the efficiency of domestic banks increased (Unite and Sullivan, 2003). Foreign banks can also use their cross-border experience to introduce innovations. Citibank responded to the scarcity of good credit information on individual firms in many

Box 9.6. **Expanding access to finance in rural areas: new approaches in India**

Firms operating in rural areas often have a hard time getting financing, but financial innovations and new technology are making a difference, as India shows. The agricultural agency model uses a third-party intermediary to coordinate the financing of inputs, the delivery of produce to the end buyer, and the repayment to the bank before the farmer receives the proceeds. The intermediary improves information by advising farmers on crop decisions that affect the quantity and quality of the produce. The intermediary can also negotiate better prices on final goods than individual farmers can. The Kisan Credit Card, offered by commercial, rural, and cooperative banks, is a technological innovation in providing credit to the agriculture sector in India, including small farmers. Since its introduction in 1998-99, some 31.6 million cards had been issued by April 2003.Though not truly credit cards, the cards have advantages for borrowers and lenders. They make it easier to get credit and renew loans, once the initial screening has been done. They reduce the number of visits to branches, and they increase the operation of accounts at designated supply branches. The increasing sophistication of financial markets is helping farmers smooth their incomes in the face of fluctuating prices and harvests. Fledgling futures markets are allowing them to fix the prices they will receive in advance. Innovations in insurance are allowing them to protect themselves from losses caused by poor weather. The payouts are based on an index measuring local weather, which allows an objective determination of the payout and maintains farmers' incentives to maximize their output despite poor weather.

Source: Hess and Klapper (2003) and World Bank (2004).

developing countries by finding other ways to assess creditworthiness. The company identifies industry segments with the potential to grow quickly and then seeks out borrowers in those segments. In India it has about 500 customers in 15 selected industrial segments.

A second concern is that foreign entry might reduce access to financing by small and medium firms, due to the adoption of different credit standards, also known as "cherry picking" (see, for example, Strahan and Weston, 1998. But there is also evidence that foreign banks do not discriminate against SMEs. In Chile and Peru, foreign banks loaned more to small firms than domestic banks did, and in Argentina and Chile, real growth in lending to small firms was higher for foreign banks.[14]

While bank-to-bank competition is important, other sources of finance can also strengthen competition. For example, firms with access to public bond financing have 35 per cent more debt (after controlling for other firm characteristics) (Faulkender and Petersen, 2003). Non-bank financial intermediaries can also broaden financial markets. For example, leasing companies and finance companies often finance start-up firms unable to raise funds from banks. As non-bank financial intermediaries develop, they often securitize their assets, further deepening securities markets (Carmichael and Pomerleano, 2002). Pension funds and contractual savings can also compete to supply funds, increasing banking efficiency and lowering the cost of capital (Impavido, 2001). Finally, commercial microfinance is beginning to have an impact on financial services for micro-entrepreneurs and poor households (Box 9.7).

How, then, to encourage the development of non-bank lenders? By not over-regulating lenders that do not take deposits, and by harmonising the tax treatment of financial

---

Box 9.7. **Commercial micro-financiers enter the market**

Micro-financiers provide thrift, credit, and other financial services of very small amounts, mainly to the poor, in both rural and urban areas. They offer an alternative to banks, which in most developing countries serve only 5-20 per cent of the population. They use non-collateralised loans to deliver short-term working capital to micro-entrepreneurs and households. One of the key characteristics of microfinance, pioneered by Grameen Bank in Bangladesh and now replicated throughout the developing world, is substituting joint liability, access to future loans, and frequent repayment periods for traditional collateral. These alternatives to collateral are especially important for borrowers who do not have assets to pledge – and for lenders who operate in countries with weak secured-lending laws and enforcement. Microfinance has demonstrated its success in reducing poverty. By 2002 more than 1 000 microfinance programs around the world had reached about 30 million borrowers, lending about $3.5 billion, with an average loan size of $280. Microfinance has helped the poor increase household income, build viable businesses, and reduce their vulnerability to external shocks. It can also empower the poor, especially women. Subsidised microfinance relying on donors, however, is unlikely to be big enough to reach all potential borrowers. That will require commercial microfinance that mobilises the savings of the general public, raising questions about the appropriate role for governments. Governments are sometimes tempted to mandate below-market interest rates, but this usually causes more problems than it solves. The removal of interest rate controls in Indonesia in 1983 allowed Bank Rakyat Indonesia to experiment with new financial products, most notably market-priced working capital and investment capital loans. By 1986 its microfinance business had turned from a chronic loss-maker to a profitable department. Governments can also eliminate unfair competition from public institutions and change regulations to facilitate competition on a level playing field. In particular, they can allow micro-finance institutions to transform themselves into licensed financial institutions and facilitate the provision of microfinance by commercial banks. In 1992 ProDem, a microfinance nongovernmental organisation (NGO), became BancoSol, the first commercial bank in Latin America dedicated to microfinance. The transformation enabled the expansion from 14 300 clients to 70 000 within five years of commercialisation, and by 1998 BancoSol was the most profitable licensed bank in Bolivia. As in other segments of the credit market, allowing the sharing of credit information among micro-lenders can foster microfinance lending, especially by commercial lenders that may not have pre-existing relationships with borrowers in rural areas. South Africa has two private credit bureaus operating in the microfinance sector. Information can be obtained by touch-tone phone, and the microfinance bureaus charge much lower fees than larger bureaus – making them affordable even for small micro-lenders.

Source: Ghatak and Guinnane (1999); Morduch (1997); Morduch, Littlefield, and Hashemi (2003); Hubka and Zaide (2004); CGAP (1997); Klapper and Kraus (2002); and *www.mixmarket.org*.

products. In Turkey, factoring companies pay a 5 per cent transaction tax while banks pay only 1 per cent (Ekmekcioglo, 2003). Pension rules can also be liberalised as capital markets mature and regulatory systems develop. For instance, investment in more asset classes, such as equities, can be allowed. Better insurance regulations can also encourage insurance providers to innovate and operate efficiently – and to create a competitive market open to new firms and the exit of insolvent firms (Impavido, 2001). Mutual funds can be developed under strong accounting and auditing rules and strict disclosure requirements.

Securing the rights of borrowers and creditors

> **What laws and regulations are in place to protect the rights of borrowers and creditors and are these rights adequately balanced? Is a registry system in place to support the use of property as collateral and to expand business access to external sources of credit? What data protection and credit reporting laws have been enacted to facilitate the flow of information and improve financial sector stability, thereby enhancing the investment environment?**

Governments can mitigate the problems for creditors and shareholders – and increase their willingness to provide finance – by ensuring that the parties have clearly defined rights and can enforce them (see, for example, Black, Jang and Kim, 2003). A strong legal environment and strong enforcement are important for access to external finance and the development of financial sectors. When creditor rights are weak, financial institutions will be less willing to extend credit to firms that have a high risk of default. When shareholders' rights are weak, investors will be less willing to provide firms with equity (Shleifer and Wolfenzohn, 2002).

Securing borrowers' property rights to assets they can pledge as collateral (including land) can increase access to financing and investment.[15] Secure property rights also allow firms to borrow longer-term and encourage more foreign lending (see, for example, Claessens and Laeven, 2003). The cost of external financing is also lower in countries with stronger property rights protection and less corruption. A study of 37 countries found that if a country improved its property rights protection from the 25th to the 75th percentile, loan spreads would decline by 87 basis points (Bae and Goyal, 2003).

Strong creditor rights – stemming, say, from laws guaranteeing secured creditors' priority in the case of default – allow lenders to reduce their risk of future losses, therefore encouraging them to make more loans. For example, one explanation offered for the low level of private credit in Mexico is that many social constituencies must be repaid before secured creditors, often leaving creditors with few assets to back their claims. Studies in the United States show that small firms are 25 per cent more likely to be denied credit if they are in states that provide creditors with less protection when the borrower is bankrupt (Berkovitz and White, 2002). The effectiveness of creditor rights also depends on strong enforcement of the laws. Russia, for example, has "imported" strong laws protecting shareholder and creditor rights, but the lack of an effective legal system to enforce these laws has been a big impediment (Claessons and Laeven, 2003). Laws and registries permitting the collateralisation of movable property can offer even greater benefits to smaller firms that are less likely to have fixed assets (Box 9.8).

Transparency and facilitating the flow of information

One way lenders can address their information disadvantage is to collect information about their customers directly through costly screening and monitoring. Lenders in most developed countries – and more now in developing countries – can also rely on reports from credit information bureaus. These reports include loan payment histories that allow lenders to use information on how borrowers met past loan obligations to predict better future loan performance. Credit reporting also improves borrowers' incentives to repay

> ### Box 9.8. **Establishing a registry for movable collateral in Romania**
>
> Legal impediments previously restricted the use of movable property as collateral in Romania and thereby limited the access to credit. First, the system did not allow lenders to access information on whether other creditors or lenders had claims on the same goods. Second, the enforcement of agreements and repossession of collateralised goods was a long process (often exceeding the economic life of the movable good). A new law, adopted in 1999, introduced a system for registering security interests. The registration, valid for five years, is required to secure new collateral. The law provides for both stronger enforcement and a new electronic archive of outstanding liens. This online collateral registry includes all registered security interests. Ten operators and 366 agents are licensed to register collateral in the electronic archive. The supervisory authority provides guidelines on the archive's operation and clarifies rules and regulations. The archive functions efficiently, allowing financial intermediaries to access information about creditors, debtors, or assets securing a commercial or civil transaction in the country. This information, accessible by people all over the world, presents huge cost-saving and time-saving opportunities – improving the investment climate.
>
> *Source:* Fleisig (1998) and Stoica and Stoica (2002).

loans promptly, because late payment with one lender can result in sanctions by many institutions (Miller, 2003).

Credit bureaus can increase bank lending and reduce default rates. They also benefit small and new firms by alleviating credit rationing based on the lack of a credit history (Galindo and Miller, 2001). In one survey more than half the credit bureaus indicated that credit history information reduced the processing time, costs, and default rates in their country by more than 25 per cent (World Bank, 2003). On average, countries without credit registries have a private credit-to-GDP ratio of about 16 per cent, those with publicly owned credit registries about 40 per cent, and those with private bureaus about 67 per cent (Love and Mylenko, 2003).

Governments can create a supportive environment for credit bureaus by enacting and enforcing data protection and credit reporting laws that allow the sharing of credit information. The laws can safeguard consumer rights by allowing consumers to obtain data about themselves, requiring disclosure of information on who gets the credit report, and providing mechanisms for resolving disputes and correcting erroneous information. Laws that allow the sharing of both positive and negative information do more to improve lenders' information and thus facilitate more lending. Credit reports that contain only negative information (such as cases of late payment) have less predictive power than reports with both positive and negative information (see, for example, Barron and Staten, 2003). Because credit reports are more important for borrowers with limited collateral, limits on data collection disproportionately harm smaller borrowers.

Controlling risk-taking

Governments limit risk-taking by banks and other financial institutions for various reasons. Limited liability can cause banks to take excessive risks and, unlike in other industries, such problems can lead to systemic crises – failure of one bank can lead to a run on other banks, undermining the payments and credit system. Deposit insurance can reduce the risk of bank runs. But unrealistic expectations of government bailouts from explicit or implicit deposit insurance can make the problem worse, by causing depositors and others to monitor banks less carefully.

Prudential oversight limits the financial risks banks can take by requiring them to diversify and maintain at least a minimum ratio of capital to loans. Prudential supervisors who monitor banks on behalf of depositors in accordance with international standards can take action to avert problems. Prudential oversight thus reduces the risk of government bailouts and systemic banking crises, but doesn't always work in practice. Host countries' authorities should also take advantage of information sharing arrangements to facilitate adequate supervision of foreign financial institutions operating in the countries.

As in other areas, choosing appropriate regulations and administering them properly requires financial resources and technical capacity that is often scarce. Further, effectively regulating risk-taking calls for a cautious approach, adapting it to fit the institutional features of the country at hand. Some studies have cast doubt on the effectiveness of prudential regulation and supervision, identifying problems with corruption and clientelism. In these situations, intensive official supervision may put a premium on the need for political connections in order to get finance, rather than the credit worthiness of the investment opportunity (see, for example, Rajan and Zingales, 2003).

Options exist that strike a balance between prudential oversight and market mechanisms that strengthen the ability of depositors and other stakeholders to monitor banks directly – for instance, through "sunshine" regulations that force information disclosure. The effectiveness of private monitoring depends on how well information disclosure regulations are enforced, whether rating agencies compete with each other, the proportion of state ownership of banks, and the nature of deposit insurance (Caprio and Hanohan, 2003).

Commercial rating companies now provide some form of rating for 439 banks in 50 developing countries. There is also evidence that market discipline can work well in developing countries. However, information constraints in many developing countries raise questions about how well market monitoring can work (Stiglitz and Yusuf, 2001) and underscore the need for prudential oversight and a focus on maintaining systemic stability.

Notes

1. The chapter on tax policy highlights the potential for a virtuous circle between private and public investment, namely that good infrastructure attracts private investment, which in turn contributes to government tax revenues, which in turn can be used to finance more efficient infrastructure. The critical question for governments is how to "break into" this virtuous circle.

2. Maritime and air transport are not discussed in this paper.

3. For a discussion of the problem and the history of private infrastructure provision, see, for example, Gomez-Ibanez and Meyer, 1993.

4. These issues are dealt with in greater detail in the chapters on investment policy, public governance, and tax policy. For empirical evidence of the effect of various features of the investment climate on infrastructure, see, for example, Bergara, Henisz and Spille, 1998; Henisz, 2002 and Henisz and Zelner, 2001.

5. On this issue, see also the chapter on investment policy.

6. See also the chapter on investment promotion and facilitation on the use of the Internet to promote transparency.

7. The chapter on competition policy deals with this issue in more detail in the context of "exclusivity" as a form of investment incentive.

8. Additional benefits of well designed private participation can also include bringing in areas of expertise in which the private sector usually has a clear comparative advantage, and more effective allocation of the various risks associated with the planning, construction and operation of the infrastructure, which are often crucial in determining whether a project is built or not, and how successfully it is operated.

9. The issue of trade in services is dealt with more extensively in the chapter on trade policy.

10. For more information on the role that competition authorities can play in avoiding abuse of dominant positions, see the chapter on competition policy.

11. See World Bank and PPIAF, 2003 for a discussion of these options.

12. For further information on this issue, see OECD (2004), *Financing Water and Environmental Infrastructure for All: Some Key Issues,* available at *www.oecd.org/dataoecd/36/53/30589212.pdf.* Additional resources are available at *http://webdomino1.oecd.org/COMNET/DCD/PovNet.nsf.*

13. See Caprio and Honohan (2003), The authors acknowledge that credit bubbles can have a negative impact on growth.

14. Clark, Cull, Peria and Sanchez (2003), Also, BIS (2004), synthesise the empirical literature on this and other issues associated with foreign bank entry.

15. This issue is further explored in the chapter on investment policy.

References and Further Policy Resources

Agarwal, Manish, Ian Alexander and Bernard Tenenbaum (2003), "The Delhi Electricity Discom Privatizations: Some Observations and Recommendations for Future Privatizations in India and Elsewhere", Washington, DC: World Bank, Energy and Mining Sector Board Discussion Paper 8.

Bae, K. and V. Goyal (2003), "Property rights protection and bank loan pricing", Korea University and Hong Kong University of Science and Technology, Seoul.

Barron, J. and M. Staten (2003), "The value of comprehensive credit reports: lessons from the US experience", in Margaret Miller (ed.) Credit Reporting Systems and the International Economy, Cambridge, Massachusetts, MIT Press.

Bergara, M., W. Henisz and P. Spiller (1998), "Political institutions and electric utility investment: a cross-nation analysis", California Management Review, Vol. 40(2).

Berger, A., A. Demirguc-Kunt., R. Levine and J. Haubrich (2004), "Bank concentration and competition: an evolution in the making", *Journal of Money, Credit and Banking*, Vol. 36.

Berkowitz, J. and M. White (2002), "Bankruptcy and small firm's access to credit", *National Bureau of Economic Research Working Paper Series 9010.*

Besant-Jones, J. and B. Tenenbaum (2001), "The California power crisis: lessons for developing countries", *World Bank, Energy and Mining Sector Board Discussion Paper*, No. 1, Washington DC.

BIS (2004), *Foreign Direct Investment in the Financial Sector of Emerging Market Economies*, Report submitted by a Working Group established by the Committee on the Global Financial System, Basel.

Black, B., H. Jang and W. Kim (2003), "Does corporate governance affect firms' market values? Evidence from Korea", *Stanford Law and Economics School, Olin Working Paper 237.*

Black, S. and P. Strahan (2002), "Entrepreneurship and bank credit availability", *Journal of Finance*, Vol. 57(6).

Boylaud, O. and G. Nicoletti (2001), "Regulation, market structure and performance in telecommunications", *OECD Economic Studies*, Vol. 32.

Burr, Chandler (2000), "Grameen Village Phone: Its Current Status and Future Prospects", Paper presented at the Business Services for Small Enterprises in Asia: Developing Markets and Measuring Performance Conference. Hanoi, Viet Nam. March 6.

Calderon, C. and L. Serven (2003), "The output cost of Latin America's infrastructure gap", in William Easterly and Luis Servén (eds.), *The Limits of Stabilisation: Infrastructure, Public Deficits and Growth in Latin America,* World Bank, Washington DC.

Cannock, Geoffrey (2001), "Expanding Rural Telephony: Output-Based Contracts for Pay Phones in Peru", In Penelope J. Brook and Suzanne M. Smith (eds.), *Contracting for Public Services: Output-based Aid and its Applications.* Washington, DC: World Bank.

Caprio, G. and P. Honohan (2003), "Can the unsophisticated market provide discipline?", Paper presented at the *Market Discipline: The Evidence Across Countries and Industries Conference*, Chicago, October 30.

Carmichael, J. and M. Pomerleano (2002), *The Development and Regulation of Non-Bank Financial Institutions*, World bank, Washington DC.

Cetorelli, N. (2003), "Life-cycle dynamics in industrial sectors: the role of banking market structure", *Federal Reserve Bank of St Louis Review*, Vol. 85(4).

CGAP (The Consultative Group to Assist the Poor) (1997), "Scaling Up in Microfinance – Evidence from Global Experience", Washington, DC: CGAP Focus Note 6.

Claessens, S. and L. Laeven (2003), "Financial development, property rights and growth", *Journal of Finance*, Vol. 58(6).

Clark, X., D. Dollar and A. Micco (2002), "Maritime transport cost and port efficiency", *World Bank Policy Research Working Paper Series*, No. 2781.

Clark, X., R. Cull., M. Peria and S. Sanchez (2003), "Foreign bank entry: experience, implications for developing countries and agenda for further research", *World Bank Research Observer*, Vol. 18(1).

Cohen, Nevin (2001), *What Works: Grameen Telecom's Village Phones*. Washington, DC: World Resources Institute, Digital Dividend Study.

Demirguc-Kunt, A., L. Laeven and R. Levine (2003), "The impact of bank regulations, concentration and institutions on bank margins", *World Bank Policy Research Working Paper Series*, No. 3030.

De Young, R., L. Goldberg and L. White (1999), "Youth, adolescence, and maturity of banks: credit availability to small businesses in an era of banking consolidation", *Journal of Banking and Finance*, Vol. 23.

Dollar, D., M. Hallward-Driemeier and T. Mengistae (2003), "Investment climate and firm performance in developing countries", *World Bank*, Washington DC.

Dubash, Navroz K. and Sudhir Chella Rajan (2001), "The Politics of Power Sector Reform in India", World Resources Institute. Washington, DC Processed.

Ekmekcioglu, R. (2003), "Development of factoring market in Turkey", *Paper Presented at the Factoring Industry as a Key Tool for SME Development in EU Accession Countries Conference*, Warsaw, October 23.

Estache, A. and J. Carbajo (1996), "Competing private ports – lessons from Argentina", *World Bank Public Policy for the Private Sector Note* 100.

Fan, Shenggen, Peter Hazell and Sukhadeo Thorat (1999), "Linkages between Government Spending, Growth, and Poverty in Rural India", Washington, DC: IFPRI Research Report 110. Available on line at *www.ifpri.org*.

Fan, Shenggen, Linxiu Zhang and Xiaobo Zhang (2002), "Growth, Inequality and Poverty in Rural China", Washington, DC: IFPRI Research Report 125. Available on line at *www.ifpri.org*.

Fan, Shenggen, Xiaobo Zhang and Neetha Rao (2004), "Public Expenditure, Growth, and Poverty Reduction In Rural Uganda", Washington, DC.: IFPRI, Development Strategy and Governance Division (DSGD), Discussion Paper 4. Available on line at *www.ifpri.org*.

Faulkender, M. and M. Petersen (2003), "Does the source of capital affect capital structure?" *National Bureau of Economic Research Working Paper Series* 9930.

Fernald, J. (1999), "Roads to prosperity? Assessing the link between public capital and productivity", *American Economic Review*, Vol. 89(3).

Fleisig, Heywood W. (1998), *How Problems in the Framework for Secured Transactions Limit Access to Credit*. Washington, DC: Center for the Economic Analysis of Law.

Galal, A., L. Jones., P. Tandon and I. Vogelsang (1994), *Welfare Consequences of selling Public Enterprises: an Empirical Analysis*, New Cork, Oxford University Press.

Galindo, A. and M. Miller (2001), "Can credit registries reduce credit constraints? Empirical evidence on the role of credit registries in firm investment decisions", *Paper presented at the Annual Meetings of the Inter-American Development Bank*, Santiago de Chile, March 16.

Gavira, J. (1998), "Port privatization and competition in Colombia", World Bank, *Public Policy for the Private Sector, Note* 167, Washington DC.

Ghatak, Maitreesh and Timothy W. Guinnane (1999), "The Economics of Lending with Joint Liability: Theory and Practice", *Journal of Development Economics* 60(1):195-228.

Gomez-Ibanez, J. and J. Meyer (1993), *Going Private, The International Experience with Transport Privatisation*, Brookings Institution, Washington, DC.

Harris, Clive (2002), "Private Rural Power: Network Expansion Using an Output-Based Scheme in Guatemala", Washington, DC: World Bank, Private Sector and Infrastructure Network, Note 245.

Henisz, W. (2002), "The institutional environment for infrastructure investment", *Industrial and Corporate Change*, Vol. 11, No. 2.

Henisz, W. and B. Zelner (2001), "The Institutional environment for telecommunications investment", *Journal of Economics and Management Strategy*, Vol. 10, No. 1.

Hess, Ulrich and Leora Klapper (2003), "The Use of New Products, Processes and Technology for the Delivery of Rural and Microfinance Loans in India", World Bank. Washington, DC Processed.

Hubka, Ashley and Rita Zaidi (2004), "Innovations in Microfinance", Background paper for the WDR 2005.

Hunt, S. and G. Shuttleworth (1996), *Competition and Choice in Electricity*, John Wiley and Sons, New York.

Impavido, G. (2001), *Assessment of Implementation of the IAIS Insurance Supervisory Principles*, World Bank, Washington DC.

India – Ministry of Finance (2003), *Economic Survey 2002-2003*, New Delhi: India – Ministry of Finance.

Inter-American Development Bank (2001), *Economic and Social Progress in Latin America 2001 Report*, IADB, Washington, DC.

Jadresic, Alejandro (2000), "Promoting Private Investment in Rural Electrification: The Case of Chile", Washington, DC: World Bank Viewpoint Note 214.

Klapper, Leora and Elke Kraus (2002), "Credit Information Infrastructure and Political Economy Issues", World Bank, Washington, DC Processed.

Klein, M. and B. Hadjimichael (2003), *The Private Sector in Development: Entrepreneurship, Regulation and Competitive Disciplines*, World Bank, Washington, DC.

Komives, K., D. Whittington and X. Wu (2003), "Infrastructure coverage and the poor: a global perspective", in T. Irwin and J. Brook, (eds.), *Infrastructure for Poor People: Public Policy for Private Provision*, World Bank, Washington, DC.

Lal, Sumir (2004), "Can Good Economics Ever Be Good Politics? Case Study of the Power Sector in India", World Bank. Washington, DC Processed.

Li, H., L. Squire and H. Zou (1998), "Explaining international and intertemporal variations in income inequality", *Economic Journal*, Vol. 108(406).

Liautaud, G. (2001), "Maintaining roads: experience with output-based contracts in Argentina", in P. Brook and S. Smith (eds.), *Contracting for Public Services: Output Based Aid and its Applications*, World Bank, Washington DC.

Limao, N. and A. Venables (2001), "Infastructure, geographical disadvantage, transport costs and trade", *World Bank Economic Review*, Vol. 15 No. 3.

Love, I. and N. Mylenko (2003), "Credit reporting and financing constraints", *World Bank Policy Research Working Paper Series*, No. 3142.

Miller, M. (2003), "Credit reporting systems around the globe: the state of the art in public credit registries and private credit reporting firms", in M. Miller, (ed.), *Credit Reporting Systems and the International Economy*, MIT Press, Massachusetts.

Morduch, Jonathan (1997), "The Microfinance Revolution", Harvard University, Cambridge, Mass. Processed.

Morduch, Jonathan, Elizabeth Littlefield and Syed Hashemi (2003), "Is Microfinance an Effective Strategy to Reach the Millennium Development Goals?" Washington, DC: CGAP Focus Note 24.

Navarrete, Camilo (2004), "Managing Investment Climate Reforms: Colombian Ports Sector Reform Case Study", Background paper for the WDR 2005.

OECD (2004), *Financing Water and Environmental Infrastructure for All: Some Key Issues*, available at *www.oecd.org/dataoecd/36/53/30589212.pdf*.

Peek, J. and E. Rosengren (1998), "Bank consolidation and small business lending: it's not just bank size that matters", *Journal of Banking and Finance*, Vol. 22.

Phillips, C. (1993), *The Regulation of Public Utilities: Theory and Practice*, 3rd edition, Public Utilities Reports, Arlington.

Pollitt, M. (2003), "Electricity reform in Chile and Argentina: lessons for developing countries", *Paper presented at the Cambridge-MIT Institute Electricity Power Autumn Research Seminar*, Cambridge Massachusetts.

PPIAF, and World Bank (2002), *Private Solutions for Infrastructure in Cambodia*. Washington, DC: World Bank.

Radelet, S. and J. Sachs (1998), "Shipping costs, manufactured exports and economic growth", *Paper presented at the American Economic Association Annual Meeting*, Chicago, January 8.

Rajan, R. and L. Zingales (2003), *Saving Capitalism from the Capitalists: Unleashing the Power of Financial Markets to Create Wealth and Spread Opportunity*, Crown Business, New York.

Ray, Amit S. (2004), "Managing Port Reforms in India: Case Study of Jawaharlal Nehru Port Trust (JNPT) Mumbai", Background paper for the WDR 2005.

Reinikka, R. and J. Svensson (2002), "Coping with poor public capital", *Journal of Development Economics*, Vol. 69, No.1.

Roller, L. and L. Waverman (2001), "Telecommunications infrastructure and economic development: a simultaneous approach", *American Economic Review*, Vol. 91, No. 4.

Rossotto, C., A. Lewin., C. Gomez and B. Wellenius (2003), "Competition in international voice communications", *Policy Paper of the Global Information and Communications Technology Department*, World Bank, Washington, DC.

Shleifer, A. and D. Wolfenzohn (2002), "Investor protection and equity markets", *Journal of Financial Economics*, Vol. 66, No. 1.

Smith, W. (1997), "Utility regulators: the independence debate", World Bank, *Public Policy for the Private Sector Note 127*.

Stiglitz, J. and S. Yusuf (eds.) (2001), *Rethinking the East Asian Miracle*, World Bank and Oxford University Press, Washington, DC.

Stoica, Christina I., and Valeriu Stoica (2002), "Romania's Legal Regime for Security Interests in Personal Property", *Law in Transition* Spring: 62-6.

Strahan, P. and J. Weston (1998), "Small business lending and the changing structure of the banking industry", *Journal of Banking and Finance*, Vol. 22.

Tanzi, V and H. Davoodi (1997), "Corruption, public investment and growth", *International Monetary Fund Working Paper*, WP/97/139.

Tomkins, Ray (2001), "Extending Rural Electrification: A Survey of Innovative Schemes". In Penelope J. Brook and Suzanne M. Smith, (eds.), *Contracting for Public Services: Output-based Aid andIts Applications*. Washington, DC: World Bank.

Trujillo, L. and T. Serebrisky (2003), "Market power: ports: a case study of post privatisation mergers", *World Bank Public Policy for the Private Sector Note 260*, Washington, DC.

Unite, A. and M. Sullivan (2003), "The effect of foreign entry and ownership structure on the Philippine domestic banking sector", *Journal of Banking and Finance*, Vol. 27, No. 12.

Wallsten, S. (2001), "An econometric analysis of telecom competition, privatisation and regulation in Africa and Latin America", *Journal of Industrial Economics*, Vol. 49, No.1.

Wellenius, Björn (1997), "Extending Telecommunications Service to Rural Areas – The Chilean Experience: Awarding Subsidies Through Competitive Bidding", Washington, DC: World Bank Public Policy for the Private Sector Note 105.

Wodon, Q., M. Ajwad and C. Siaens (2003), "Lifeline or means-testing? Electric utility subsidies in Honduras", in P. Brook and T. Irwin, (eds.), *Infrastructure for Poor People: Public Policy for Private Provision*, World Bank, Washington, DC.

World Bank (1996), *Morocco-Socioeconomic Influence of Rural Roads: Fourth Highway Project*. Washington, DC: World Bank, Operations Evaluation Department.

World Bank (2003), *Doing Business in 2004 – Understanding Regulation*, Washington DC.

World Bank (2004), *World Bank Policy Research Report 2004. Reforming Infrastructure: Privatization, Regulation, and Competition*, New York: Oxford University Press.

World Bank (2005), *World Development Report 2005: A Better Investment Climate for Everyone*, Chapter 6. Finance and Infrastructure, Washington DC.

World Bank and PPIAF (2003), *Port Reform Toolkit: Effective Decision Support for Policymakers*, Washington, DC.

World Energy Council (2001), *Pricing Energy in Developing Countries*, London, UK.

Zhang, Y., D. Parker and C. Kirkpatrick (2002), "Electricity sector reform in developing countries: an econometric assessment of the effects of privatisation, competition and regulation", University of Manchester, Centre on Regulation and Competition, *Institute for Development Policy and Management Working Paper 13*.

ISBN 92-64-02586-3
Policy Framework for Investment
A Review of Good Practices
© OECD 2006

Chapter 10

Public Governance*

*   This background document was prepared by Janos Bertok, Elodie Beth, Josef Konvitz, Delia Rodrigo and Christian Vergez of the OECD Directorate for Public Governance and Territorial Development and Nicola Ehlermann-Cache of the Anti-Corruption Division of the OECD Directorate for Financial and Enterprise Affairs.

10.1. Introduction: the relationship between public governance and investment

The debate on the links between public governance, investment and development has taken on greater urgency as the interconnectedness of economies intensifies. Investment decisions of citizens and foreigners are directly influenced by their understanding of how public policies and laws are formulated and enforced. Just as there is no single model for good public governance in developed countries, there is no single model with fixed stages of transformation for developing countries. Nevertheless, there are commonly accepted standards of public governance to assist governments in assuming their roles effectively.

The challenge is that to accomplish their roles, governments must mobilize co-operation within the administration, between the national government and others levels, and between the public sector and others actors, principally in the private sector and civil society. In OECD and non-OECD countries, the means by which government intervenes to guide and promote social and economic development no longer depend on rigid "command and control" mechanisms, but on more flexible and indirect forms of rule-making, guidance, evaluation and persuasion.

A key test of good public governance in the investment context is when the actions of government are credible, i.e. when it can be trusted by investors and stakeholders and be held accountable. This chapter addresses two key dimensions of public governance which matter for attracting and maximising the benefits of investment: i) regulatory quality, ii) public sector integrity, including the contribution of international co-operation.

Poor public governance poses major risks for investors. Surveys by the OECD, the World Bank and other organisations consistently identify uncertainty about the regulatory actions of policymakers, corruption and weak judicial systems as among most important considerations for investors. Corruption undermines the integrity of governments and business enterprises, by distorting the allocation of public and private resources, making the public administration unreliable, and destroying investor confidence in whole countries. It is therefore essential that governments enact and implement effective anti-bribery legislation, develop an encompassing approach that promotes regulatory quality and integrity within public organisations. Conversely, good public governance has been consistently associated with positive investment performance. OECD work shows a positive relationship between the quality of the regulatory framework and foreign investment for instance across a sample of countries (see Figure 10.1).

It is also widely recognised that the rule of law is fundamental to the link between good governance and investment. The issue of property rights figures prominently in the historical literature: access to land, security of tenure, and provision of housing have been cited for the assurance they give that the fruits of initiative will not be confiscated or jeopardised. Protection against arbitrary action is consistent with the legitimacy of legal measures binding on all. Weak implementation and/or enforcement of law, limited knowledge of rights, and a lack of access to affordable legal representation all compromise

Figure 10.1. **The relationship between inward FDI and the quality of governance**

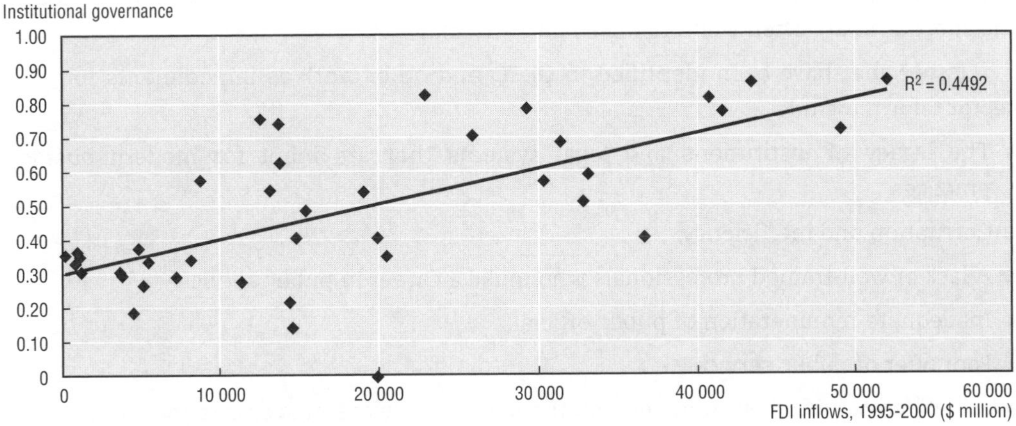

Source: OECD (2002) Foreign Direct Investment: Maximising Benefits, Minimising Costs, page 180.

rule of law. The question of security is also linked to an acceptably low level of domestic violence and theft, and to the absence of civil war (see Box 10.1).

Box 10.1. Stability and security

The importance of taking state fragility and conflict into account is underlined by statistics. In 2003, 14 wars, 21 severe crises and 45 crisis situations unfolded around the world. Data on 2004 shows that 2003 was no anomaly: major political violence affected 18 countries. While states move in and out of a dangerous situation, it is estimated that some 40 to 50 countries are considered to be fragile or failing, accounting for about 14% of the world's population but nearly a third of the world's poor and 41% of all child deaths. A focus on helping states to improve the most basic security, justice, economic and service delivery functions is key (see OECD/DAC draft Ten Principles of Good International Engagement in Fragile States).

The perception of risk can have nearly as much of a negative impact as the actual level of insecurity. Even where there is investment activity, foreign and domestic firms may incur significant costs to protect their premises, products and personnel; they may also face demands for payment of protection money or "customs" tariffs to militias or organised criminal gangs. Inadvertently, businesses can act in ways that perpetuate this cycle of exploitation, violence and corruption. For the private sector as much as for external donors, more in-depth analysis and awareness of conflict and peace dynamics are essential, whether at the sub-national, national or regional levels. The security and justice systems in developing countries must provide conditions in which people and businesses have confidence in their personal security and investments. [See the DAC Guidelines: Security System Reform and Governance: Policy and Good Practice (2004).]

10.1.1. Context for reform

Public sector reforms compete for attention with other policy objectives. Good public governance is however one of the more complex and arduous agendas for a government because: 1) it takes time, and must be supported consistently; 2) it calls for additional resources, particularly to recruit better-trained professionals and offer them competitive pay; 3) those who benefit from better governance are often scattered throughout the society and are poorly organised to express support, whereas 4) those who stand to lose in the short term are often well-organised and articulate.

Issues that have been identified in OECD and other work as impediments to public sector reform include:

● The legacy of institutions and legal systems that are inapt for modern business practices.

● Corruption and inefficiency.

● A lack of well-trained professionals who make a career in public service.

● Inadequate remuneration of public officials.

● Poor offer of public services.

● A ineffective judicial system and enforcement, and delays in access to the courts.

● Information and communication deficiencies.

Therefore, a sound regulatory framework is strongly linked with promoting a good investment climate.

Many countries have learned through experience that successful legal and regulatory reform requires support at the highest political levels, and that responsibility for such reform in particular should be located in a governmental unit at the centre, often attached to the office of the prime minister or president. Comprehensive reform works better than piecemeal reform. These and other aspects of public governance are inter-related: weakness in one aspect compromises the whole; equally, efforts to improve are likely to be mutually reinforcing. But comprehensiveness does not mean that all changes must occur at the same time. A successful reform policy will need a strategy establishing transitional steps. Often, the commitment to change is strongest during and immediately after a crisis. The challenge comes in setting up a process for reform in the absence of a crisis.

Much of what needs to get done to set a durable framework for good governance is a matter of domestic policy and institutions, leadership supported by civil society, and of cultural and social norms. There is no single model, nor is there agreement on the steps or sequencing of reform to improve governance. There is, however, a consensus that sequencing does matter, but the specific measures and the pace of progress (including in relation to time-bound targets according to which governments make themselves accountable to achievements) need to be adapted to each country's context. The international community can however help in several respects: 1) international agreements often call for implementation and compliance measures, which in turn shift resources and attention to governance; 2) "soft laws" help set standards and create expectations, and pressures from investors; and 3) capacity-building measures can be strengthened by contributions from intergovernmental organisations, private and other non-governmental organisations, and bilateral co-operation.

10.2. Regulatory quality

Regulatory quality refers to regulations that are efficient in terms of cost, effective in terms of having a clear regulatory and policy purpose, transparent and accountable. Regulatory policy is broadly defined as an explicit, dynamic, continuous and consistent "whole-of-government" policy to pursue regulatory quality. An effective regulatory policy that helps to improve the framework for investment is made up of three components that are mutually reinforcing: policies, institutions and tools.

Regulatory policies should aim at facilitating the operation of efficient markets. Regulations can create benefits for enterprises by setting market frameworks in which commercial transactions can take place in a pro-competitive and low cost environment. Regulations which are poorly designed or applied can slow business responsiveness, divert resources away from productive investments, hamper entry into markets, reduce job creation and generally discourage entrepreneurship.

The advantages of an effective regulatory system are multiple:

- it can help to encourage competition rather than protection;
- it bears down on costs from the accretion of rules over time, removing complexity, red tape, and inconsistencies;
- it encourages new or previously unheard stakeholders into the policy debate, so that policy is better grounded; and
- it promotes timely and necessary change to support economic and social renewal, quickly and at least cost.

The way regulatory quality can be built up in practice is affected by values, public policy goals, institutions and legal systems across countries. They have deep roots in historical, cultural and political development, as well as geography. Regulatory policy, tools and institutions must therefore be adapted, and differences acknowledged, as these are integral part of distinctive societies, globalisation notwithstanding. Regulatory policy is not a question of "one size fits all". The value systems and governance of a country may be reflected and taken forward in regulatory systems and processes, which can be unhelpful for or contribute positively to regulatory quality. Over time, competitive pressures will call attention to differences in regulatory regimes and capacities.

10.2.1. Regulatory policy

> **Has the government established and implemented a coherent and comprehensive regulatory reform framework, consistent with its broader development and investment strategy?**

Regulatory policy is an explicit policy for a dynamic, continuous and consistent "whole of government" approach to pursue regulatory quality. Regulatory policy is about the process by which regulations are drafted, updated, implemented and enforced, set in a broader context of public policy objectives.[1] The evaluation of policy therefore includes not only the social, environmental and economic impact of regulations, but the links between regulatory processes or systems on the one hand, and those outcomes on the other. Nothing contributes more to investor scepticism about regulation than regulatory failures: the impression that rules respond to special interest pressures, and the recognition that rules often do not achieve their objective. Mistakes can be avoided. A forward-looking perspective is therefore important.

OECD experience with regulatory reform suggests that government intervention should be based on clear evidence that government action is justified, given the nature of the problem, which has to be correctly defined. Giving clear evidence of its nature and magnitude, as well as explaining why it has arisen (identifying the incentives of affected entities) is the first step to propose regulations.

From an investors' perspective, regulatory policies should preferably take the form of a statement setting out principles that provide strong guidance and benchmarks for action by officials, and also what the investors can expect from government regarding regulation. Thus domestic and foreign stakeholders would have a statement of government policy for reference, in addition to other obligations that may govern regulatory action.

The regulatory environment where citizens and business people operate is composed of complex layers of regulation stemming from sub-national, national and local levels of government. For example, land use and construction are typically handled at county or municipal level, and many administrative procedures such as licenses to open a business are processed at sub-national level. Where the capacity to handle such matters quickly and transparently is lacking, corruption, local anti-competitive measures, and costly delays often follow. Where regulatory powers are shared between levels of government, co-ordination may be an essential element of successful reform. Formal policies or mechanisms for co-ordination within and between governments on regulation and its reform can be set up to maximise the benefits of reforms and reduce internal regulatory barriers to trade and investment.

Regulatory processes should be structured so that all regulatory decisions rigorously respect the "rule of law"; that is, responsibility should be explicit for ensuring that all regulations are authorised by higher level regulations and consistent with treaty obligations, and comply with relevant legal principles such as certainty, proportionality, and applicable procedures mechanisms.

It is often believed that OECD and non-OECD countries live in an age of deregulation. In fact, regulation has moved into many new areas, the complexity of rules has increased, and regulations have been added whenever the state has withdrawn from direct provision of services, to create markets. Attempts to promote regulatory quality, which began with important areas of low-quality regulation, are now undertaken on many fronts simultaneously. But these efforts are hampered by the fragmentation of responsibility for regulation, and by poor coordination when developing regulatory policies, tools and institutions. Change depends crucially on promoting a better regulation culture within government.

10.2.2. Regulatory institutions

What mechanisms are in place for managing and co-ordinating regulatory reform across different levels of government to ensure consistency and a transparent application of regulations and clear standards for regulatory quality?

Diversity in institutional systems and institutional traditions has an impact in regulatory policy. Nevertheless, during the regulatory process, the need for some form of central mechanism to promote regulatory quality appears to be essential if durable progress is to be made. An oversight body that works as an "engine of reform" can help to focus the interest of investors in support of regulatory quality development. To avoid duplications and contradictions, all appropriate official bodies should be informed and consulted when preparing a new measure or planning a reform.

Quality regulation that enhances investment needs a strong involvement and a sense of "ownership" by regulators in charge of their design and implementation. Special interests, close identification with the objectives of outdated regulation, countervailing pressures from different parts of society, and coherence when applying regulations and regimes across multiple areas, are challenges for regulatory institutions.

A regulatory quality framework that promotes investment in a transparent and accountable way benefits when responsibility is shared between regulators and a central quality control entity. Budget transparency is an example among others (see Box 10.2).

Box 10.2. **OECD Best Practices for budget transparency**

OECD experience suggests that budget transparency is a constituent part of a regulatory environment which provides predictability for informed investment decisions. The Best Practices are designed as a reference tool for member and non-member countries to use in order to increase the degree of budget transparency in their respective countries. The Best Practices are organised around specific budget reports for presentation purposes only. It is not meant to constitute a formal "standard" for budget transparency since states have different reporting regimes and may have different areas of emphasis for transparency. The Best Practices have been used as a benchmark in country reports on budget transparency.

Source: OECD (2001), *OECD Best Practices for Budget Transparency*, Paris.

The establishment of a central oversight body, backed by political support with whole-of-government responsibilities, is one of the most visible signs of the integration of regulatory reform into government management systems. Private-sector and civil society forces for reform, such as advisory bodies or private initiatives, can also be helpful in identifying priorities, proposing specific reforms and providing advocacy for reform in general.

A principal role of the oversight body is to review regulations and improvements in regulatory quality. This body should be competent to assess the substantive quality of new regulation and have the capacity to ensure that ministries achieve the goals embodied in the assessment criteria. Regulatory Impact Assessment (RIA) is the most important mechanism for this role. To be effective, the oversight body must be able to question the quality of RIA and regulatory proposals. An oversight body needs the technical capacity to verify the impact analysis and the political power to ensure that its view prevails in most cases.

Independent regulators are also part of the regulatory structure in many countries. They include economic regulators for network industries, or regulators set up to support civil liberties and foster administrative transparency. Independent regulators have become more significant over the last decade.[2] When such regulators are responsible for making rules or interpreting them, they should operate under the same disciplines as other rule-makers, notably as regards RIA (see Box 10.3). Some countries achieve the benefits of reform while regulating from within line ministries.

Box 10.3. **Independent regulators**

In most OECD countries, economic structural reforms, promoted in part by international commitments, have prompted the establishment of independent regulatory agencies and the redesign of existing regulators. These institutions are intended to provide neutral regulatory oversight in liberalised or privatised sectors, and prudential oversight of competitive markets. The design and management of such regulatory agencies constitute an important component of regulatory management. Key issues in this respect include considerations on how to establish institutions that are:

- competent, accountable and independent;

- at arms length from short-term political interference;

- capable of resisting capture by interest groups, but still;

- responsive to general political priorities; and

- have decision-making procedures that take into account the particularities of the area being regulated, while at the same time maintaining transparency and accessibility for all stakeholders.

Source: OECD (2004), *OECD Reviews of Regulatory Reform – Germany. Consolidating Economic and Social Renewal,* Paris.

Strong and effective institutions require expert staff and resources to provide all core functions. Expertise and experience need to be developed and maintained over time so that officials responsible for policy development and institutional design are more aware of and better able to identify what is necessary for high quality regulation that provides a better framework for investment. Synergies among regulatory institutions are crucial for policy coherence and effective coordination.

10.2.3. *Regulatory tools: Regulatory Impact Assessment (RIA)*

> **To what extent are regulatory impact assessments used to evaluate the consequences of economic regulations on the investment environment? Are the results of these assessments made public on a timely basis?**

Regulatory Impact Assessment (RIA) examines and measures the likely benefits, costs and effects of new or changed regulations. It is a useful regulatory tool that provides decision-makers with valuable empirical data and a comprehensive framework in which they can assess their options and the consequences their decisions may have. A poor understanding of the problems at hand or of the side effects of government action can undermine regulatory efforts and result in regulatory failures. RIA is used to define problems and to ensure that government action is justified and appropriate in economic, social and environmental terms.

RIA recognises the need to assess regulations on a case-by-case basis to determine whether they contribute to strategic policy goals. For RIA to achieve concrete results, it must be based on a long-term perspective. It is also crucial that a culture of acceptance and commitment to the process be developed and nurtured in the public and private sectors, and among the general public. Communicating the results of RIA is an essential part of the process of improving regulatory design.

The OECD experience reveals that RIA may take various forms depending upon policy agendas of governments or even social and cultural background of countries.[3] RIA is best understood as one "decision method" among several used to reach regulatory decisions. The methods used by regulators to reach effective and efficient decisions can be classified as follows:

1. Expert – The decision is reached by a trusted expert, either a regulator or an expert, who uses professional judgment to decide what should be done.

2. Consensus – The decision is reached by a group of stakeholders who reach a common position that balances interests of all concerned with the proposed regulation.

3. Political – The decision is reached by political representatives based on consensus view of the issues of importance to the political process.

4. Benchmarking – The decision is based on reliance on an external model, such as international regulation.

5. Empirical – The decision is based on research, fact-finding and analysis that defines the parameters of action according to established objective criteria.

A regulatory decision is supported by a mix of these decision methods, differing according to specific characteristics such as national culture, political conditions and administrative style.

Many OECD countries rely on RIA to avoid unnecessary investment restrictiveness. The RIA process provides a systematic approach for assessing the impacts of a proposed regulation and helps inform regulatory decision-making. Where appropriate, therefore, investment impacts would normally be assessed in the mix of other factors deemed relevant in a given regulatory scenario. In the absence of a broader requirement to assess

Figure 10.2. **Aspects of regulatory impact assessments in OECD countries**

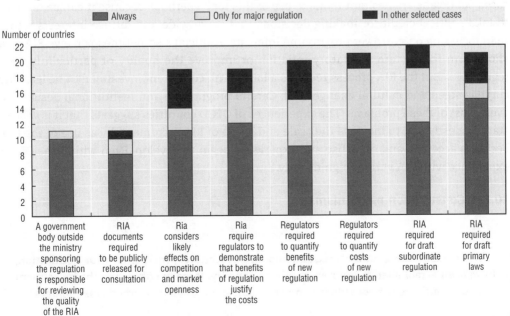

the impacts of a proposed regulation on market openness (or indeed an explicit requirement to select a regulatory approach based on market openness considerations), RIA thus emerges as a potentially useful tool for considering investment impacts of various regulations. Policy guidelines for improving the regulatory framework, such as the APEC-OECD Integrated Checklist on Regulatory Reform, are also important for evaluating the consequences of economic regulation on the investment environment.

RIA exposes the merits of decisions and the impacts of actions. For this reason, RIA is closely linked to processes of public consultation. Public involvement in RIA has several significant benefits. The public and especially those affected by regulations, can often provide much of the data that are needed to complete the RIA. Consultation can furnish important information on the feasibility of proposals, on the range of alternatives considered, and on the degree to which affected parties are likely to accept the proposed regulation. RIA can also improve the involvement and accountability of decision-making at ministerial and political levels. It fosters an understanding of the impacts policies will have and demonstrates how government decisions benefit society. By emphasising openness, RIA favours policies that serve the interests of society as a whole, rather than just those of special groups.

Designing and applying effective RIA requires special consideration of a number of different issues, the relative importance of which can change depending upon a country's level of development. First, methodological and operational difficulties can easily arise in the decision-making processes of developing countries. Second, in many cases the use of regulatory tools requires a high level of expertise and access to extensive resources and information which may not be immediately available and need to be built up. Finally, common political practices can make better political oversight and more attention to consultation a challenge. Policy-makers in these countries have to evaluate and assess the weight of the tools they have available, and determine how to best use and combine them to achieve concrete results.

RIA provides policy makers with a great deal of invaluable information, but in many cases politicians are hesitant to make use of this tool – perhaps because it can be difficult to take political credit for making decisions that serve wide and diffuse interests rather than focussing on narrower programme interests. Politicians sometimes perceive RIA as a short-term fix to stem regulatory inflation or improve the quality of particularly poor regulations. But the RIA process requires a long-term, consistent investment. The learning curve is steep and cultural change vital. Careful programme and institutional design can avert most of these problems. The experiences of OECD countries suggests that it is wise to start modestly and to increase the scale and scope of RIA incrementally as use of the tool becomes accepted and expertise and experience begin to develop. Even within the OECD, experience with RIA various significantly.

10.2.4. Consultation mechanisms

> **What public consultation mechanisms and procedures, including prior notification, have been established to improve regulatory quality, thereby enhancing the investment environment? Are the consultation mechanisms open to all concerned stakeholders?**

Regulations should be developed in an open and transparent fashion, with appropriate procedures for effective and timely inputs from interested national and foreign parties. This should of course include potential domestic and foreign investors as well as affected business, trade unions, civil society, wider interest groups and other levels of government.[4] The way comments from interested parties are handled by government enhances the credibility of the process and the prospects of regulatory compliance by the economic actors.

Consultation is important to ensure that affected parties understand the nature of new regulations, why it is needed and what is expected of them. Inadequate consultation may result in poor quality regulation and/or uncertainty among businesses and investors about how they will be affected.[5] This is likely to deter new investment as potential investors seek our opportunities where there is more regulatory certainty and quality.

10.2.5. Administrative simplification and responsiveness

> **To what extent are the administrative burdens on investors measured and quantified? What government procedures exist to identify and to reduce unnecessary administrative burdens, including those on investors? How widely are information and communication technologies used to promote administrative simplification, quality services, transparency and accountability?**

Administrative simplification is the most commonly used regulatory reform tool. It is aimed at reducing and streamlining government formalities and paperwork – the most visible component of which is often permits and licences. There is evidence in many countries that the administrative burden imposed on businesses is significant, with small to medium size enterprises particularly affected. It is also important to consider the cumulative effect of all the regulations to which enterprises are subject, not just those that have been introduced recently. Increasingly, governments are making use of information and communication technologies as means of reducing administrative burdens. Enabling administrative simplification has become in many countries a key driver of their e-government programmes.

Excessive "red tape" adds to business costs, can impede market entry, reduce incentives to innovate and reduce competitive pressures within the economy.[6] In addition, it creates uncertainty which can disrupt business planning and hinder the ability of businesses to respond quickly to new market opportunities. Ultimately, this discourages new investment, both domestic and international, weakens competitive pressures within the economy and economic performance will suffer.

This is not to imply of course that all regulation and administrative measures should be removed. Well designed and implemented government formalities are necessary for the implementation of policy and the attainment of policy goals. An administrative simplification program should focus on poorly designed, implemented or outdated formalities. Reforming these formalities removes a substantial burden from business, and encourages new investment while ensuring that the remaining formalities help, rather than hinder, the government's policy agenda. Administrative simplification programmes, by providing a framework for transparency and accountability, also contribute to broader goals such as promoting integrity and preventing corruption.

Administrative simplification programs can help encourage an evaluation culture within government. These programs focus attention on the need to specify the objectives of regulation clearly and explore both positive and negative impacts on the target group and other groups in society. The use of *ex ante* tools to evaluate the effects of regulatory measures before they are introduced, and *ex post* measure to review regulations in place, can help identify administrative burdens, which impact adversely on business and hinder investment and economic progress. An initial focus on administrative simplification can help build a culture that feeds into broader regulatory policy goals and leads to a regulatory environment that is more conducive to attracting new investment.

10.2.6. International co-operation on regulatory reform

Better-quality regulation is a key goal of public-sector management reform and is fundamental to the functioning of society and the economy. Most countries now recognise that regulatory quality is crucial to economic performance and to improving the quality of life of their citizens. This has motivated a number of international initiatives.

The APEC-OECD Integrated Checklist for Regulatory reform is one such example. The Checklist is a joint effort of OECD and APEC member countries and economies, designed to

---

Box 10.4. **A short history of regulatory reform at the OECD**

In March 1995, the OECD established a Recommendation on Improving the Quality of Government Regulation – the first internationally accepted set of principles concerning regulatory quality.[1]

Attempts to improve regulatory quality initially focused on identifying problem areas, advocating specific reforms and scrapping burdensome regulations. But policy makers soon recognised that makeshift approaches to reform were insufficient. The reform agenda of OECD countries began to broaden, to include a range of explicit overarching policies, disciplines and tools. In 1997, the *OECD Report on Regulatory Reform* outlined an action plan with policy recommendations that included seven "Principles of Good Regulation" and a set of ten best practices in the design and implementation of RIA systems.

From 1998 to 2004, the OECD completed 20 country reviews of regulatory reform.[2] These include more than 1 000 specific policy recommendations and approximately 120 chapters, each focussing on regulatory reforms in selected areas. Taken as a whole, the reviews demonstrate that a well-structured and well-implemented programme of regulatory reform contributes to better economic performance and enhances social welfare. The OECD has taken stock of the progress made in OECD member countries and released the 2005 "OECD Guiding Principles for Regulatory Quality and Performance", which highlight the dynamic, forward-looking process by which regulatory policies, tools and institutions are adapted for the 21st century.

1. At the time of the Recommendation on Improving the Quality of Government Regulation, only a minority of member countries had formal regulatory policies to ensure that such principles could be systematically implemented. By 2000, 24 of the 30 OECD member countries had adopted regulatory policies. In at least ten of those countries, the policy had been introduced within the previous five years OECD, (2002), *Regulatory Policies in OECD Countries. From Interventionism to Regulatory Governance*, Paris.
2. Canada, Czech Republic, Denmark, Finland, France, Germany, Greece, Hungary, Ireland, Italy, Japan, Korea, Mexico, Netherlands, Norway, Poland, Spain, Turkey, United Kingdom, United States.

---

help countries to self-assess their progress toward regulatory reform. The *Integrated Checklist* translates the general statements found in the already agreed-upon APEC and OECD Principles into concrete, practical terms that can be applied in different contexts. The Checklist is a self-assessment tool that integrates three policy areas – competition, rule-making and market openness – to provide a coherent whole-of-government view. Furthermore, it integrates governance perspectives of transparency, accountability and performance, key elements that contribute to investment promotion (see Annex 10.A). Bilateral co-operation through training programmes, seminars and exchange of experts helps to promote regulatory reform and improve the investment promotion and legal structures (see also Box 10.4 on the evolving treatment of regulatory reform at the OECD).

10.3. Fostering public sector integrity

Fostering a corruption-free environment for investment is essential for private sector development, promotion of foreign investments and sustained economic growth. This requires implementing international anti-corruption and integrity standards in the public service, effectively applying and enforcing them in practice, ensuring compliance through monitoring, and engaging in international co-operation for fighting corruption.

10.3.1. *Implementing international anti-corruption and integrity standards*

> **To what extent have international anti-corruption and integrity standards been implemented in national legislation and regulations? Do penal, administrative and civil law provisions provide an effective legislative and regulatory framework for fighting corruption, including bribe solicitation and extortion as well as promoting integrity, thereby reducing uncertainty and improving business conditions for all investors?**

Anti-corruption and integrity standards include both preventive as well as repressive measures. Governments should enact provisions, mostly in criminal law but also in the civil and administrative codes, to prevent and sanction corruption of domestic public officials. Over the last decade, the international community has become aware of increasing economic and political evidence of the detrimental effects of corruption. Since the adoption in 1997 of the OECD Convention on Combating Bribery of Foreign Public Officials in International Business Transactions, an increasing number of governments have strengthened their legal framework for fighting corruption (Box 10.5).

Creating and sustaining good governance arrangements that support high standards of conduct in the public sector is a complex task for governments. They have made substantial efforts to develop an "Ethics Infrastructure" in their domestic administrations, a system of supportive laws, institutions and procedures to promote integrity and prevent corruption. For example, in the 1998 OECD Recommendation on Improving Ethical Conduct in the Public Service (see Box 10.6), OECD countries strongly acknowledged that globalisation and the development of international relations, particularly trade and investment, demand high recognisable integrity standards in the public service. In the last decade, many governments have updated the core values of their public service and modernised expected standards of conduct on the part of public officials, particularly at senior levels, to ensure the predictability and integrity of public decision-making. The

> ### Box 10.5. **International anti-corruption Conventions**
>
> **OECD Convention of Combating Bribery of Foreign Public Officials, 1997:** The Convention, along with the revised Recommendation on Combating Bribery in International Business Transactions and the 1996 Recommendation on the Tax Deductibility of Bribes to Foreign Public Officials, are the core instruments through which OECD and non-OECD members of the anti-bribery group co-operate to stop the flow of bribes for the purpose of obtaining or retaining international business. In Mai 2005, 36 countries were Party to the Convention, which is open to accession.
>
> **United Nations Convention against Corruption (UNCAC)** which was adopted by the United Nations General Assembly in October 2003, provides a very broad blueprint for anti-corruption systems, including concepts and principles that are relevant for the public sector, for private business and for other actors in national anti-corruption systems.

> ### Box 10.6. **1998 OECD Recommendation on Improving Ethical Conduct in the Public Service**
>
> With the 1998 Recommendation on Improving Ethical Conduct in the Public Service, OECD countries committed to take action to ensure well-functioning institutions and systems for promoting ethical conduct in the public service, in particular by:
>
> - updating legislation and internalisation of core ethical standards, for instance in the form of codes of conduct;
> - political leaders as well as managers demonstrating commitment to ethics and serving as role models;
> - providing incentives for integrity in human resource management (*e.g.* merit-based recruitment and career promotion, adequate remuneration, etc.);
> - enabling prevention (*e.g.* through increased transparency and disclosure systems), detection and investigation of misconduct (*e.g.* clear rules and procedures for "whistle blowing");
> - providing guidance to help public officials apply ethical standards in concrete circumstances particularly at the interface of the public and private sectors; and
> - ensuring transparency and accountability in the decision-making process and facilitating scrutiny.
>
> In order to provide a strategic tool to help countries review their mechanisms for promoting public service ethics and better integrate integrity measures within the broader governance environment, a reference checklist – a set of twelve Principles for Managing Ethics in the Public Service – was also agreed upon.
>
> *Source:* OECD Recommendation on Improving Ethical Conduct in the Public Service (1998).

approach favoured has been to combine both aspirational standards for public officials as well as control and accountability mechanisms for ensuring compliance in daily behaviour.

Over the last decades, many governments have developed specific standards of conduct to address conflicts between public officials' individual private interests and their public duties. Governments originally focussed on traditional sources of influence, such as gifts or hospitality offered to public officials, and personal or family relationships. Due to the increased co-operation between the public and private sectors, many countries have also established in recent years specific standards of conduct for tackling other forms of conflict-of-interest such as business interests (*e.g.* in the form of partnerships, shareholdings), affiliations with other organisations and post-public employment (see Figure 10.3). In order to address risks to good governance arising from conflicts of interest, the OECD has developed a framework for reviewing and modernising a country's conflict-of-interest policy with the 2003 Recommendation on Guidelines for Managing Conflict of Interest in the Public Service, as well as a Toolkit to help public officials put them into practice (see Annex 10.A).

Figure 10.3. **Activities and situations holding potential for conflicts of interest for public officials in OECD countries**

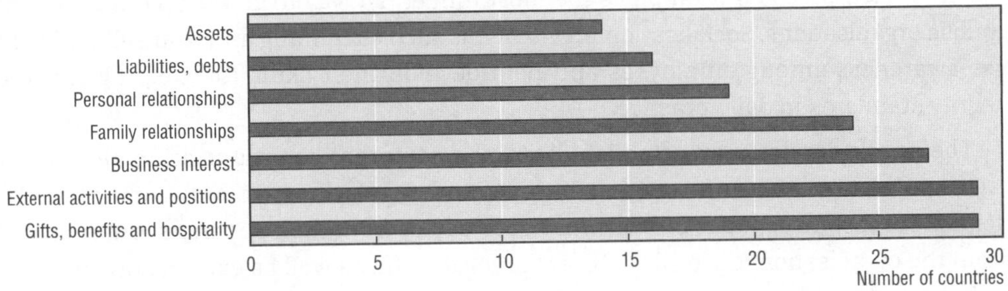

Source: OECD (2003), Managing Conflict of Interest in the Public Service: OECD Guidelines and Country Experiences, OECD, Paris.

10.3.2. Application and enforcement of international anti-corruption and integrity standards

While the implementation of international anti-corruption and integrity standards is necessary, it is not sufficient for establishing an investment favourable environment. Adequate application in practice and enforcement by all parts of government, including public administrations, is a major, subsequent, challenge. Governments should develop policies and practical steps to help in the application of laws and regulations concerning standards of conduct in the public service including in the areas of detection and whistle blowing. Government action alone, however, is not enough. Complementary and mutually supportive actions by the business community, trade unions and civil society actors are recognised to be increasingly important.

> **Do institutions and procedures ensure transparent, effective and consistent application and enforcement of laws and regulations on anti-corruption, including bribe solicitation and extortion and integrity in the public service? Have standards of conduct by public officials been established and made transparent? What measures are used to assist public officials and to ensure the expected standards are met? Are civil society organisations and the media free to scrutinize the conduct of public officials' duties? Are "whistle-blower" protections in place?**

Application and enforcement of laws and regulations on anti-corruption and integrity involves many institutions across the public service. In order to turn specific arrangements into a coherent and efficient system, co-ordination mechanisms have been set up to promote integrity and prevent corruption that may take various forms – such as central government agencies, parliamentary committees or specially created bodies.

Furthermore, agency specific guidelines and practical measures (e.g. staff rotation, specific training or briefing, etc.) may need to be developed to enforce anti-corruption and integrity standards in parts of the public service that are particularly exposed to corruption. Specific risk areas include law enforcement, public procurement, export credit, development assistance as well as customs and tax administration.

Codes of conduct are often developed to provide standards of conduct in a single concise document. These should be made available and adequately communicated to all public officials. Managers should play a role model for other employees in applying ethical standards, their personal example is the most influential way to create an ethical culture in public organisations. Socialisation mechanisms such as training and counselling further raise awareness among employees and help develop their skills for meeting expected integrity standards in daily practice.

The public service may establish internal or external communication channels to assist application and enforcement of laws and regulations on anti-corruption and integrity. For instance, public officials may seek advice from their superiors, other persons within the organisation (e.g. ethics officers or legal staff), as well as external organisations (e.g. independent commissions, ombudsman, or ethics offices).

Transparent procedures within the administration, such as setting standards for timeliness and requesting reasons for decisions also contribute to creating trust and credible decision-making in the public service. In addition, human resource management policies should provide suitable conditions and incentives for public officials, such as basing recruitment and promotion on merit, providing an adequate remuneration and taking ethical considerations into account in recruitment and performance appraisal.

Reporting suspicion of misconduct by public officials can be either required by law and/or facilitated by organisational rules. Whistle blowing, the act of raising concerns about misconduct within an organisation, is a key element of good governance to ensure transparency and accountability. A range of institutions and procedures such as Ombudsman, Inspector General, complaint procedures and help desks or telephone lines could enable public officials and citizens to expose wrongdoing. Their effectiveness also depends on public confidence that people who make *bona fide* reports about wrongdoing receive proper protection against retaliation.

Detection of violations of anti-corruption and integrity laws and regulations call for actions by many. On the one hand, governments are encouraged to develop a general framework for disciplinary procedures that both allows managers to impose timely administrative actions and guarantees a fair process for public officials. Administrative disciplinary sanctions may be foreseen; they usually range from warning and reprimand through material penalty to temporary or final dismissal, which is the most severe disciplinary consequence. On the other hand, violations are pursued by the domestic investigative and prosecutorial bodies that ultimately should impose effective, proportionate and dissuasive sanctions.

Parties to the OECD Convention hold regular consultations with the private sector, trade unions and civil society to discuss anti-corruption standards and policies. The consultations provide for an opportunity to administrations to learn about the complementary and mutually supportive actions by the business community, trade unions and civil society actors. Increased awareness of the different anti-corruption standards encourages managers to introduce self-regulatory systems aimed at compliance. Many businesses have indeed stepped up their anti-corruption efforts through development of codes of conduct and internal compliance programs. Business also liaises with key players in specific sectors or on a horizontal business federation level to prevent bribery through developing and adopting common standards. Companies with high governance and integrity standards may, due to improved public trust, be in a better position to attract investors.

10.3.3. Role of internal and external reviews

Do review mechanisms exist to assess the performance of laws and regulations on anti-corruption and integrity?

Solid and independent review is essential to help ensure enforcement of laws and regulations on anti-corruption and integrity. In general, the legislative branch undertakes reviews of public service activities. Other common types of evaluation range from external independent investigation by the Ombudsman or the Inspector General to specific judicial or ethics reviews. Additionally, monitoring compliance may be based on internal controls, widely used to detect individual irregularities and systemic failures and is likely to be accompanied by independent scrutiny. This scrutiny keeps public officials accountable for their actions, ultimately, to the public.

Transparency in government operations is considered both as an instrument for ensuring accountability and combating corruption, and for promoting democratic participation by informing and involving citizens. In recent years, citizens' access to official information has significantly improved, in particular with the development of Freedom of Information legislation and the growing use of electronic procedures. Coupled with an increasingly active media and well-organised interest groups, this has led to more vigilant public scrutiny over public officials' behaviours.

10.3.4. Ensuring compliance through monitoring and international co-operation

Is the government a party to international initiatives aimed at fighting corruption and improving public sector integrity? What mechanisms are in place to ensure timely and effective implementation of anti-corruption conventions? Do these mechanisms monitor the application and enforcement of the anti-corruption laws implementing the conventions?

Governments have realised that corruption cannot be addressed at the domestic level alone. Only concerted, internationally coordinated action can make a meaningful contribution to eradicating corruption. Governments have consequently adopted a number of international and regional anti-corruption instruments (see Box 10.4 and Box 10.6). Although these instruments may have different focuses, they generally aim at ensuring a

> ## Box 10.7. **International and regional anti-corruption initiatives**
>
> **Organization of American States (OAS): Inter-American Convention against Corruption, 1996:** The Inter-American Convention against Corruption (IACC) is the first international Convention against corruption ever adopted (from 6 March 1997). It has been ratified by 29 countries, and is broader in scope than the European and OECD instruments. The IACC provisions can be broadly classified into three groups: Preventive Measures, Criminal Offences and Mutual Legal Assistance.
>
> **Council of Europe Criminal Law Convention on Corruption, 1999:** The Convention is drafted as a binding legal instrument and applies to a broad range of occupations and circumstances. It contains provisions criminalising a list of specific forms of corruption, and extending to both active and passive forms of corruption, and to both private and public sector cases. The Convention also deals with a range of transnational cases: bribery of foreign public officials and members of foreign public assemblies is expressly included, and offences established pursuant to the private-sector criminalisation provisions would generally apply in transnational cases in any State Party where a sufficient portion of the offence to trigger domestic jurisdictional rules had taken place.
>
> **Council of Europe Civil Law Convention on Corruption, 1999:** This is the first attempt to define common international rules for civil litigation in corruption cases. Where the *Criminal Law Convention* seeks to control corruption by ensuring that offences and punishments are in place, the *Civil Law Convention* requires States Parties to ensure that those affected by corruption can sue the perpetrators civilly, effectively drawing the victims of corruption into the Council's anti-corruption strategy. The Civil Law Convention is narrower that its criminal law counterpart in the scope of the forms of corruption to which it applies, extending only to bribery and similar acts. It came into force in November 2003.
>
> **SADC – The Southern African Development Community Protocol on Corruption, 2001:** SADC – The Southern African Development Community Protocol on Corruption was adopted by all 14 SADC Heads of States and Governments at the Summit held in Malawi in August 2001. It represents the first anti-corruption treaty in Africa and was ratified by 8 of 14 SADC members States. It promotes the development of anti-corruption mechanisms at national level and the harmonization of anti-corruption legislations in Africa as well as the cooperation between States in the fight against corruption.
>
> **African Union Convention on Preventing and Combating Corruption and Related Offences, 2002:** African heads of state adopted the African Union Convention on Preventing and Combating Corruption at the Second Ordinary Session of the Assembly of the African Union in July 2003. Its main objectives are to strengthen the laws on corruption by listing offences that should be punishable by domestic legislation; to outline measures to be undertaken to enable the detection and investigation of corruption offences; to indicate mechanisms for the confiscation and forfeiture of the proceeds of corruption and related offences; to organize mutual assistance in relation to corruption and related offences; and to encourage the education and promotion of public awareness on the evils of corruption.

holistic approach that encompasses preventive measures as well as repressive provisions to fight domestic and foreign corruption. Moreover, they contain provisions regarding mutual legal assistance, which facilitate the detection, the investigation and sanctioning of corruption.

In order to ensure compliance with international anti-corruption standards, it is essential that systematic monitoring be established to ensure effective enforcement of the relevant Conventions. The OECD regularly releases reports on the effectiveness of the enforcement of the laws and regulations in countries for implementing the Convention on Combating the Bribery of Foreign Public Officials in International Business Transactions. Through its ongoing monitoring process and by promoting high standards, the Convention has contributed to levelling the competitive playing field for companies doing transborder business.

Regional initiatives against corruption and in support of public sector integrity serve to help governments establish similar rules and to level the playing field, which in turn is beneficial for the investment climate. This is particularly important in an age of globalisation when the internationalisation of illegal transactions calls for increased international co-operation of governments, notably through the adoption of clear mutual legal assistance provisions and procedures. Through the establishment of similar rules to provide level playing fields, regional initiatives can also serve to highlight instances of non-compliance or non-enforcement and provide avenues for peer review of a government's efforts for improving the public governance framework.

International co-operation in the fight against corruption is an example of the interface of private and public sector integrity where home countries have made a contribution to public sector integrity in host countries by targeting the "supply side" (see Box 10.7). For example, the OECD Convention of Combating Bribery of Foreign Public Officials in International Business Transactions aims to stop the flow of bribes to public officials in host countries.[7]

Other intergovernmental organisations such as the United Nations, the World Bank, the Asian Development Bank and the International Monetary Fund have also developed policies aimed at fostering good governance and sanctioning corruption and related malpractices, variously addressing both the "demand" and "supply" sides.

Notes

1. Especially important in the context of investment is the extent to which regulatory policy is transparent and mechanisms established to ensure fairness, efficiency, accountability, and credibility. Many of these issues are dealt with in greater detail in the sections 1 and 2, on transparency and protection, of the chapter on investment policy.

2. For a recent discussion on the set up of independent regulators see OECD (2005), *Designing Independent and Accountable Authorities for High Quality Regulation*, Working Party on Regulatory Management and Reform, OECD, Paris, also available at: *www.oecd.org/dataoecd/15/28/35028836.pdf*.

3. While some countries assess business impacts, others require it for administrative and paperwork burdens. Some countries use full-fledged benefit-cost analysis based on social welfare theories. Environmental impact assessment is used to identify potential impacts of regulations in environmental quality. Other regulators assess how proposed rules affect sub-national governments, or aboriginal groups, or small business or international trade.

4. See also the treatment of public consultation in the chapter on investment policy, especially Box 2.

5. See OECD (2005), *Public Sector Modernisation: Open Government* (OECD Policy Brief).

6. See also the chapter on investment promotion and facilitation.

7. The OECD Guidelines for Multinational Enterprises, which is part of the broader OECD Declaration on International Investment and Multinational Enterprises, is another such example, given their comprehensive anti-bribery provisions, which apply wherever multinational enterprises may operate.

References and Further Policy Resources

OECD (2005), OECD Guiding Principles for Regulatory Quality and Performance.

OECD (2005), Designing Independent and Accountable Authorities for High Quality Regulation, Working Party on Regulatory Management and Reform.

OECD (2005), Public Sector Integrity: A Framework for Assessment.

OECD (2005), Managing Conflict of Interest in the Public Sector: A Toolkit.

OECD (2005), Evaluating Public Participation in Policy Making.

OECD (2005), Policy Brief. Public Sector Modernisation: Open Government.

OECD (2004), OECD Reviews of Regulatory Reform – Germany. Consolidating Economic and Social Renewal.

OECD (2004), Governance in China.

OECD (2003), Public Sector Transparency and the International Investor.

OECD (2003), Managing Conflict of Interest in the Public Service: OECD Guidelines and Country Experiences.

OECD (2003), Annual Report on the OECD Guidelines for Multinational Enterprises: Enhancing the Role of Business in the Fight Against Corruption.

OECD (2003), From Red Tape to Smart Tape: Administrative Simplification in OECD Countries.

OECD (2002), Regulatory Policies in OECD Countries: From Intervention to Regulatory Governance.

OECD (2002), Foreign Direct Investment: Maximising Benefits, Minimising Costs.

OECD (2002), Public Sector Transparency and Accountability: Making it Happen.

OECD (2001), OECD Best Practices for Budget Transparency.

OECD (2001), Citizens as Partners: Information, Consultation and Public Participation in Policy-making.

OECD (2000), Trust in Government: Ethics Measures in OECD Countries.

OECD (2000), Policy Brief. Building Public Trust: Ethics Measures in OECD Countries.

OECD (1998), OECD Recommendation on Improving Ethical Conduct in the Public Service.

OECD (1998), Policy Brief. Principles for Managing Ethics in the Public Service: OECD Recommendation.

OECD (1997), Regulatory Quality and Public Sector Reform.

OECD (1997), Regulatory Impact Analysis: Best Practices in OECD Countries.

OECD (1997), The OECD Report on Regulatory Reform: Synthesis.

OECD (1997), The OECD Report on Regulatory Reform, Volume II: Thematic Studies.

World Bank (2002), Reforming Public Institutions and Strengthening Governance: A World Bank Strategy, Implementation Update, Part 1.

ANNEX 10.A1

The APEC-OECD Integrated Checklist on Regulatory Reform

Note: the place of the cells has no relation to the order of the rows.
That is, questions H4, A4, B4 and C4 are not related

H. Integrated policies (horizontal dimension)	A. Regulatory policy	B. Competition policy	C. Market openness policies
H1. To what extent is there an integrated policy for regulatory reform that sets out principles dealing with regulatory, competition and market openness policies?	A1. To what extent are capacities created that ensure consistent and coherent application of principles of quality regulation?	B1. To what extent has a policy been embraced in the jurisdiction that is directed towards promoting efficiency and eliminating or minimising the material competition distorting aspects of all existing and future laws, regulations, administrative practices and other institutional measures (collectively "regulations") that have an impact upon markets?	C1. To what extent are there mechanisms in regulatory decision-making to foster awareness of trade and investment implications?
H2. How strongly do political leaders and senior officials express support for regulatory reform to both the public and officials, including the explicit fostering of competition and open markets? How is this support translated in practice into reform and how have businesspeople, consumers and other interested groups reacted to these actions and to the reforms in concrete terms?	A2. Are the legal basis and the economic and social impacts of drafts of new regulations reviewed? What performance measurement instruments are being envisaged for reviewing the economic and social impacts of new regulations?	B2. To what extent do the objectives of the competition law and policy include, and only include, promoting and protecting the competitive process and enhancing economic efficiency including consumer surplus?	C2. To what extent does the government promote approaches to regulation and its implementation that are trade-friendly and avoid unnecessary burdens on economic actors?
H3. What are the accountability mechanisms that assure the effective implementation of regulatory, competition and market openness policies?	A3. Are the legal basis and the economic and social impacts of existing regulations reviewed, and if so, what use is made of performance measurement instruments?	B3. To what extent does the Competition Authority or another body have i) a clear mandate to advocate actively in order to promote competition and efficiency throughout the economy and raise general awareness of the benefits of competition, and ii) sufficient resources to carry out any advocacy functions included in its mandate?	C3. To what extent are customs and border procedures designed and implemented to provide consistency, predictability, simplicity and transparency so as to avoid unnecessary burdens on the flow of goods? To what extent are migration procedures related to the temporary movement of people to supply services transparent and consistent with the market access offered?

H. Integrated policies (horizontal dimension)	A. Regulatory policy	B. Competition policy	C. Market openness policies
H4. To what extent do regulation, competition and market openness policies avoid discrimination between like goods, services, or service suppliers in like circumstances, whether foreign or domestic? If elements of discrimination exist, what is their rationale? What consideration has been given to eliminating or minimising them?	A4. To what extent are rules, regulatory institutions, and the regulatory management process itself transparent, clear and predictable to users both inside and outside the government?	B4. To what extent are measures taken to neutralise the advantages accruing to government business activities as a consequence of their public ownership?	C4. To what extent has the government established effective public consultation mechanisms and procedures (including prior notification, as appropriate) and do such mechanisms allow sufficient access for all interested parties, including foreign stakeholders?[1]
H5. To what extent has regulatory reform, including policies dealing with regulatory quality, competition and market openness, been encouraged and co-ordinated at all levels of government?	A5. Are there effective public consultation mechanisms and procedures including prior notification open to regulated parties and other stakeholders, including non-governmental organisations, the private sector, advisory bodies, accreditation bodies, standards-development organisations and other governments?[2]	B5. To what extent does the agency responsible for the administration and enforcement of the competition law (the "Competition Authority") operate autonomously, and to what extent are its human and financial resources sufficient to enable it to do its job?	C5. To what extent are government procurement processes open and transparent to potential suppliers, both domestic and foreign?
H6. Are the policies, laws, regulations, practices, procedures and decision making transparent, consistent, comprehensible and accessible to users both inside and outside government, and to domestic as well as foreign parties? And is effectiveness regularly assessed?	A6. To what extent are clear and transparent methodologies and criteria used to analyse the regulatory impact when developing new regulations and reviewing existing regulations?	B6. If the competition law reserves a role for governmental bodies other than the Competition Authority under the competition law, to what extent is this role transparent, for example, regarding factors taken into account by such decision-maker, and their relative weighting?	C6. Do regulatory requirements discriminate against or otherwise impede foreign investment and foreign ownership or foreign supply of services?[3] If elements of discrimination exist, what is their rationale? What consideration has been given to eliminating or minimising them, to ensure equivalent treatment with domestic investors?
H7. Are the reform of regulation, the establishment of appropriate regulatory authorities, and the introduction of competition coherent in timing and sequencing?	A7. How are alternatives to regulation assessed?	B7. To what extent is there a transparent policy and practice that addresses the relationship between the Competition Authority and sectoral regulatory authorities?	C7. To what extent are harmonised international standards being used as the basis for primary and secondary domestic regulation?
H8. To what extent are there effective inter-ministerial mechanisms for managing and co-ordinating regulatory reform and integrating competition and market openness considerations into regulatory management systems?	A8. To what extent have measures been taken to assure compliance with and enforcement of regulations?	B8. To what extent does the competition law contain provisions to deter effectively and prevent hard-core cartel conduct, abuses of dominant position or unlawful monopolistic conduct, and contain provisions to address effectively anti-competitive mergers? To what extent does the broader competition policy strive to ensure that this type of conduct is not facilitated by government regulation?	C8. To what extent are measures implemented in other countries accepted as being equivalent to domestic measures?

1. This Question could be further integrated, in particular with elements of Question H6 and Question A5.
2. This Question could be further integrated for instance moving it to the Horizontal section and merging it with Question C4.
3. This Question could be further integrated, in particular with elements of Question H4.

H. Integrated policies (horizontal dimension)	A. Regulatory policy	B. Competition policy	C. Market openness policies
H9. Do the authorities responsible for the quality of regulation and the openness of markets to foreign firms and the competition authorities have adequate human and technical resources, to fulfil their responsibilities in a timely manner?		B9. To what extent does the competition law apply broadly to all activities in the economy, including both goods and services, as well as to both public and private activities, except for those excluded?	C9. To what extent are procedures to assure conformity developed in a transparent manner and with due consideration as to whether they are effective, feasible and implemented in ways that avoid creating unnecessary barriers to the free flow of goods or provision of services?
H10. Are there training and capacity building programmes for rule-makers and regulators to ensure that they are aware of high quality regulatory, competition and market openness considerations?		B10. To what extent does the competition law provide for effective investigative powers and sanctions to detect, investigate, punish and deter anti-competitive behaviour?	
H11. Does the legal framework have in place or strive to establish credible mechanisms to ensure the fundamental due process rights of persons subject to the law, in particular concerning the appeal system?		B11. To what extent do firms and individuals have access to i) the Competition Authority to become apprised of the case against them and to make their views known, and ii) to the relevant court(s) or tribunal(s) to appeal decisions of the Competition Authority or seek compensation for damages suffered as a result of conduct contrary to the domestic competition law?	
		B12.In the absence of a competition law, to what extent is there an effective framework or mechanism for deterring and addressing private anti-competitive conduct?	

ANNEX 10.A2

Identifying and Managing Conflict of Interest

The OECD Guidelines on Managing Conflict of Interest set four core principles for public officials to follow in dealing with conflict-of-interest situations in order to maintain trust in public institutions: serving the public interest; supporting transparency; promoting individual responsibility; and creating an organisational culture that does not tolerate conflict of interest.

Serving the public interest

Public officials should make decisions and provide advice without regard for personal gain. The religious, professional, party-political, ethnic, family or other personal preferences of the decision-maker should not affect the integrity of official decision-making. At the same time, public officials should dispose of, or restrict the operation of, private financial interests, personal relationships or affiliations that could compromise official decisions they are involved in. Where this is not feasible – an official can hardly be expected to abandon her relationship with her husband or children in the interests of her job – a public official should abstain from involvement in official decisions that could be compromised by private interests.

Public officials should also avoid taking improper advantage in their private lives from "inside information" obtained in the course of official duties that is not available to the public. Therefore public officials should not engage in a private financial transaction which involves the use of confidential information obtained at work. In addition, public officials must not misuse their position and government resources for private gain, such as awarding a contract to a firm in the hope of obtaining a job with that firm on leaving public office.

Supporting transparency and scrutiny

The Guidelines state that public officials and public organisations are expected to act in a way that will bear the closest public scrutiny. Public officials should disclose any private interests and affiliations that could compromise the disinterested performance of public duties when taking up office and afterwards if circumstances change, to enable adequate control and management of the situation.

Public organisations and officials should also ensure consistency and openness in resolving or managing conflict-of-interest situations, for example by providing up-to-date information about the organisation's policy, rules and administrative procedures regarding conflict of interest, or by encouraging discussion on how specific situations have been handled in the past and are expected to be handled in the future. Organisations should also promote scrutiny of their management of such situations, perhaps by involving employees in reviews of existing conflict-of-interest policy or consulting them on future preventive measures.

Promoting individual responsibility and personal example

Public officials, particularly public office holders and senior managers, should act at all times in a manner that demonstrates integrity and thus serves as an example to other officials and the public. When dealing with individual cases, senior officials and managers should balance the interests of the organisation, the individual and the public. Public officials should also accept responsibility for arranging their private affairs so as to prevent conflicts of interest, and for identifying and resolving conflicts in favour of the public interest when a conflict does arise. So an official could sell a relevant financial interest, or declare an interest in a particular issue and withdraw from the decision-making process.

Creating an organisational culture that does not tolerate conflict of interest

The Guidelines also call on public organisations to create an organisational culture that does not tolerate conflict of interest. This can be done in a number of ways, such as raising awareness by publishing the conflict-of-interest policy, giving regular reminders, developing learning tools to help employees apply and integrate the policy and by providing concrete advice when need arises. Organisational practices should encourage public officials to disclose and discuss real, apparent or potential conflict-of-interest cases, and provide reasonable measures to protect them from retaliation. Public organisations should also create and sustain a culture of open communication and dialogue to promote integrity, while providing guidance and training to promote understanding.

The Guidelines provide the following key policy recommendations on how to identify, prevent, manage and resolve conflict-of-interest situations.

Box 10.A2.1. **Key recommendations for managing conflict of interest**

1. Identify relevant conflict-of-interest situations:

- Provide a clear and realistic description of what circumstances and relationships can lead to a conflict-of-interest situation.

- Ensure that the conflict-of-interest policy is supported by organisational strategies and practices to help identify concrete conflict-of-interest situations at the workplace.

2. Establish procedures to identify, manage and resolve conflict-of-interest situations:

- Ensure that public officials know what is required of them in identifying and declaring conflict-of-interest situations.

- Set clear rules on what is expected of public officials in dealing with conflict-of-interest situations, so that both managers and employees can achieve appropriate resolution and management.

3. Demonstrate leadership commitment:

- Managers and leaders in the public service should take responsibility for the effective application of conflict-of-interest policy, by establishing a consistent decision-making process, taking decisions based on this model in individual cases, monitoring and evaluating the effectiveness of the policy and, where necessary, enhancing or modifying the policy to make it more effective.

4. Create a partnership with employees:

- Ensure wide publication, awareness and understanding of the conflict-of-interest policy through training and counselling.

- Review "at-risk" areas for potential conflict-of-interest situations.

- Identify preventive measures that deal with emergent conflict-of-interest situations.

- Develop and sustain an open organisational culture where measures dealing with conflict-of-interest matters can be freely raised and discussed.

5. Enforce the conflict-of-interest policy:

- Provide procedures for establishing a conflict-of-interest offence, and consequences for non-compliance, including disciplinary sanctions.

- Develop monitoring mechanisms to detect breaches of policy and take into account any gain or benefit that resulted.

- Co-ordinate prevention and enforcement measures and integrate them into a coherent institutional framework.

- Provide a mechanism for recognising and rewarding exemplary behaviour related to consistent demonstrated compliance with the conflict-of-interest policy.

6. Initiate a new partnership with the business and non-profit sectors:

- Involve the business and non-profit sectors in elaborating and implementing the conflict-of-interest policy for public officials.

- Anticipate potential conflict-of-interest situations when public organisations involve persons representing businesses and the non-profit sector through boards or advisory bodies.

- Include safeguards against potential conflict-of-interest situations by making other organisations aware of the potential consequences of non-compliance and reviewing together high-risk areas.

OECD PUBLICATIONS, 2, rue André-Pascal, 75775 PARIS CEDEX 16
PRINTED IN FRANCE
(20 2006 02 1 P) ISBN 92-64-02586-3 – 55193 2006